SOLDIERS' STORIES

Yvonne Tasker

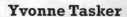

SOLDIERS' STORIES

MILITARY WOMEN IN
CINEMA AND TELEVISION
SINCE WORLD WAR II

Duke University Press
Durham and London
2011

© 2011 Duke University Press

All rights reserved.

Printed in the United States of America
on acid-free paper ∞

Designed by Heather Hensley

Typeset in Warnock Pro by Tseng Information Systems, Inc.

Library of Congress Cataloging-in-Publication
Data appear on the last printed page of this book.

In memory of
Elspeth Snodgrass,
1964–2003

CONTENTS

FIGURES

ACKNOWLEDGMENTS

First and foremost I want to thank the staff at Duke University Press and in particular Ken Wissoker, who has been a supportive, incisive, and patient editor throughout this process. Over the ten years or so that I have worked on and around images of military women, I have presented papers and received enthusiastic, helpful, and probing responses from audiences in the U.K. and the U.S. Thanks are due to all those who listened and debated with me on these issues, though I particularly want to thank Christine Gledhill for her incisive commentary. Many others have discussed this project with me, read segments, helped out, or loaned materials; among others, my thanks go to Charles Barr, Jane Bryan, Shelley Cobb, Steve Cohan, Richard Crockatt, Bob Eberwein, Gwendolyn Audrey Foster, Christine Gledhill, Hannah Hamad, Mike Hammond, Christine Holmlund, Bill Luhr, Linda Mizejewski, Kristian Moen, Margaret Montgomerie, Lawrence Napper, Diane Negra, Sarah Projansky, Lindsay Steenberg, Tim Stephens, Sue Thornham, Linda Ruth Williams, Nadine Wills, and Elizabeth Young.

Immense thanks are owed to the Library of Congress staff, notably Madeline Matz, who tracked down film prints, enthusiastically identified new titles for me to peruse, and was so very welcoming during my stay in the U.S. Thanks also to the staff at the National Archives in Washington, the film archive at the Imperial War Museum, the National Film Archive in London, and the Television News Archive at Vanderbilt University. The U.K.'s

Arts and Humanities Research Council supported archival work and funded a period of sabbatical leave to enable the completion of the initial manuscript. The University of East Anglia has supported the project throughout its development, and I am grateful to colleagues, both academic and administrative, in the current School of Film and Television Studies and the former School of English and American Studies. As ever, my partner, Rachel Hall, has been my most valued advisor, editor, and support.

A PROVOCATIVE PRESENCE

Military Women in Visual Culture

Among the advertisements for cosmetics and cigarettes in an issue of the British fan magazine *Picture Show* in 1953 the (young) female reader is addressed directly in this way: "There's a place for YOU in the W.R.A.F." (figure 1).[1] A WRAF member, Joan Pears, smiles while the text informs us, "She wanted to stand on her own feet; to meet different people; to travel abroad." Having left her civilian training as a hairdresser in favor of her new role as a fighter plotter in an operations room, Pears suggests the exciting possibilities of military service for women, a potential migration from feminized labor (hair and beauty) to a position of agency and responsibility (an "important life"). Historians have demonstrated that the place offered to women after the Second World War was a rather contradictory and in many ways limited one; it was nonetheless a place, one officially sanctioned at that, within the male institutions of the postwar military. While I use the term *postwar* conventionally here to denote the period after the Second World War, it is worth noting that this recruitment ad ran just three months after the end of the Korean War, a reminder of the extent to which Western military forces, U.S. forces in particular, would continue to be involved in wars and conflicts in the postwar era. As an exemplary young recruit, Joan Pears works in precisely the kind of clerical and communications role the expansion of which led to increased utilization of (and indeed dependence on) women in the military. The laws and cus-

1. Recruitment ad for the WRAF as featured in the British movie magazine *Picture Show* (1953).

toms of patriarchal society and the open misogyny in much of the popular culture of the 1950s worked to put women (back) in "their place," that is, a position of subordination. The figure of the military woman, however, suggests another sort of place, a different ordering of gender and power.

The particular character and location of this ad suggests another set of questions for the reader. How might we make sense of this address to female *cinemagoers*, for instance, and how might that invocation be qualified by the familiar and powerful discourses of domestic femininity operating in the 1950s, or by the postwar films and novels which celebrated the bravery and wartime sacrifices of women? Social class is also clearly pertinent; Joan Pears is a worker rather than a customer at the salon and is thus positioned within the emergent service sector, a woman for whom the economic benefits of military service are centralized. Implicitly the "absorbing, important life" outlined by the recruitment drive is counterpoised to the limits and (feminine) triviality of her role as hairdresser. Moreover the example of this young Scottish woman suggests that military service provides an opportunity to actually experience the sort of mobility (social and geographic) delivered as entertainment by the cinema. In an ad nestled in the back pages of a movie magazine, the military woman is here an iconic sign of economic opportunity, movement, and adventure.

This book begins with a relatively straightforward question: How have military women been represented in the cinema and subsequently in television? In answering this question, I aim to provide a comprehensive study of military women in American and British cinema and television from the Second World War to the present. My goal is both to make the military woman a more visible figure within film and television history, and feminist media studies more broadly, and to suggest ways we might understand the formations of gender and power that she thematizes. How have film, television, and popular narratives framed the ambitions and desires of the military woman? At times normalized, at times deviant, often peripheral, and typically controversial when she takes center stage, the military woman is a contradictory icon of modernity and continuity. To make sense of both her iconicity and her contradictory character, I analyze fictional military women through a series of histories: the institution and contested character of women's services in the U.S. and the U.K.; an evolving discourse of duty and opportunity through which recruiters have sought to enlist women (unlike men, in the period I survey here women have not been subject to the draft); feminism as a prominent public discourse of the late 1960s and 1970s; the emergence of a postfeminist media culture in the late 1980s; and the specificity of those film and television genres in which the military woman finds a place.

Thus my account of military women in film and television proceeds from both real-world concerns and representational histories. That the two are complexly bound together is fundamental to my argument. A concern with the military woman's *image*, a desire to exploit and contain her association with modernity recurs in policy debates, recruitment materials, and other forms of official discourse. In popular imagery and narratives too the military woman represents a particular sort of gender trouble. As Thomas Doherty writes with respect to representations of military women during the Second World War, "A military uniform betokened a sanctioned dominance that undermined gender subservience."[2] The peculiarity of this *authorized subversion* of hierarchies is evident; in many of the examples I explore we find an accompanying under-lying anxiety that the military woman might escape such limits, tipping ordered military life into anarchic misrule. Thus I argue, for instance, that gendered discourses of the military woman as potentially masculinized (a recurrent trope) have informed not only fictional representations, but public, military, and policy debates regarding the "proper" utilization of women in the armed forces. It follows that although film and television are my major focus, an understanding of the cinematic and televisual career of the military woman cannot be separated from an exploration of the wider discursive deployment of this figure.

Soldiers' Stories builds on feminist scholarship within the humani-ties, drawing on sources from women's history and politics to feminist media studies. Scholars working in sociology as well as women's, mili-tary, and nursing history have done much to map women's role in the Second World War and other conflicts and have explored in detail their ongoing struggles for equality within various military institutions. The analysis of film and television texts presented here speaks to and supple-ments such social, cultural, and historical work in which an awareness of the contested image of the military woman has long been central. In her analysis of the formation and early years of the Women's Army Corps (WAC), Leisa D. Meyer identifies a "cultural inability to reconcile the cate-gories of 'woman' and 'soldier'" lying at the heart of opposition to the proposed women's corps.[3] This cultural common sense underpins many of the representations explored in this book, and I return to its terms re-peatedly. The significance of the dislocation between these terms has to do, of course, with gender; to the extent that soldiering is understood as a masculine business, the female soldier is a troubling category. Conversely, to the extent that the female soldier demonstrates her capability in sol-diering, her masculinity (or at least her manliness) is at issue. Across the period considered here popular narratives work to address the anxiety that attaches to the military woman's troublesome gender, whether she is portrayed as manly, masculine, or failing to effectively perform an appro-priate femininity.

Representations of military women produced during the Second World War, as well as those generated in more recent times, reveal a preoccu-pation with the policing of gendered behavior and appearance. Assump-tions about, say, women's inability to work together, men's reluctance to take orders from women, and the likelihood that women will respond hysterically (and on occasion heroically) to danger are played out in the narratives I examine. Physical appearance remains a constant concern, whether narratives emphasize the conventional femininity, even glamour, of military women, showcase their sexy if thereby problematic bodies, or underline their physical strength, capacity for endurance, and capability.

To the extent that popular narratives and imagery insist that women cannot *really* be soldiers, they speak to a hierarchical opposition between combatants (male soldiers) and noncombatants (female soldiers). Such a distinction has proven extremely difficult to pin down. As Meyer's analysis shows, the U.S. Army's contradictory attempts to preserve the distinctiveness of the male soldier as combatant during the Second World War and to treat female soldiers as noncombatants, whatever task each was performing, became increasingly strained. Particular sites of tension were situations in which official policy explicitly distinguished between female civilians (who were not permitted to work in active combat areas) and female soldiers (who were). For the policy to make sense female soldiers must be regarded as either not really soldiers or not really women. Meyer continues, "The differentiation between male soldiers as combatants and 'female soldiers' as noncombatants was also undermined by the general blurring of combat and noncombat areas that began to occur during World War II."[4] With civilians, including women and children, coming under regular, intensive attack during artillery and air raids, the notion that policy might be motivated by a desire to keep military women *as women* out of harm's way seemed increasingly unviable.[5] What, then, was being protected or preserved here? The answer has to do with a pressing desire to shore up cultural formulations of gender which the organization of working, family, and civic life was increasingly calling into question. Such questions remain current, as is evident in attempts to restrict the combat roles of female troops even as their labor remains vital.

In exploring the contradictory characterization of the female soldier as a boundary-crossing figure—not really a woman and not really a soldier—this book addresses a range of issues to do with gender, agency, and female heroism. In this process the heavily mediated image of the military woman forms a productive point of reference. Consider the following chain of events and images. In wartime Britain young women were conscripted into the armed forces, industry, or other service, and other British women were actively involved in Air Raid Precaution duties, fire services, and voluntary assistance of various kinds. In a controversial move, members of the Auxiliary Territorial Service (ATS) who worked in anti-aircraft duties on mixed battery units took on a limited but nonetheless significant combat role operating predictors, range finders, searchlights, and at times (albeit unofficially) the guns themselves. Concurrent debates in the U.S. Congress on the advisability and shape of a women's Army corps reflected an awareness of the part that soldiering (quite specifically the right to bear arms in defense of the nation) played in the Constitution. Significantly Meyer suggests that a public fascination with the military work of British women, as represented in popular forums such as *Life* magazine, provided one model of advocacy for developing a military role for American women.[6] The feature from 1941 that accompanies the cover reproduced in figure 2 proclaims, "[British women] have demanded the right to do something, anything, so long as it hurts Hitler. . . . [Their energy] gives American women an idea of what they can do, should the U.S. go to war."[7] The ATS women featured in photo spreads could, it seems, be imagined (both visualized and narrativized) as defending the home, and by extension the nation, in appropriate feminine or maternal terms. That appropriately gendered appearances be kept up was vital for both cultures. Yet the evident propaganda potential of military women—the mobilization of their images—is telling with respect to their subsequent deployment in film and later television fictions.

To further clarify some of the issues at stake in the figuring of the military woman, we can consider a brief yet indicative sequence from the RKO film *Marine Raiders* (1944). In a scene staged at the Marine Corps base in San Diego two experienced soldiers comment, in familiar generic terms, on a batch of youthful male recruits: "Recruits? They still got fuzz on their cheeks!" The two men are posed together in the center of the frame, facing the camera; one comments in concerned tones, "Well, *what* won't they be taking into the Marine Corps next?" As if in wordless answer, a group of female Marines appear from behind the pair, marching toward the camera; they do not so much pass the men as force their way through. These drilling women keep resolutely in formation, and the sound of their marching feet loudly announces their precision and presence, in contrast to the young civilian men we have just seen. And yet the impression is one of disorder as well as order, the women dividing the two men, literally disrupting the frame as they come toward us, brushing past the camera (figure 3). Our two male Marines are taken quite by surprise; one pushes

LIFE

BRITISH WOMEN

AUGUST 4, 1941 **10** CENTS
YEARLY SUBSCRIPTION $4.50

2. *Life* magazine
(August 1941)
circulates the
image of British
military women
for American
audiences.

his cap back on his head; the other, doffing his cap in a gentlemanly fashion, comments wryly after the women have passed, "We've been outmaneuvered."

This short sequence nicely captures the sense in which the military
woman was, and indeed remains, a disruptive, even startling presence
in popular representations. To introduce another set of themes explored
in this book, I'll highlight three aspects of this sequence. First, it indicates how often the disruption associated with military women is expressed in comic or whimsical terms. Indeed it exemplifies the "battle
of the sexes" format that would become perhaps the established frame
for representing military women in the postwar period. Given the cultural uncertainty associated with the figure of the military woman in the
U.K. and the U.S., it is perhaps not surprising that comedy emerges as an
important generic site for her representation. It is not simply that she is

3. In *Marine Raiders* (1944) military women are pictured disrupting the frame and the expectations of male Marines.

a source of amusement by definition, although this is undoubtedly the case in some popular images and narratives. Rather comedy allows the potential staging of female unruliness (whether assuming authority over men or a cruder sexual freedom) in a rule-bound situation. Second, the appearance of this group of military women is framed primarily in terms of their *impact on military men*, an emphasis that will be repeatedly employed in the years that followed. The musicals I explore in chapter 3, for instance, juxtapose the confidence and dexterity of military women with male protagonists whose masculinity is in some way compromised. An implicit (or explicit) suggestion that the two are related—that the military woman has disarmed or unmanned her male counterpart—is a recurrent theme. Third, the Marine's use of the pronoun *what* rather than *who* is indicative of military women's boundary-crossing status; military women are transformed into "things" rather than recognized as citizen-soldiers. Defined in negative terms, as not (white) men, they are human perhaps, but neither comfortably recognizable nor welcome. While the youthful men glimpsed in this sequence (also referred to as *what*) will no doubt be drilled into shape (cinemagoers are familiar with that story, after all), military women represent a rather different sort of problem—one that evidently has to do with gender. That is, drilling female recruits into shape raises the disconcerting specter of female masculinity, of an eradication of difference, and of men "outmaneuvered" by marching women.

In making sense of the contradictory cultural formulation of the military woman, I theorize two recurrent tropes: the military woman as *auxiliary* and as a *provocative presence*. Both figures work to foreground aspects of the gendered anxiety with which this study is concerned.

The novel visibility of the military woman as citizen-soldier in wartime is premised on a quite specific understanding of her role as temporary and as an auxiliary. Peripheral but visible, striking and at times even glamorous in her uniform, the military woman is an important iconic figure in representations of the Second World War. Her involvement signals the "total war" which the conflict was frequently described as, an allusion both to the unprecedented (in scale at least) bombing of civilian targets and the scale of mobilization. Typically constructed in terms of youth and modernity, she functions as a marker—on occasion quite explicitly—of the role that women might play in public life. In the British context the extent to which women's new wartime role signaled a change in their status is nicely summed up in the figure of the mobile woman. As Antonia Lant explains, "'Mobile' and 'immobile' were Ministry of Labour classifications designating women who could either be moved to work anywhere in the country (mobile) or who had to work locally because they had dependents or were married (immobile)."[8] The military woman is thus a figure of social mobility; functioning independently, she is associated with traditionally masculine activities such as traveling, driving, or working with machinery. Alongside her literal mobility she demonstrates an ability to traverse social categories. In films of and about this period the boundary crossing of these military women is not only explained by national emergency, but mediated through comedy or by an emphasis on military women as nurturing nurses, somehow distant from the business of war (again, somehow not *really* soldiers).

In film and television fictions military women serve as auxiliaries in a different sense, typically playing supporting rather than leading roles. Their auxiliary status is more than a metaphor, although it also clearly works on this level. The First World War had seen the establishment of women's services, conceived as auxiliary forces, not required in peacetime and without the medical and other benefits associated with male military service. By the end of the Second World War, women's services were no longer defined as fundamentally auxiliary either in the U.K. or the U.S., though they remained more vulnerable than the men to job cuts. Yet contemporary popular culture and media imagery continue to reiterate the lack of fit between *woman* and *soldier*, whether in narratives that emphasize women's vulnerability to sexual violence, in those that underline their isolation within a hostile (male or masculine) institution, or even, or perhaps especially, in media coverage that continues to express surprise at and fetishistic interest in military women. Thus despite the significant extension of peacekeeping and combat roles for women in both the British and the American military, the debates played out since at least the Second World War remain resonant today. The high visibility of contemporary military women has not swept away the intensity of that cultural common sense which tells us that women are not *really* soldiers.

Consider, for instance, an Army recruitment spot that aired on British television in 1998. The spot deploys a handheld camera and eerie music in a style derived in equal parts from horror cinema and photojournalism. We are led through a devastated home in which a raped woman fearfully clutches her small child. The immediate context is the British involvement in Bosnia and the developing situation in Kosovo which led to UN action the following year, specifically media attention to mass rapes during the Bosnia war of 1992–95. The text informs us, "The last thing she wants to see is more soldiers," then adds, "But not all soldiers are men." As the camera closes in on the woman's fearful face, another woman speaks the comforting words, "It's over now. You're all right" (figure 4). The military woman isn't seen at all in this spot, but is implicitly contrasted to both military men (who pose a potential threat) and victimized civilian women. Here the female soldier's seeming difference is exploited, both to boost recruitment and to bolster the desired perception of the British military as a peacekeeping force.

The figure of the auxiliary contains the military woman by emphasizing her supporting and ultimately subservient role. The second term I make reference to in this study, the military woman as *provocative presence*, has a different set of valances. I take the phrase from an account, written under a pseudonym, of a military woman's time as a West Point cadet. She writes that she and her female peers "worked so hard not to be

4. "But not all soldiers are men": this recruitment ad for the British Army suggests that military women can supplement the violent military masculinity experienced by a rape victim.

provocative in any way."[9] Her observation demonstrates an awareness of the troubling character of the female presence within institutions which until recently had been all-male and which remained defined and organized in terms of military masculinity. While gender trouble features in numerous films from the 1940s and 1950s centering on military women, disruption takes a different form in the film and television culture of a later period, after gender integration and, arguably, after feminism's initial influence. Here women's proximity to men continues to produce humor, but increasingly we also see a marked shift toward a suggestion of danger or the potential for violence. Military women are seen as isolated, even besieged; they are routinely cast as victims of rape, harassment, violence, and hostility from male peers. In the context of high-profile scandals (Tailhook, Aberdeen) and political debate on combat exclusions, film and televisual culture frequently features a barely contained disgust at female bodies. Despite the ostensible liberalism of many texts featuring military women, women's bodies seem to serve as a recurrent sign of provocation. Rape and sexual assault as well as deception and betrayal function as central narrative terms. Where military women *are* figured as credible soldiers they are almost invariably mannish or masculine, effectively de-emphasizing their (potentially provocative) femaleness.

These images take us a long way from my starting point, the WRAF's recruitment strategy of comforting inclusion in the mid-1950s. It is important to underline that the military woman in that image does not inherently figure as disruption and misrule. More complexly, the military woman is both conformist and challenging. In film and television narratives she signals transgression (in stepping outside the bounds of femininity) and conformity (in her desire to belong to a conservative, military community) in equal measure. It is this contradiction that allows M*A*S*H's Maj. Margaret Houlihan simultaneously to be ridiculed for an excessive sexuality (her nickname is "Hot Lips") and to represent the ultimate in military conformity against which the show's male doctors rebel.

Formulations of the military woman as both auxiliary and a provocative presence help us make sense of her place in popular film and television genres. Those narratives featuring military women may portray them in a male-dominated and highly regulated hierarchy, yet their location is also quite distinctive in generic terms. When Lawrence H. Suid writes that "the typical heroine in a Hollywood military movie is submissive, long-suffering and long-waiting, a woman who satisfies her man's desires and provides loving care and relaxation from the true excitement of combat," he does not distinguish between military and civilian women.[10] Military women do love and wait in many of the narratives explored here, but their significance as a sign of modernity and agency, whether welcomed or troubling, also repays our attention. The heroine of the film *Flight Nurse* (1954), for instance, is both loving and waiting in line with Suid's dictum. Yet she is also the protagonist, and the majority of the film is devoted to scenes of her working; she ultimately chooses her military identity over civilian life and marriage. (That she has to choose is not, of course, without significance, as I discuss in chapter 2.) If accounts such as Suid's suggest that the specificity of military women is insignificant, they also imply that female characters involve an unwarranted, and even inappropriate, intrusion in generic terms.[11] Thus the purity of the combat film is compromised by the attempt to integrate female characters, whether civilian or military, and by the combat-romance hybrid films considered in chapter 1 of this book or the women's picture variants explored in chapter 2.[12]

In this context it is perhaps not surprising that the process of mapping representations of military women has led me to such diverse genres and subgenres as the musical, the melodrama, the legal drama, and boot camp films. Embodying a categorical contradiction, the military woman promotes generic hybridity. Investigating these images reveals the *trans-*

generic articulation of the military woman as a figure of agency, modernity, and anxiety.

FEMINISM, SOLDIERING, AND CITIZENSHIP

As a provocative presence the military woman has an evident, though far from straightforward, relevance for feminism. Contemporary debates relating to military service foreground women's access to professional opportunities and advancement, opportunities from which, it can be argued, there is no reason beyond custom and practice to exclude women. Popular imagery, however, retains a fascination with the exotic, even erotic associations of the armed military woman; she is a figure of fantasy and anxiety, a subject of comment rather than a naturalized or normalized cultural presence. Cynthia Enloe, whose pathbreaking work on women and militarization provides an important reference point for this study, speculates whether "the very inclination to dwell on women as soldiers is a reflection of our own militarized imagination."[13] Her remarks contextualize the celebratory images of military women frequently deployed in news media. In essence Enloe cautions us to be aware of just how compelling mediated images of military women can be.

During the Second World War the governments of both Britain and the U.S. overcame initial doubts and open expressions of hostility about the need for women's involvement in the war effort on any scale; ultimately they were to channel significant energies toward the goal of recruiting young women into military service, as well as other nontraditional forms of work such as industry and agriculture. In the process the military woman emerged as a sign of modernity, both compelling and troubling. "THIS IS MY WAR TOO!" proclaims a recruiting poster for the U.S. Women's Army Auxiliary Corps in 1943 (figure 5).[14] The patriotic imagery and confident claim of shared ownership speak to the connections drawn between the military woman's service and her status as citizen. As men and women were called on to work for the war, questions about the nature of democracy and the rights and responsibilities of citizenship were also foregrounded. As Richard Crockatt writes, "Democratic citizenship in war is a heightened form of the identification which citizens in democracies are invited to make with their national communities in the normal course of events."[15] Such intense forms of national identification serve, if anything, to underscore the inequalities of class, race, and gender that structured the democracies of Britain (an imperial

5. "This is my war too": both patriotic endeavor and gender inclusion are central to this recruitment poster from 1943.

power) and the U.S. in the war period. An insistent question emerges in wartime political and cultural discourse as to whether, or when, Britain and the U.S. would fully bestow citizenship on all its subjects.

The Second World War has been popularly regarded as a watershed in both British and American social history; indeed it is a commonplace to assert that this particular war changed women's place in society irrevocably and in a manner different from other wars.[16] However, as Christine Gledhill and Gillian Swanson argue, it pays to be cautious in our approach to history. "The war," they write, "can be seen as both a catalyst for changes already in the making and an incitement to energies directed towards preserving traditional gender differences."[17] Moreover, as Penny Summerfield makes clear, much depends on precisely *which* women are referred to in such formulations.[18] As I show in chapter 1, both wartime British cinema and American films about Britain concerned themselves with the inequities of a class system regarded as well past its expiration date. An expectation that the postwar world would be more equitable was increasingly apparent in British popular culture toward the end of the war. Yet for women, and for racial minorities and colonial subjects of both sexes, democracy and citizenship are complex questions.

Anne Phillips writes that, in Western democracies, "the conventional assumption of a non-gendered, abstract citizenship" operates "to centre the male."[19] The possibility that the status of (predominantly white) women in British and American society might also change forms an explicit element of wartime political and cultural discourse relating to military women; whether expressed in policy, cartoons, comedy, or other forms of the era's popular culture, the modernity of the military woman is clearly troubling. In this context Lant points to the changed value of women's work in wartime Britain such that women "now had to be figured as part of the nation's political body."[20] Lant's project of mapping the shifting construction of women in wartime British cinema takes on the implicit, subtle, and even unconscious ways in which popular culture and official discourse of the period constituted women's military service (and indeed women's war work more generally) as necessary, virtuous, patriotic, temporary, but *troubling* nonetheless. Let me be clear here: though women's military service was evidently culturally troubling, I do not argue in this book that it is inherently transgressive or subversive. Though alive to the military woman's deployment as a sign of modernity, we should not romanticize or simply celebrate her. It is clear that to a large extent a place appears for military women as and when their labor is required. In our current historical context of open-ended war and ongoing military interventions, that labor has been integral to American assertions of military authority.

From her perspective as a military woman, Billie Mitchell (a pseudonym) writes, "Feminists are right to be bewildered and even ambivalent about military women. On the one hand, military women are fighting the good fight for equality. On the other, they have been co-opted into accepting not only a male standard of success but one that professionalizes violence, has been responsible for the misery and death of women and children across all time and space, and glamorizes violent and demeaning sexual imagery as symbols of both victory and death. Feminists have every right to ask military women, 'Are you for us or against us?'"[21] More recently Enloe urges us to question any easy equation between military service and citizenship. Across a variety of national and cultural contexts, she writes, "yoking citizenship to military service has been a deliberate political enterprise."[22] The status and benefits given to veterans in the U.S. and the withholding of those benefits from female auxiliaries underline the civic valorization of military service. Feminist historians have produced fascinating work on the development, contested character, and issues faced by the women's services, including the policing of class, race, and sexuality, and by military women within the gender-integrated military that followed the disestablishment of the WAC in 1978. This study asks a different set of questions concerning the ways an analysis of visual culture might complement or contradict that history.

Soldiers' Stories pursues a telling trajectory across genres and historical periods with respect to the representation of military women. The cultural anxieties, romantic narratives, and endorsement of a vital but temporary military service during the Second World War is explored primarily in part 1. Part 2 focuses on musicals and comedies of the Second World War and the postwar period, underlining the framing of the cinematic (and televisual) military woman in terms of a series of comic variations on the "battle of the sexes," from Esther Williams as a raucous member of the WAVES in *Skirts Ahoy!* (1952) to Sgt. Joan Hogan as Bilko's love interest and nemesis in *The Phil Silvers Show* (1955–59). This section of the book also analyzes voyeuristic sex comedies, the long-running CBS series *M*A*S*H* (1972–83), and the feminist-informed (albeit somewhat superficially) articulation of the military woman in the film *Private Benjamin* (1980). Part 3 points to the gradual reworking of comic and dramatic narratives in recent decades, a reworking marked by a turn to trauma against the cultural context of postfeminism. Here I engage with texts clearly informed by more recent debates concerning military women's role in combat and dealing with the impact of a variety of scandals relating to sexual harassment. I show how film and television fictions from the late 1980s onward foreground sexual violence against military women, as well as detail their personal and professional isolation.

Popular narratives of this period see the development of a figure I characterize as an *exemplary military woman*. We encounter this figure in various contexts; her skills and professionalism may mark her as exceptional (and at times as not *really* a woman), but she is rarely portrayed in terms of the comradeship or teamwork that characterizes male military representations. In mapping this discursive shift toward the pessimism of contemporary narratives, evident even in those texts that in many ways seek to celebrate the military woman, *Soldiers' Stories* engages with widely circulating, popular, and political discourses of postfeminism. In constituting military women as exemplary but lonely and subject to sexual violence, many recent narratives speak to the wider issues facing women working in male-dominated institutions. That the masculinity and misogyny of military culture is in many ways officially sanctioned renders the incorporation of military women into that culture, and the narratives that represent or valorize it, a particularly acute site of contest over gender and power.

PART ONE

These chapters establish the framework for my analysis of representations of military women. With its unprecedented levels of mobilization, the Second World War has been absolutely central to the representation of the military woman and as such provides a starting point. Chapter 1 focuses on this period, detailing the ways British and Hollywood films of the period portrayed the military woman as an auxiliary figure, a temporary necessity awkwardly incorporated into a male military. I situate these films in the context of contemporary recruitment campaigns and wider discourses to do with the status and character of military women's service. Chapter 2 explores the figure of the military nurse specifically since it is as a nurse that military women are most often represented in both British and American films and television shows. The discussion of representations of military nursing begins with films produced during the war and those that look back on this period (although much could be said about the First World War and even earlier conflicts in this context). I then consider portrayals of military nursing during the Korean and Vietnam wars, ending with a discussion of *China Beach*, a series that explicitly aimed to make the figure of the female veteran visible within contemporary media culture.

Both chapters in this section explore how cultural concerns with women's military service are enmeshed with their gender identity, as film after film asks, Are military women still women, still feminine? Themes of personal transformation and of military service as an opportunity—whether for travel, escape, change, or fulfilling (or at least patriotic) work—are centralized in many of the narratives considered here. Equally central, though, are romance narratives, crucial in signaling the military woman's continuing commitment to femininity. As the focus moves from the emphasis on necessary but temporary service which characterizes the period during the Second World War, it becomes clear that narratives featuring military women orchestrate a tension between professional and romantic possibilities. Thus these films and television shows can be placed within the larger cultural context of the postwar period in which the value and purpose of women in any form of work, not just in professions strongly associated with men and masculinity, were keenly contested.

To the extent that they were auxiliaries, women were not fully members of the armed forces in the Second World War.[1] Yet the term also clearly has a metaphoric significance—one not lost on politicians at the time—which serves to qualify the potent image of the military woman as a sign of modernity. Feature films, newsreels, documentaries, and recruitment materials relating to the war repeatedly underlined the *supportive* role of the military woman. From a contemporary vantage point, this coding of the military woman's agency as fundamentally supportive of male and national endeavors emerges as the key contradiction of the wartime imagery which entreated women to enter the services or gave contemporary audiences glimpses of their lives after enlistment. Put simply, the military woman is cast as a figure of agency and modernity simultaneously framed by traditional, patriarchal cultural assumptions. Thus the modern woman is also in the parlance of the time a "girl." Consider, for instance, an Auxiliary Territorial Service recruitment poster depicting a young female soldier astride a motorcycle, the text informing us, "The motor cylist messenger, roaring across country from Headquarters to scattered units is now an ATS girl" (figure 6).[2] Previously, we must assume, such a task would have fallen to a male soldier. The image underlines the novelty of the role and celebrates the uniformed ATS girl-woman calmly conducting her duty under difficult circumstances.

A rhetoric of girlishness works to mediate the shock of the

ATS CARRY THE MESSAGES

The motor cyclist messenger, roaring across country from Headquarters to scattered units is now an ATS girl

6. Beverley Pick's ATS poster emphasizes women in a vital and modern military role. Reprinted by permission of the Imperial War Museum.

military woman in such imagery, both infantilizing her and emphasizing her status as not yet a woman. She is not neglecting the responsibilities of adult womanhood, but rather channeling her youthful energies into the (temporary) service of the nation. Such images were produced by teams mindful of a contemporary context in which many responded to the idea of women's military service with skepticism and even hostility. Some characterized women as unsuitable and unqualified for military duties; others were repelled by the supposedly unfeminine character of such work, whether that was manifest in mannishness or in sexual immorality, both of which were attributed to military women in the U.K. and U.S. at different points during the war. In short the military mobilization of women was regarded by many as deeply problematic, with military women themselves doomed to failure, whether in their performance of soldiering or of femininity, or both. Ambivalent responses to women's military service were prominent features of the war period in both Britain and the U.S., informing policy and shaping popular representations in a number of important ways. In the debate over legislation to establish the Women's Army Auxiliary Corps (WAAC), Leisa Meyer reports, "Republican Congresswomen Rogers (Mass.) and Bolton (Ohio) assured their male colleagues that military women would not be usurping the positions of male soldiers. They and other supporters depicted women's role in the military as one of 'assisting,' not 'displacing,' those in combat, particularly by filling jobs considered 'women's work' in civilian life."[3] Such rhetoric underlines the extent to which the work performed by military women and men needed to be distinct in order to maintain sexual difference. To this end, roles such as driver and dispatch rider could be, and indeed were, recast as women's work, defined as auxiliary to and supportive of the manly endeavors of command and combat.

At issue here is the fundamentally contradictory character of discourses of femininity, discourses in which women are both weak and frivolous figures in need of male protection and yet powerful when supporting men or defending their home, children, or nation. Such discourses allowed politicians to claim that they were "protecting" women's femininity by denying them the benefits of military status, for instance. In the process, we might argue, policymakers also sought to ensure that women would not gain equality as citizens (or as subjects in the British context) through their service. Equally they allowed advocates of military women to press their case on terms clearly less threatening to male interest and privilege.[4] These contradictions are clearly in evidence in the British short film *Airwoman* (1941), which depicts the day-to-day work of women in the Women's Auxiliary Air Force; WAAFs are seen working as messengers, drivers, secretaries, and telephone, wireless, and teleprinter operators.[5] They also prepare food for male aircrews who are about to depart on a bombing raid. We see them cooking and waiting at table on the men's return; in an evocation of more traditional domestic responsibilities, a male voice-over describes this activity as one of the many "worthwhile jobs an airwoman can do: look after those hungry men." Sponsored by the Air Ministry and the Ministry of Information, *Airwoman* is organized around the story of one woman and the success of a bombing raid in Bremen in which she has effectively played a part. ("Behind every story," we are told, lies "woman's cooperation.") While the drama of the mission itself is enacted, the WAAFs relax and wait; waiting, as we will see, is a key function for women (both military and civilian) in wartime representations.

The closing recruitment appeal describes the WAAF as a "vital part of the Royal Air Force," its personnel sharing in the men's trials and triumphs. In the film's stirring final declaration, "Airwoman, we salute you!," the WAAF is lauded and included but also clearly auxiliary to the work of military men, remaining firmly on the ground, never threatening to displace these heroic figures.

In this chapter I consider the representation of the military woman as auxiliary in terms of the rhetoric of support she provides the (male) institutions of the (male) military and the individual soldiers, sailors, and airmen. During the war period such rhetoric is central even when the narrative focuses almost exclusively on the training or work of military women. I also address the construction of military women in supporting roles, focusing in particular on a routine association with romance. In focusing on representations of the Second World War I explore in detail a historical moment associated with unprecedented levels of female military service in both the U.S. and the U.K. I deal directly with the peripheral status of the military woman as enacted on screen, exploring how she is addressed and constructed as war worker, as part of a romantic couple, as a figure who waits, and as one who works close to the field of battle. I consider the alternately, or even simultaneously, celebratory and trivializing or patronizing treatment of military women in recruitment and other film materials, detailing the ways the military woman functions as a contradictory sign of modernity (her public role, the iconicity of women in uniform, the potential for romantic and sexual encounters) and continuity (feminine service, ideologies of romance, military service as a temporary disruption of domesticity). As much as my analysis points to the visual and narrative work put into containing military women within a supportive or auxiliary role, so evident in *Airwoman* and numerous other instances of representations of the war, I also foreground the aspirational and glamorous connotations of this figure.

Consider in this context the controversial wartime satire *The Life and Death of Colonel Blimp* (1943), in which Deborah Kerr plays three women, each encountered by the protagonist at different stages of his life. One of her incarnations is Angela "Johnny" Cannon, a driver for the Mechanized Transport Corps. Questions of woman's place in relation to men, the home, and the nation during war pervade *Colonel Blimp*. In a film that stages the drama of a man (Blimp) who has been left behind by history, Kerr's three characters function as signs of both continuity and modernity: as a governess in Berlin in 1902 she is frustrated by the limits placed on middle-class women; as a nurse during the First World War she is dreamy rather than feisty; as a driver during the Second World War she is a masculinized and militarized modern woman.[6] Johnny is associated with technology and a novel female mobility: "I never drove before the war," she remarks. She is also plainly an auxiliary figure, supportive and caring for the sentimental, outmoded Blimp.

The Life and Death of Colonel Blimp suggests how much can be gleaned from a consideration of military women in such supporting roles; indeed both in cinema and on television military women are frequently found on the periphery rather than at the center of the narrative. A. L. Kennedy writes of the film that Johnny has "taken a male name and does a male job," suggesting a sort of transvestism.[7] Yet I believe this figure highlights not only the gender confusion that regularly accompanies the military woman (her implicit manliness), but also the extent to which she thematizes and embodies a powerful trope of *transformation*. Before the war, we learn, Johnny was a photographer's model, a spectacle of femininity; her movement from model to driver is nicely evocative of wartime mobility and of the transformative character attributed to military service. Moreover although Kerr plays Johnny with appropriate military bearing, she is also a vivid, lively figure, dodging furniture in a scuffle, employing exaggerated facial expressions and body language. Johnny signals female mobility at a number of levels: in her role as a militarized driver; in Kerr's lively performance; and in her construction as emblematic new woman (figure 7). *Colonel Blimp* is both deeply critical of the British class system and marked by a sense of profound loss at its seeming dissolution. Kerr's modern manifestation as military woman is equally ambivalent, simultaneously a figure of energy and vitality against Clive Candy's aging body and ideals and a cause for lament.[8] The war has transformed Johnny just as, the film implies, Britain must be transformed and modernized.

In addressing the various ways the military woman is imagined as auxiliary, this chapter lays the groundwork for the analysis presented in the book as a whole. The understanding of the military woman's role as auxiliary depends on her status as not male and not a soldier, an equation that has been challenged by subsequent demands for armed services that are more equal and effectively integrated but that remains very much in evidence. I address the conundrum of the military woman, the ways in which she poses a culturally troubling figure even when her service is called

7. In *The Life and Death of Colonel Blimp* (1943) Johnny (Deborah Kerr) incarnates the modern mobile woman.

for unequivocally. Unsurprisingly that problem of representation centers primarily on gender, but it also turns on other important categories of identity, most particularly class, but also national, regional, racial, and ethnic identity. The chapter begins with an exploration of the imagery and rhetoric of American and British recruitment campaigns directed toward women, analyzing the ways gendered discourses of respectability and duty frame appeals to self-interest and personal opportunity. I then explore themes of transformation through an analysis of films which describe the forging of disparate groups of women into soldiers. Finally I turn to themes of romance, exploring war films that center on a military woman's developing romance with a military man. Overall I aim to elucidate the ways representations of the Second World War figured the military woman in relation to gendered norms of appropriate femininity.

RESPECTABILITY, OPPORTUNITY, AND DUTY:
RECRUITING WOMEN IN THE SECOND WORLD WAR

Wartime recruitment materials framed an invitation to and inclusion of auxiliary military women in rather contradictory and intriguing terms. As forms of official discourse such recruitment materials provide insight into the emergence of an institutionalized and culturally acceptable place for military women. The rhetoric of the Second World War insistently emphasized that the enlistment of women would enable more male soldiers to serve as combatants, thus reinforcing the distance between the roles of male and female personnel. The invitation "Be a Marine: Free a Marine to Fight" typifies this strategy (figure 8). The poster effectively captures a scene of action and movement; under her marine-green cap, the woman's hair billows out behind her, giving the image dynamism even as the clipboard and pen she holds emphasize the clerical or administrative tasks undertaken by the female soldier. There is a significant distinction between a (military) woman becoming or being a Marine and the male Marines who are "freed" to fight through her work. The imagery and language of substitution and support were also widely used in the U.K. Such appeals clearly imply that women are a temporary and lesser substitute for men. Yet even a cursory look at recruitment materials addressed to women in the war period suggests that a more complex set of appeals is at work. True, recruitment materials appeal to duty and patriotism, but they also promise personal opportunities, speaking directly to the self-interest of potential recruits. While military life is by definition routine and subject to discipline, recruitment materials were not slow to pick up on the adventurous and even glamorous associations of service in the forces. A poster for the Women Appointed for Voluntary Emergency Service (WAVES) from July 1944 prominently features an urban skyline, suggesting a life involving female companionship, smart uniforms, and personal opportunity (figure 9). Such a presentation of service as a route to travel and excitement is indicative. Given the voluntary nature of women's service, recruitment appeals needed to manage the promise of worthwhile labor and opportunity with some care. (Even under conscription in the U.K. women could opt to work in industry.)

A fascinating insight in this regard is provided by a pamphlet published in 1943, "How to Enlist More Women in the U.S. Navy," designed to supplement the training of naval personnel involved in recruitment.[9] The pamphlet makes explicit use of civilian marketing techniques in the form of "selling psychology." It includes a summary of the benefits of naval service which the recruiter might offer to her "prospect." The first of these is, of course, serving her nation and contributing to the war effort. Next in line comes shared responsibility with men, involving an implicit invitation to full citizenship for women. Third is material benefits, and fourth opportunity. The fifth advantage relates again to public esteem: the new recruit will be both recognized and admired. Advantages six and seven

8. For military women, being a Marine means an auxiliary role. An iconography of freedom, service, and support inform this recruitment poster.

9. Recruitment posters frequently emphasized military service as providing women with opportunities for travel, professional training, and advancement, as well as patriotism and duty.

relate to personal development and appearance. Two final and provisional advantages are included, the italicized *may* indicating that these are only possibilities: the recruit "*may* receive valuable technical training" and "*may* be assigned to an exciting, thrilling job." Recruiters must clearly be careful not to *promise* excitement, but to offer it as a possibility.

Contradictory demands and cultural forces are clearly in play here, since many people believed that women's military service was simply inappropriate, in part due to the consequent mobility of young women who, away from their families, lived and worked in proximity to military men. (In contrast to military women, the sexual promiscuity of military men was, if not encouraged, at least sanctioned.) In this context Meyer traces the extensive internal conflicts over WAC recruitment campaigns, in which the director, Col. Oveta Hobby, argued consistently that "military service for women should not be portrayed as 'glamorous,' but rather as a 'selfless' act consistent with women's traditional patriotic duties."[10] Hobby's concerns seemed to stem from personal conviction and also, crucially, from a desire to establish the legitimacy of the WAC, an endeavor for which the patriotic motivation of young servicewomen was vital. By contrast, the advertisers who advised WAC recruiters insisted that "'duty' is not an effective advertising appeal." Meyer consequently reports an effective shift in late 1943 from Hobby's favored strategy of patriotism combined with guilt to a stress on "the attractive jobs and material advantages women gained joining the WAC."[11]

An explicit alignment between women's service and the nation is suggested in a short film produced in 1940 entitled *Britannia Is a Woman*. Sponsored by the British Council, produced by British Movietone News, and distributed in the U.S. by 20th Century Fox, *Britannia Is a Woman* provides an early instance of the themes and images that would become familiar features of representations of the war. As a mediation of the "war effort of British women" aimed at international audiences, the film focuses primarily on the (unpaid) work of the Women's Voluntary Service (WVS). However, the first section concerns women in the services, including images of ATS, Women's Royal Naval Service (WRNS, whose recruits were called Wrens), and WAAF personnel, segueing into the section detailing the work of the WVS serving the "demands of civil defence." Thus a kind of continuum is established, with military women at one end, uniformed women in various nursing and civil defense duties somewhere in the middle, and women performing voluntary labor at the other end. With both a national and an international audience in view the film is at pains to emphasize the patriotism, competence, and respectability of British military women who are seen marching, cooking, and typing. (Recall Meyer's contention, discussed in the introduction, that popular images of British military women proved influential in an American context, providing a reference point for the necessity and value of such service.)[12]

The film's (male-voiced) commentary underlines the extent to which the training and work of military women allow military men to perform more manly tasks: "This is the object of women's enrollment in the services: to enable more men to be spared for the sterner duties of war." It is in this context that women's supposed feminine frivolity is set aside for the duration; as ATS personnel fall in for drill we are informed that the "khaki uniform replaces the peacetime diversity of fashion," a comment that nonetheless functions to underline woman's function as spectacle: while falling in, these women are also, in effect, modeling the uniform for our approval. *Britannia Is a Woman* concludes its military section with a few brief images of women of the Air Transport Auxiliary.[13] These female ferry pilots are portrayed in an informal group; we see them standing beside their planes, smoking and laughing. They wear boots and greatcoats, but we also see them in full flight gear, ready for duty as the voice-over intones, "[This is] surely one of the most adventurous jobs which has so far fallen to the fair sex." Here the commentary touches on the possibility of a new role for military women; not only telephony and typing, cooking and cleaning, waiting and supporting, but more "adventurous" work associated with the command of machinery and suggesting the possibilities of movement.[14]

These images of women fliers, framed so explicitly in terms of adventure, are no isolated instance. The best-selling author and creator of the pilot-hero Biggles, Capt. W. E. Johns, created his WAAF pilot character Worrals in response to a direct request from the Air Ministry to aid recruitment of women to the service.[15] Yet young women joining the WAAF would have had almost no opportunity to fly in the manner of Worrals; instead their function was to serve alongside and support the "men who fly."[16] As Beryl E. Escott writes in her history of the wartime WAAF, its personnel "did not fly (except by luck, accident, or to carry out air checks)."[17] Both the girlish fictional figure of Worrals and the imagery of female ferry pilots celebrated in *Britannia Is a Woman* exploit the suggestion that women's military labors might open up nontraditional avenues. Part recruitment film, part propaganda geared to a United States as yet outside the war, *Britannia Is a Woman* celebrates the modernity of the British military woman, glossing over her exceptional status while exploiting her iconic function.

Aside from highlighting patriotism, economic benefits, and career opportunities, wartime recruitment materials directed at women drew on notions of personal fulfillment. There are opportunities for the individual woman to find or develop herself, whether through travel or acquiring new skills. This emphasis feeds the trope of transformation which is so central to wartime feature films centered on military women. Indeed opportunity and transformation are routinely harnessed together in recruitment films, which use editing and other visual strategies to suggest the positive transition from civilian to military life. Recruitment campaigns thus frequently seek to marry tropes of personal transformation to the themes of supportive female service outlined above.

Where recruitment posters focus on iconic images of women in uniform, the cinema is particularly suited to an evocation of transition and transformation, deploying dissolves and montage sequences within and alongside basic narrative scenarios (the preparations for battle, waiting, and return seen in *Airwoman*, for instance). To illustrate the point I'll refer to two recruitment films developed in 1943 for the SPARS, the women's branch of the U.S. Coast Guard, *Coast Guard Spars* and *Battle Stations*.[18] Both films explicitly endorse the military woman as noncombatant replacements for men. *Coast Guard Spars* outlines opportunities for travel through possible postings at a number of American cities, along with the chance to "release a man for the sea." Two sequences employ editing to enact the transformative character of women's military service. In the first of these we see massed women transformed in appearance; initially dressed in civilian clothes, the women turn to face the camera smiling, a wipe replacing the image with a shot of the group in uniform. Another wipe replaces this shot with one showing the SPARS recruits marching. The voice-over addresses the potential recruit directly, observing, "You learn to take orders and to carry them out," thus stressing teamwork and personal development. It is also made clear that pay begins during training, emphasizing the economic rewards of service. Over the elaborate, even elegant drill that follows comes a further endorsement of military life as a route to personal fulfillment: "You acquire new vigor, new confidence. You learn to march with others and to work with others." The language, dynamic montage, and dynamic movement combine to suggest the *active* nature of service.

The second evocative image of transformation featured in this recruitment film enacts the trained SPARS personnel replacing men. From a rack holding many Guardsmen's caps a man selects one; a dissolve now shows a woman stowing her cap among those of other SPARS personnel. Female caps replace male caps and women replace men, effectively visualizing the men's militarized mobility. Detailing the jobs a SPARS recruit might take on and the training she might receive, the film speculates on her enhanced employability in the postwar workplace (again suggesting personal progression and economic opportunity). The camera closes in tantalizingly on a door marked "Office of the Commandant"; as the image dissolves to a man seated at a desk, a woman at his side, the promise of advancement is both offered and strictly contained: "You won't get to be an admiral, but you may be the admiral's secretary." This endorsement of a traditional female role as a new opportunity, presented with no discernible irony, suggests a need for reassurance as to the continuing validity of gender norms.

Battle Stations, produced by the Office of Strategic Services, maintains the gendered divide established in *Coast Guard Spars*. In addition to its official, anonymous male voice-over, the film enlists the services of the Hollywood stars Ginger Rogers and James Cagney to speak the parts of a SPARS recruit and a Guardsman. Cagney and Rogers are thus simultaneously extraordinary and ordinary figures, bringing the glamour of celebrity to the work of servicemen and servicewomen. A combination of stock footage, editing, and voice-over constructs a dramatic narrative in which an enemy submarine is defeated by a combination of grounded military women and mobile—in this instance, seafaring—military men. Following the action, the message of separate but equally important contributions and spheres of action is made explicit through dialogue in which Cagney's Guardsman praises teamwork. The film's final sequence shows a SPARS recruit running to convey orders to the pilot of an amphibious airplane. While Cagney's voice-over gives his personal dedication, she watches the plane's departure, her arm raised and eyes lifted up in an iconic pose of the war. Such an image of the grounded woman watching the skies also concludes *Airwoman*, underlining the auxiliary, supportive function of the military woman.

Perhaps the key visual element used to portray the transition to military service as transformative is the uniform. As Antonia Lant writes, "The potential for glamour and self-confidence associated with a uniform lent itself . . . readily to screen spectacle."[19] The uniform marks the military woman as a professional figure, potentially erasing other differences between women and allowing mixing across previously clear class (though not racial) boundaries. The glamorous associations of uniformed service are nicely summarized (and punctured) in a short sequence of the extremely popular British film *Millions Like Us* (1943). Having received her call-up, Celia fancifully imagines herself as, successively, a WAAF, a Wren, an ATS recruit, a land girl, and a nurse; in each role she appears to herself as elegant and sophisticated, though the film implies that she is slightly ridiculous, as she fawns at the attentive men who accompany her in these imaginary scenarios. The interview that follows is a disappointment; since she cannot type and does not wish to cook, the WAAF has no openings. The WRNS and the ATS too want only cooks, so Celia reluctantly opts for work in a factory. In a film that stresses ordinary, everyday commitment and sacrifice on the part of British men and women, Celia's sexualized fantasies of uniformed service as a shortcut to romance and adventure are gently mocked. Moreover the shortfall between the glamorous promises of recruitment posters and the role of typist or cook that the services actually offered women speaks to a cynicism born of experience. Designed to boost recruitment for industrial workers, *Millions Like Us* exploits that shortfall, pointing out that the WRNS and the WAAF are no more fertile grounds for female advancement than civilian service. *Millions Like Us* effectively debunks the recruitment imagery used in posters directed at wartime British women, but this gentle debunking is double-edged; it acknowledges the contrast between recruitment appeals and the reality of military service for women, but it also aligns Celia's fanciful daydreaming with, and thereby ridicules, a sexual confidence which military women had already come to signify. Bringing Celia back to earth is also about putting her back in her place.

One poster in particular is frequently cited as exemplifying the contested meaning of images of female military service. This is the ATS poster dubbed by the press "the Blonde Bombshell." Designed by Abram Games in 1941, it was withdrawn by the War Office after debate in Parliament condemned it for its undue glamour (figure 10). To Lant this decision "suggests the War Office's (understandable) lack of faith in glamorized images of women for speaking to real women of national need. The risk that a female audience would not recognize itself in this imagery—that it would remain a fantastic, unattainable femininity—was indeed too great."[20] And yet it was *politicians* who objected most vocally to the image, and implicitly to the self-confident, modern sexuality it represented. This much is acknowledged in a contemporary cartoon featuring a spoof recruitment poster for the ATS, depicting a large, distinctly unglamorous (even mannish) woman. The cartoon lampoons both bureaucracy and the stuffiness of politicians with regard to the withdrawal of "the Blonde Bombshell." Its caption reads, "After long and careful consideration this new ATS-recruiting poster has been accepted ('That's the stuff . . .'—comment by Woman M.P.)."[21] That it is a female member of Parliament who voices a critique of female glamour is doubly damning: the joke plays on an assumption that of course such a woman, herself seeking an inappropriate position of power and authority, would appreciate the mannish caricature on display. Ironically the intent behind Games's poster was precisely to *contest* the dour public image that had become associated with the ATS. The woman in the withdrawn poster sports a new-style cap specifically designed to "dispel the dowdy image" of the service. Catherine Moriarty comments on the approved poster that served as a replacement: "Lacking the sexuality of Games' design, it was felt to attract 'the right sort,' something Games' recruit, exhibiting worrying independence and self-assurance clearly was not."[22]

The controversy over "the Blonde Bombshell" indicates just how contested the image of the military woman was in the war period. The volatility of the military woman as a sign of modernity associated with an unregulated female sexuality functioned as a site of cultural disruption. Attracting "the right sort" of woman to military service involved recruiters in a complex cultural exercise, in which they emphasized the importance of duty as well as the respectability and excitement of military life in differing degrees. It is thus no surprise that posters, recruitment films, and indeed those narrative feature films that center on military women in the war period so explicitly countered widely circulated myths and rumors concerning the effectiveness, femininity, and morality of military women. With respect to their *effectiveness*, recruitment materials routinely emphasized the equal importance of women's role in relation to men's, noting for instance that they would be serving *alongside* men in furthering important national goals. The implicit equality of such appeals

10. Appeals to glamour were contentious in a British context. Abram Games's "Blonde Bombshell" poster (1941), designed to boost recruitment to the ATS, notoriously fell foul of Parliament.

effectively serves to address women as full citizens, notwithstanding their status as temporary replacements for men. An extension of such professional equality forms an explicit part of other wartime recruitment materials which emphasize the perks, benefits, good salary, and training opportunities as well as the chance to serve one's country and assist male loved ones. Thus we are told that WAVES will earn the same as regular Navy men,[23] or that the Army and Navy offer a number of different job roles and training opportunities for women.

Turning to cultural preconceptions regarding the *femininity* and *morality* of military women, the mobility and opportunities emphasized in some representations of the war read somewhat differently. Traditionalists clearly regarded both the femininity and the morality of military women to be potentially compromised by their labor, mobility, and proximity to men. Maintaining the respectability of the female soldier against assumptions of (hetero)sexual promiscuity or lesbianism was an ongoing concern for the British ATS and the American WAC.[24] The ATS formed the "prime target for allegations of immorality in the women's services which swept Britain during the first two years of the war."[25] Meyer details a comparable slander campaign, ultimately traced to male servicemen, in relation to the WAC.[26] Both services battled with a problematic public image characterized by a combination of condescension and moral condemnation. Although military women might be admired for their patriotism, suggestive comments pervaded popular discourse, whether in relation to an assumed excessive femininity that rendered them unsuitable for the job, an excessive sexual interest in men that posed a danger for male soldiers (the vamp who spreads venereal disease), or a mannish persona that made their presence in an all-female context suspicious (lesbian). In the aftermath of Oveta Hobby's first press conference as director of the WAAC, John Costello observes a media "unable or unwilling to resist the temptation to run pictures under captions labelled 'Whackies,' 'Powder Magazines,' and 'Fort Lipstick.'" One columnist, he writes, "compared the WAACS with 'the naked Amazons . . . and the queer damozels of the Isle of Lesbos.'"[27] Here the implication of sexual impropriety, excessive femininity, and incompetence are effectively collapsed together. Such salacious coverage provides the context for a WAC poster featuring a smiling silver-haired mother figure standing between her equally beaming uniformed son and daughter (figure 11). In the figure of a mother who equally endorses the service of both her children, the poster speaks to a normalizing of military service for young, white American women.[28]

Though supporters of the WAC constructed female soldiers precisely in these terms of patriotism and duty, those who sought to denigrate the service saw Army women in terms of deviance from gender norms (mannishness), a deviance also linked by rumor to inappropriate sexuality, whether heterosexual activity or lesbianism. The perceived need to maintain the femininity of female soldiers is a persistent feature of the discourses surrounding military women; it is also evident in internal debates over the styling of uniforms, the moral regulation of behavior, and the appropriate development of physical strength.[29] One of the questions a reluctant civilian is envisaged as posing to her recruiter in the pamphlet "How to Enlist More Women in the U.S. Navy" has to do with physical demands: "Is the training strenuous?" The answer suggested is indicative: "Not at all. You keep healthy and fit with moderate exercise." Not only that, but boot camp, the recruit is promised, "will make [her] feel like a

11. The implication of an equivalence between male and female service is coupled with the need to legitimate the military woman, who was often taken as a sign of unwanted modernity.

million." The Navy, she is reassured, "doesn't believe in rigorous athletics": "We don't want our WAVES to be 'amazons.'" As this language makes clear, the Navy wanted neither combatants nor lesbians. The Army, as Meyer reports, aimed to screen out women whose behavior "suggested sexual deviance."[30] Elsewhere in the Navy pamphlet the recruiter is advised to emphasize to the recruit and her parents that members of the WAVES will "lead a normal, religious life." Toward the end one of an inventory of questions designed to test the recruiter on her skills asks, "Do I and other WAVES in my office attend church regularly and show interest in religious organizations?" A little farther down the list, however, we find a rather different question: "Do I see that the WAVES in our office are seen with attractive men occasionally?" Thus not only is it important to insist on the respectability of naval service, but strategically recruiters must also allow for the opportunity to meet attractive men (occasionally) and the need to insist that WAVES are still women attractive *to* and attracted *by* men. In addressing objections from hypothetical parents, men (whether in uniform or out of it), and the individual herself, the recruiter's pamphlet makes explicit just how extensive objections to women's military service were in the U.S. during the war.

In such a context it is not surprising that discernable hierarchies emerged in the war period, effectively distinguishing between approved and culturally acceptable images of the military woman and alternative or disreputable images. Such distinctions were by no means fixed, as the instance of "the Blonde Bombshell" demonstrates; in that attempt to feminize the ATS some believed that the image of blonde glamour carried troubling overtones of sexual freedom, rendering the image disreputable. Distinctions between the services also played a part in regulating military women as appropriately feminine national subjects. That it was the ATS rather than the WRNS that needed a makeover is significant in this context. In both Britain and the United States service in the Navy was widely perceived (and indeed operated) as select; entry requirements were higher, numbers admitted smaller.[31] ATS Joan Stewart's comments point to the class dimensions of the hierarchy between the services in Britain: "People, even soldier friends, begged me not to join, to consider the WRNS or the WAAF. The ATS certainly had a very bad press at the time, though I'm blessed if I know why, unless it was that there were more jobs of a lowly nature to be done."[32] The working-class associations of the ATS ("jobs of a lowly nature") compared to the WRNS are also clear in another ATS servicewoman's comment on Princess Elizabeth's decision to join the service: "I was absolutely staggered because we had all taken it for granted that she would go into the Navy as a Wren."[33] Indeed it seems clear that the unimpeachable class and gender status of the future monarch was effectively deployed to shore up the respectability of the ATS and to signal the hands-on involvement of the ruling elite in the war.

Race figures alongside class to moderate the respectable or disreputable femininity of the military woman. It may be that, as Meyer speculates, the elite status of the WAVES was underlined by not only the higher entrance requirements than for the WAC, but the fact that for most of the war it was an all-white force. (It was not until December 1944 that African American women were permitted to join the WAVES, and then in response to a direct presidential order.)[34] This is not to imply that the WAC was particularly welcoming to African American women; as both Brenda L. Moore and Meyer document, its policies with respect to the maintenance of segregation and the allocation of duties reflected and were structured by the racism of the wider military culture.

Personnel shortages prompted initially reluctant civil and military authorities to back an accelerated recruitment of military women throughout the war period, yet the service of African American women in the U.S. military and black West Indian women in the U.K. seemingly represented an immovable problem of representation. At times the service of such women was actively discouraged. Meyer reports the difficulties faced by African American women seeking to enlist.[35] In a British context, Delia Jarrett-Macauley notes that for a War Office happy to recruit white West Indians, the recruitment of black women was a highly contested question; only the ATS accepted black colonial women.[36] Ben Bousquet and Colin Douglas recount that the thirty black West Indian women who traveled to Britain to serve in the ATS in 1943 were admitted to service only following a lengthy period of wrangling between the War Office, which was resolutely opposed to their presence, and the Colonial Office, which was keen to avoid the political consequences of such overt racial discrimination.[37] Particularly relevant for this study is Jarrett-Macauley's emphasis on the extent to which white authorities may have understood the issue as one of visibility: "Colonial subjects had played a significant role in the economic development of Britain and were educated to view England as their country. However, attempts to bring them *into view* alongside white British women or their white peers from the dominions went against the long-held colour bar which placed black people at the bottom of the social pile" (emphasis added).[38] Black and Asian colonial women were recruited into separate local units, such as the Women's Royal Indian Naval Service, formed in 1944; although their labor was required, visualizing these women, or acknowledging their service, was a different matter. Though photographs of the West Indian ATS women were published in the *Picture Post* on their arrival in the U.K., the women do not appear in films of the period.[39] This problem of visibility highlights the ways in which discourses of class and race were used to shore up the supposedly problematic femininity of the military woman, with military leaders drawing on presumptions of the "respectability" of white, middle-class women in defining the "right sort" of recruit.[40] Moreover it has a direct impact on the films considered in this chapter, whether produced in the war period or subsequently. Whatever the actual policies of different services with respect to segregation and recruitment of black women, the military women represented in the narratives of the Second World War discussed in the remainder of this chapter are all white.

Despite her new visibility, the white military woman is in many senses a disruptive figure in wartime culture, requiring regulation. She is not only a working woman, but a woman who works in a sphere of action traditionally reserved for men. Even though her supportive role is repeatedly emphasized in recruitment materials and fictional narratives, representations of the military women stepped into an arena marked as both distinctly *female* and yet *unfeminine*, if not implicitly masculine. Moreover it is apparent that questions of class and race play a key part in securing the potentially compromised femininity of the military woman. In the remainder of this chapter I explore the different ways feature films of the period negotiate these contradictions using themes of comradeship, duty, transformation, and romance.

TRANSFORMATION THROUGH SERVICE:
FEMININITY, COMRADESHIP, AND THE FEMALE
SOLDIER IN CINEMA OF THE SECOND WORLD WAR

Biographical accounts of women's military service during the Second World War confirm the importance of those elements foregrounded in recruitment materials: teamwork, pride and professionalism, the opportunity to undertake work previously off-limits to women, and the chance (for some at least) to travel and to function independently from the restrictions experienced at home.[41] Such positive perspectives certainly find expression in war films centered on military women; recurrent elements include the formation of friendships, a sense of pride in belonging, and the development of independence, self-worth, and professional skills. Yet as we've seen, the military woman is also a potentially disruptive figure in wartime culture, and this too is evident in feature films. This section explores how two films, one British (*The Gentle Sex*, 1943) and one American (*Keep Your Powder Dry*, 1945), dramatize the themes of contemporary recruitment campaigns, championing military women as both capable and respectable.[42] Both films deal with the integration of civilian women into military life and the transformative potential of military service for women.

Given its support from both the War Office and the ATS and its stated goal of boosting recruitment for the latter, it is not surprising that *The Gentle Sex* stages so many of the tropes of contemporary recruitment materials.⁴³ The film follows seven recruits drawn from different class, national, and regional backgrounds, demonstrating their ability to overcome conflict and work together as a team. A considerable box-office success in Britain, particularly with women, *The Gentle Sex* was welcomed by critics as both "a well-deserved tribute" and "good entertainment."⁴⁴ *The Star*'s reviewer observed, "Whenever in future I pass any member of the ATS I shall feel inclined to raise my hat respectfully."⁴⁵ The trade press too celebrated *The Gentle Sex* as a testament to British womanhood, describing the film as "a true picture of our women at war" and "a fine and timely tribute to the women of Britain."⁴⁶ Such responses point to the film's success in documenting and celebrating the work of the ATS. In a fashion similar to the recruitment campaigns it sought to bolster, the film is a tribute, but it is also an assertion directed at those skeptical of the capability of military women and their value to the British war effort. Thus to Lant the film seems "above all ... to want to speak to men."⁴⁷ To this end it is characterized by a peculiar double address. On one hand *The Gentle Sex* speaks directly to an important domestic female audience, championing the work of the ATS and the strength of women in time of war. Women are shown working in two of the most unfamiliar or nontraditional roles, as drivers and performing anti-aircraft duties. On the other hand the film raises and then counters assumptions of women's limited potential. Central here is the director Leslie Howard's peculiarly patronizing and at times intrusive commentary, which is heard throughout the film.

From their initial cramped encounter in a railway carriage, the seven women who represent the "gentle sex" bond, battle, and adapt themselves to military life. Despite the suspicions wartime culture might have attached to a young woman's desire to join the military, both *The Gentle Sex* and *Keep Your Powder Dry* emphasize the value of female comradeship. Feature films of this period visualize female collaboration and comradeship in two ways. First, the togetherness of military women is portrayed in off-duty scenes where they relax and socialize together, either within the private space of the barracks or in more public social spaces (even bars on occasion). Second, scenes in which military women march and work together underline their shared participation in military life and culture. Both recruitment and feature films regularly deploy scenes of women drilling; such images emphasize women's newly acquired military identity and their capacity to work effectively together. One former ATS recruit recalls her pleasure in the coordinated movement: "It felt good

12. Members of the ATS serve as spotters in the climactic scenes of *The Gentle Sex* (1943).

to move as one body, each pair of feet doing exactly the same."[48] Drilling serves to foreground unity rather than difference, just as the uniform (potentially at least) serves to erase class differences. In this regard, drilling epitomizes the logic of basic training, which "demands a suppression of individual difference and exacts conformity in all outward actions and dress."[49] *The Gentle Sex* makes use of both these strategies for showcasing female comradeship, concluding with sequences of professionalized teamwork and shared leisure. We see women working as part of a mixed battery unit, demonstrating their capability under fire during an air raid (figure 12). Following the excitement and tension of combat the film closes with more mundane images of service and companionship, as men and women eat bread and drink mugs of tea in a field, the original group of seven reunited. The easy realist style of these sequences serves the film's attempt to normalize as well as celebrate women's military service. In line with recruitment goals, such imagery underscores the vital nature of women's service while simultaneously foregrounding the pleasures of comradeship.

While the military requires the conformity represented by uniforms and drills, narrative development typically requires conflict and the play of differences. Thus conflict between women forms an important strand within both movies. In *The Gentle Sex*, Joan is both brusque and ambitious; she rejects the sentimentality of the female companion who sees her off at the train station and is consistently unfriendly toward the other women, exercising petty tyranny once promoted to corporal. At one point she even expresses admiration for Nazi efficiency, producing a scathing and impassioned response from Erna, whose direct experience of fascism has shaped her bitterness and desire for revenge. Ultimately, however, Joan acknowledges her underlying shyness and is admitted into the group, demonstrating teamwork triumphing over individual rivalries. Conflict structures *Keep Your Powder Dry* much more centrally and explicitly; Val Parks (Lana Turner) and Leigh Rand (Larraine Day) take an instant dislike to each other, and their bitter personal feud drives the narrative forward. The two are united, however, in their affection for fellow recruit Ann Darrison and ultimately agree to overcome their differences as a result. The film ends with the three confidently marching together, ready to ship out.

The portrayal of conflict within the group clearly feeds off negative stereotypes which suggest that women are not able to productively work together. At the same time the films draw on what Jeanine Basinger identifies as a basic and highly flexible dynamic of the combat films of the Second World War: a competitive, adversarial relationship between two characters whose "conflict becomes representative of a differing attitude toward combat, toward politics, toward life—whatever."[50] While recruitment rhetoric and uplifting montage sequences might celebrate the military unit, narrative traces the movement toward that unity, turning the processes by which a team is formed into drama. Thus both *The Gentle Sex* and *Keep Your Powder Dry* use the metaphor of a journey, featuring train stations as points of departure or arrival. Such a scene forms the opening sequence of *The Gentle Sex*, as the women bid farewell to their loved ones and embark on a new adventure. As if he were both a recruiter identifying prospects and a somewhat leering male observer, the director's voice-over picks out and comments on the seven women whose lives are "about to be turned upside down" and whose stories the film will tell: Betty and her overprotective mother; the colonel's daughter Anne; thrifty Scot Maggie; Dot, who bids goodbye to her shady boyfriend, talking of her need for a change; Erna, a Czech refugee motivated by hatred; and the seemingly unfeeling Joan, a former dancing teacher who, we are told, looks "pretty hard to please" (and is thus, in the film's terms, failing in femininity). The late arrival of the working-class, Cockney waitress Gwen completes the group. The first meeting of the three female leads in *Keep*

Your Powder Dry—the spoiled heiress Val, the Army brat Leigh, and the military wife Ann—similarly takes place on the station platform, where they assess each other and await instructions. Both groups are visually and narratively in transit, moving from civilian life and preoccupations to a military identity that will define them in new ways.

A narrative trajectory of self-discovery and personal transformation, allied to a realization of the primacy of the group, serves as a defining convention of the war movie during this period. Thus the class, ethnic, and regional diversity of the women in *The Gentle Sex*, the different backgrounds (though all are white and middle class) of the trio in *Keep Your Powder Dry*, and the antagonism between individuals in both films are set up in order to be transcended, as the women learn to work together and to sublimate their own desires and emotions to the needs of service. Transformation is evoked by the replacement of civilian clothing with military uniforms (in the manner of contemporary recruitment films, such as *Coast Guard Spars*). Both films show the women being equipped and trained. In *The Gentle Sex* they are also assigned to and seen undertaking their duties, both the mundane and familiar and those more removed from their civilian roles. The importance of their work to the war effort is emphasized, as is the active participation of women from all walks of life. Gwen's dissatisfaction with her initial assignment as a mess orderly (she was a waitress in civilian life and wants to escape this service role) is played for comic effect, but she nonetheless succeeds in qualifying as a telephone operator and joins the other women at a mixed battery unit, suggesting mobility and opportunity.

The Gentle Sex explicitly compares the opportunities and challenges facing the modern woman of the early 1940s with the limited and highly demarcated lives of an earlier generation of middle-class women. Over a sequence showing ATS drivers being transported back to barracks in the cargo area of a train, making their beds as best they can, Leslie Howard's voice-over addresses the audience directly in these terms: "Do you realize, my friend, that before the battle of Waterloo, the officers' ladies put on pretty evening dresses and had a ball? That's as near as they ever got to the war. The soldiers' girls couldn't even get as near as that. Now it looks to me as if without the women we shouldn't carry on at all." It is the film's project to both insist on and qualify the nation's dependence on female labor. As Lant explores in some detail, the ironic evocation and rejection of a nineteenth-century femininity (envisaged as archaic) in the embroidery sampler–style graphics of the credit sequence speaks to a context of profound uncertainty relating to women's new social role. Thus the first frame reads, "1838. The Gentle Sex. In whatever station in life a woman is placed, a spirit of modesty, humility, obedience and submission will always be required of her," to be replaced by a new image which frames the film itself as concerned with "the gentle sex" from "1938 onwards." The war is clearly the marker of a new phase in British women's lives. Nonetheless the words of the final mock embroidery frame of the credit sequence are "Woman, when I behold thee flippant, vain, inconstant, childish, proud and full of fancies." It is in many ways the project of the film to challenge such views, to tackle what Lant describes as "the powerful notion of femininity as incompatible with cohesion, rationality, and public dependability."[51] And yet Howard's words, not only presented graphically but heard in his distinctive voice-over, seem to simultaneously reiterate this now outdated view of femininity. Indeed Lant suggests that the film as a whole is engaged in spanning that contradictory evocation of embroidery and Victorian ideals of (middle-class) womanhood with the modern military woman who works with weapons and machines. In the process, an insistence on continuing femininity effaces class differences between the women. (Working-class women had a rather different relationship to paid labor, after all.)[52] We might recall here the images of female ferry pilots in *Britannia Is a Woman*. The commentary ("surely one of the most adventurous jobs which has so far fallen to the fair sex") is absolutely characteristic of a rhetorical move surrounding military women in a range of wartime materials. The suggestion of innovation and agency is accompanied by an archaic use of visual and verbal language in relation to women and femininity, not simply terms like *girl* to describe young women—that was after all common usage at the time—but references to the *fair* or *gentle sex*, for instance. The rhetoric of recruitment emphasized the positive features of a modern world in which women were free to undertake work associated with men and male privilege. At the same time, however, the culture of the period strongly suggests that change was felt and figured as disconcerting, necessitating a reassuring glance backward in history.

Effectively *The Gentle Sex* presents as a problem not the capabilities of military women but the attitudes of civilian and military men; at the same time it voices what were widespread concerns about the consolidation of women's position within the services. In one of the film's most interesting sequences with respect to its assertion of necessary social change, the complacent assumptions of two of the ATS recruits (Anne and Maggie) are challenged as they learn of the war work undertaken by a previous generation of women. Visiting Mrs. Sheridan, the mother of her lover, Anne confidently asserts, "Probably for the first time in English history, women are fighting side by side with the men." Mrs. Sheridan subsequently reveals that she had met her pilot husband during the First World War and that she had been wounded while working as an ambulance driver. The sequence draws out the cultural invisibility of women's prior wartime work and a new generation of women seemingly complicit in this invisibility. The scene also presents British women's service in the Second World War as significantly different from that of women in the First, with the older woman endorsing the importance of a postwar change in the opportunities available to women. Of her own generation's experience Mrs. Sheridan remarks, "We didn't really know what we wanted, but I believe you do, and I believe you'll get it." In this way the war work of an earlier generation is recognized, and an argument about the importance of longer term changes is also advanced. The transformation of women because of their military service suggests a changed place for women in a putative postwar society.

Such generational contrasts are also interestingly foregrounded in *Women on the March*, a recruitment film produced in 1942 for the Australian Women's Army Service. In addition to the usual direct-address documentary techniques, the film features a framing device involving a conversation between two women. One is already in the AWAS; the other, Lois, is about to join but is apprehensive about military life. The older hand talks the new recruit through the process, praising the uniform, the "open-air life," the value of camaraderie, and the importance of the work. A picture of Lois's great-grandmother as a young woman leads to reflections on the different roles that modern women take on in time of war. "The women in those days were so helpless," comments Lois, as we cut to a shot of her earlier incarnation, pictured looking down on the parade ground where men in period uniforms drill. "When Grandpa marched off to war all she could do was knit. I wonder how Grandma would feel if she could see the barracks square today?" The camera pans from the Victorian figure on the balcony to the sight of women drilling below, a scene presented as both vital and modern. At the close of the film Lois has set her doubts aside and embraced the opportunity to "do a man's job." The photo of her grandmother, adorned in the fashions of a decorative femi-

ninity, dissolves into an image of the younger woman in uniform, marching one among many.[53] In this contrast the new mobility of women is
invoked as a benefit of wartime service, substituting the image of a feminized woman spectator with a military woman drilling, taking up her role
on a public stage.

Simultaneously looking forward and backward in this manner allows
wartime imagery to effectively manage cultural anxieties about the pace
of change. As we've seen, much anxiety centered on the perception of a
potential for immorality associated with military women's mobility. While
The Gentle Sex is largely concerned with demonstrating military women's
capability, *Keep Your Powder Dry* seems more preoccupied with picturing
women's service as not only respectable but healthy and moral. Thus the
film condenses its acknowledgment of skeptical men to a single sequence
in which the recruits fix an incredulous general's new car. "Amazing—and
such pretty girls too," he blusters to the WAC colonel. Instead the film's
energies are devoted to portraying the military as a site in which women's
bodies and behaviors can be appropriately regulated. To this end it carefully mediates the seeming discrepancy between the female body (feminine, allied with glamour and sensuality) and the military body (disciplined, but potentially masculine or mannish).

Val Parks is introduced in the opening sequence of *Keep Your Powder
Dry* in a tracking shot that reveals discarded items of clothing (shoes,
luxurious lingerie), halting on Lana Turner's tousled blonde hair. Hung
over, Val recoils at her own image in the mirror, hinting at her subsequent
rejection of a decadent (uncontrolled) femininity in favor of regulated
military life. We learn that she cannot take possession of a substantial
legacy until all the trustees are satisfied that she "is conducting herself
in a manner typical of the finest traditions of American womanhood."
Urged to set aside her playgirl lifestyle, Val determines to join the WAC
as a testament to her good character, declaring, "Whatever I have to do
to get this money, I'll do it." Thus equipped with a selfish, financial motivation for service, Val is set up as a character in need of transformation. After a brief scene introducing the virtuous Ann Darrison and her
husband (both about to depart for war), we meet the self-defined "Army
brat," Leigh Rand. Her father the general pronounces his view that she
will be "the all-fired best soldier to ever wear a skirt," then adds a quiet
warning that she should not try to run things. Leigh does not heed the
warning, and her evident enthusiasm for rules and regulations quickly

alienates her from her fellow recruits. Leigh, like Val, emerges as a character with much to learn. On the first night she challenges Val, sneering, "I don't think you'll ever survive basic training," thus providing Val with an additional (though no less self-centered) motivation to stick it out. Ultimately Leigh will learn that leadership must be earned, and Val that duty is more important than personal quarrels or concerns. (Having convinced the trustees of her respectability, she no longer wishes to lead the glamorous life she had sought to fund.)

Lant characterizes the British experience in terms of a "deglamorization of the national heroine" in the context of wartime hardship, reading British realism as explicitly defined against the Hollywood glamour of the sort embodied by Lana Turner in *Keep Your Powder Dry*. British films "worked to redefine femininity," she writes, "but they had, by their very focus, to dramatize its concurrent disintegration" as women engaged in forms of labor associated with men, machinery, and modernity.[54] While traditionally feminine glamour might well be at odds with women's labors (and their mobility) in the war period, as we have seen, military service and specifically the uniform are frequently represented as glamorous.[55] With Val's glamorous public femininity juxtaposed to Leigh's militarized tomboy status, the conflict between the two women is thoroughly gendered, enacted in terms of an opposition between feminine glamour and military masculinity. However, although she is defined by her seemingly inappropriate (even decadent) femininity, Val takes to military life almost immediately, excelling in basic training. She is capable of being both a good soldier and a desirable woman, while Army life (and Army clothes) endow her with respectability.

As discussed earlier, gendered discourses of behavior and respectability played an important part in the management of military women's sexuality in the war period. It is not surprising, then, that in wartime cinema, and indeed popular culture of the period more widely, physical appearance and clothing (just as much as behavior) became established as important mechanisms for visualizing and working through the problematic femininity of the military woman (problematic because, while femininity remained central to contemporary definitions of womanhood, the values associated with it were widely perceived as incompatible with military service). In different ways *The Gentle Sex* and *Keep Your Powder Dry* demonstrate the subjection of women to the masculine regimes of military discipline while assuring audiences of their continued femininity. Thus as civilian women are transformed before our eyes into military women—through generic scenes of kitting out, mess halls, drilling, and sports—that process is also regulated by the deployment of assumptions to do with femininity.

Val's redemption comes through a confrontation with her dissolute former friends and a realization that she has developed a new sense of purpose and commitment in the Army. In a scuffle her uniform is torn; knowing that her appearance is a sign of impropriety, Val persuades Leigh to cover for her, convincing her enemy of her sincerity with the plea "Being a WAC means more to me than anything." The torn uniform symbolizes the intrusion of Val's former life onto her newly regulated existence. Her aspirations to a glamorous, pleasure-seeking life are firmly rejected in favor of military comradeship. Yet the film does not set aside Val's (or Lana Turner's) desirability. Ironically it is Leigh herself who resurrects it in an anguished speech to Ann which reveals the complexity of her feelings (jealousy, desire) toward her rival: "From the first time I ever saw her, she was everything I wanted to be—all my life. A girl in high heels and furs; a girl who knew her power as a woman; the kind of girl who lived in the pages of *Vogue* and *Town and Country*, not in an army camp in boots and breeches. I just couldn't bear to see a girl from her world make good in mine." A point-of-view shot makes us privy to Leigh's first glimpse of Val: a shot of her legs as she adjusts an unmilitary shoe before stepping off the train. Conflict follows almost immediately. In the jostling initiated by Leigh (eager to impress the approaching colonel, she encourages the women to form a line) the heel of Val's shoe is snapped off; Leigh apologizes, qualifying the gesture by adding, "But, after all, we were told to wear low-heeled shoes." In this way Leigh attempts to use her conformity to regulations—sensible footwear—against Val's "high heels and furs." Although she is by no means mannish, when set against Val, Leigh appears masculine. (Gender is, after all, defined in relational terms.) And while *Keep Your Powder Dry* is concerned to valorize the transformation of civilian women into military women, the mixture of desire, envy, and contempt with which Leigh views Val's glamorous femininity underlines her own deviant (military and masculine) gender status. As such moments remind us, the indeterminacy of gender identity is repeatedly at issue in narratives showcasing military women.

Lant suggests that it is possible to regard *The Gentle Sex* as "a variant of the cross-dressing genre, that is, of films that probe the rigidity or

flexibility of gender identity by detaching gender signifiers from the expected biological sex."[56] Though Lant's point has clear rhetorical power,
I am reluctant to construe cinematic military women as cross-dressers,
for reasons including the long history of the term in a military context
and the continued relevance of gender as a question in relation to military women.[57] As Pat Kirkham reminds us, while "the wearing of military
uniform by women . . . represented a 'masculinisation' of female dress,"
it nevertheless "remained female dress."[58] Yet Lant is certainly right to
identify the uncertainties about gender and sexual identity that are associated with military women during the Second World War. Given that
the desire to join the services potentially rendered a woman suspicious
(as mannish or potentially lesbian), and the fact that military women
were not regarded by many (even their supporters) as real soldiers, it is
understandable how charged questions such as women's uniform became
and have remained. Writing of more recent negotiations on the style of
women's service attire, Enloe summarizes the contradictory forces at
work: "Women in the military must not be mistaken in public for soldiering men. Neither, however, should women in military uniforms be mistaken for bar waitresses or flight attendants. Women soldiers must look
like representatives of the state's military. Women soldiers must be attired
in a matter that enables them to do their job effectively for that military.
This four-side fashion mantra has not been easy to satisfy."[59]

Scenes of women receiving their uniforms and equipment, foregrounding clothes and the body, are a core element of recruitment films
and also feature prominently in many fictional narratives concerning
military women. Sometimes the process is described at length, as in *The
Gentle Sex*, while in other films it may simply be suggested in montage
sequences juxtaposing women in civilian clothes and military uniform.
Along with barrack room sequences, such scenes show military women
in between their two identities, as well as offering the opportunity for
glimpses of women in states of partial undress. Writing on *The Gentle Sex*,
Lant draws our attention to the film's frequent scenes of dressing, groom-
ing, and mirrors—"shots show women squeezing in and out of skirts,
practicing hat angles, and checking the effects in mirrors"—suggesting
that the film "needs to assert over and over again the presence of a female
body beneath the uniform."[60] It could equally be asserted that the repetition of this imagery enacts the containment of the troublesome female
body by the military uniform and the masculine authority it represents. In

either view such imagery points to the perceived contradiction, embodied by military women, between an "unruly" femininity and an orderly yet gender-inappropriate (masculine) service.

A preoccupation with appearance and reflection is, in this context, not surprising. Military women are frequently depicted viewing their reflection in the mirror, an image that suggests female narcissism and a process of transformation in equal measure; the uniformed woman posed before a mirror offers a potent evocation of duty coupled with pleasure. The trope appears in recruitment and feature films, in war and postwar imagery. In *Airwoman* both uniforms and the mirror device feature prominently in the opening sequence. The credits run over an image of a hat and gloves, panning up to a uniformed woman who reads in the paper a report of a successful air raid and how credit should go to all involved. We cut from a close-up of her face to a shot which centers the woman's reflected image in the mirror. She looks up at her reflection, saying "Everyone" with evident pleasure at the thought that this category includes her. Thus the WAAF's seeming pride in her appearance reinforces her professional pride and sense of belonging to the military and the war effort. Mirrors and kitting out scenes continue to feature in postwar recruitment materials, as well as feature films concerning the training of military women. *Someone Special*, a twenty-minute information film produced for the WRNS in 1966 features a fetishistic tracking shot along a line of stocking-clad female feet stepping into military-issue court shoes.[61] Another shot shows a Wren looking at her reflection in the mirror, while a second, seen in the midground, is shown smiling at the first (and us), complicit in her narcissistic pleasure. The voice-over emphasizes the pride that comes with wearing a naval uniform: "From your smart court shoes to your sailor's hat, you are a Wren." As we cut to a close-up of the recruit's reflection she and we are told, "And to the Navy, you're someone special." The uniform brings uniqueness and anonymity in equal measure. For the female recruit, contemplation of her own image is an affirmation; for the audience, it affirms appropriate (feminine) associations with fashion and appearance, mitigating the disruptive aspects of the military woman even while her transformation is foregrounded.

Before shifting from narratives of personal transformation to narratives of romance, it is useful to consider a British film which effectively harnesses both, suggesting the extent to which associations of service with sexual freedom and geographic mobility had become firmly established by the mid-1940s. *Perfect Strangers* (1946) commences with the dull routines of married life in wartime as lived by the film's two dull protagonists, Robert Wilson (Robert Donat) and Cathy Wilson (Deborah Kerr). After Robert departs for the Navy, Cathy decides to ignore her husband's traditionalist injunction against work and joins the WRNS. Military service is transformative for both parties; living separate, independent, and challenging lives for three years, they vow not to return to their preservice state and instead to seek a divorce.[62] Ultimately the two are reconciled, their reunion a recognition of the positive transformations undergone by both men and women in wartime. For Cathy it is, significantly, a combination of the uniform, military service, and female comradeship that turns her into a more confident, attractive, even glamorous woman. It is not her induction into military life that we see, but rather the transformation of her appearance, tutored by fellow Wren Dizzy. Dizzy both polices Cathy's appearance ("You can't come out looking like that") and tutors her in glamorous femininity. It is Cathy's friendship with Dizzy, as much as a developing romance, that enables her to speak her desires, to realize the limitations of her preservice married life. If these comments suggest that only appearance is at stake, it is worth noting that Cathy's military service, albeit shown only briefly, clearly denotes her new professional confidence: we see her proficiency and bravery as she navigates a launch to deliver a message while guns fire and bombs fall around her. Moreover Dizzy's appearance is correct within the codes of both the military uniform and womanliness, suggesting once again that the two are, after all, compatible. In a film produced in the immediate aftermath of war, *Perfect Strangers* valorizes military women's (temporary, auxiliary) service as energizing from a vantage point that assumes it is no longer required. Though both parties have been transformed, the demobilized couple must come to terms with each other in (postwar) civilian life.

WOMEN AND ROMANCE IN WARTIME: WORKING AND WAITING

Movies which couple war and romance narratives provide an enhanced role for military women. Romance functions as a generic space within which audiences, whether in the war period or in the years since, might reasonably expect female characters to play a significant part. Romance narratives also cast women in familiar and even traditional terms. But what, if any, is the specific significance of the *military* woman in romance narratives? I've argued that her presence as a figure in uniform, serving her country, is often explicitly taken as a sign of modernity (as in *The Life and Death of Colonel Blimp*). How is this reconciled with the more familiar, and highly gendered, terrain of romance and couple formation? In both British and Hollywood feature films the work undertaken by military women is often, like the women themselves, both integral and yet in some way auxiliary. Similarly romance narratives function to center the military woman at the same time that they emphasize her distance from what cinema understands as the real work of war: combat. Because military women are defined primarily as noncombatants, whether or not they are near the front, their work is downplayed against the spectacular scenes of combat that showcase the work of military men, who are almost always defined primarily as combatants. In this way the romance plot is contradictory in its effect in films of and about the Second World War. On the one hand it opens up a potentially much larger space for military women as characters; on the other hand that greater presence within the narrative may have little to do, directly at least, with their military status. Indeed the romance plot repeatedly positions military women as women who wait, a passive pursuit primarily associated with civilian women and the home front.

Though routine in peacetime, the formation of a romantic couple provides an unsatisfactory resolution in war films since loving relationships are frequently disrupted by death or duty. "War is never very kind to lovers," muses Leslie Howard's voice-over in *The Gentle Sex* as Anne learns that her fiancé is missing and presumed dead; the couple's romance is emotionally involving, but the loss is no great surprise in generic terms. The juxtaposition of love and death is a recurrent theme in representations of the war. In *Force of Arms* (1951) Sgt. Joe Peterson (William Holden) first encounters WAC Lt. Eleanor McKay (Nancy Olsen) following hard combat in the battle of San Pietro; appropriately enough they meet in a cemetery.[63] Set during the Second World War, the film was released during the Korean War, simultaneously looking back while covertly acknowledging the contemporary context of the Korean conflict. The romance in *Marine Raiders* (1944), similarly wrapped around combat sequences (this time in the Pacific), is rather edgier. The couple are not reunited in the film's closing scenes, as WAAF Lt. Ellen Forster is left to wait and Marine Capt. Dan Craig to fight. Such uncertainty is central to the whimsical film by Michael Powell and Emeric Pressburger, *A Matter of Life and Death*, made and released shortly after the end of the war (in late 1946). June, an

American operator makes contact with RAF pilot Peter Carter in what both assume will be his final moments; there is an immediate and intense attraction between the two. Vivid Technicolor juxtaposes Peter in his burning plane with June, who works in a communications tower, her face illuminated by a red glow. June represents life and vitality against Peter's imminent death. In contrast to the bold color of these opening shots, the film's bureaucratic afterlife, staffed by women in military-style uniforms, is pictured in austere black and white. Miraculously—indeed by heavenly oversight—Peter survives the crash of his plane; the couple meet the following morning as June bicycles across the sands back to her barracks. The love that develops between Peter and June in *A Matter of Life and Death* is both rapid and intense, a product of the heightened situation in which they find themselves.

In a film lushly celebrating the primacy of love, the relationship between Peter and June is clearly metaphoric for new relations between the U.K. and the U.S.[64] Here the New World is as much temporal as geographic, new not only in relation to Europe, but also to the extent that it functions as a sign of modernity. Newness in both senses is signaled by June in her youth, enthusiasm, and capacity for passion, but also her military status. The couple are brought together through her work as a military woman, aligning the role with intimacy, spontaneity, and romance. She is not only a military woman, but as a radio operator she is a point of contact between land and air. She is both a figure of agency, taking the initiative, and a figure who waits, frozen in time while playing table tennis and, later, as a spectator during Peter's crucial surgery. Her spirited attitude, her "mobility," in wartime terms, is in this way explicitly counterposed with more passive constructions of femininity prevalent in the war period (the woman who waits). What is perhaps most striking about representations of military women in the Second World War as both mobile and waiting (with all the connotations of fixity that position involves) is that these qualities rarely generate dramatic conflict; that is, they are not evidently contradictory. The war films explored in this section emphasize the romantic and erotic possibilities of military service, suggesting that the transformative qualities of military life can be recuperated for more conventional postwar domesticity. While such narratives clearly mobilize conventional patterns of femininity, these hybrid films of war and romance also insist on the modernity and independence of the military woman.

Force of Arms and Marine Raiders are exemplary of such hybrids. Set during the Second World War, both films demonstrate the ways the romance narrative brings the military woman into the action while attempting to deal with the disruption that she represents within this masculine world. Both films open with scenes of combat in which the hero demonstrates his courage, followed by a brief period of leave in which he encounters the military woman with whom he will become involved. In each case the hero is embittered by what he has seen or endured during the recent combat, a fact that makes the couple's encounter particularly intense. In Force of Arms their meeting is antagonistic as a result of Joe's bitterness following combat, their different ranks, and Eleanor's reluctance to become sexually involved. By contrast, there is an instant bond between Dan and Ellen in Marine Raiders. In line with the generic conventions of romance, both films place obstacles in the path of the couple: misunderstandings, the interventions of well-intentioned friends, sheer physical distance, and of course the different roles they perform as military men and women. Force of Arms ends with the couple reunited in a liberated Rome; the ending of Marine Raiders is open, with the war in the Pacific continuing in its intensity and the couple uncertain as to their future.

Both films stage the meeting of the romantic military couple away from the fighting at the front, thus reinforcing the contemporary view that military men and women occupy distinct and separate spaces. Yet neither couple meets on home ground (that is to say, in the United States), but abroad—in Italy and Australia—suggesting that the mobility associated with wartime involves romantic potential as well as danger. In effect these movies exploit the very erotic possibilities that so troubled traditionalist opponents of women's military service, staging opportunities for intimacy between men and women as a consequence of the women's mobility.

The dangers of the foreign spaces to which women's mobility leads them are underlined by scenes in which the couples come under unexpected attack from the air. In Marine Raiders Japanese planes strafe the beach as Dan and Ellen drive along the coast road, having decided to marry. They dive into a foxhole to take cover together, Dan heroically attempting to take over an anti-aircraft gun and sustaining a head injury in the process. In Force of Arms the couple share their first consensual kiss during a bombing raid. The attack serves to remind them of the perils of

13. In *Battle of Britain* (1969) Harvey (Susannah York) surveys the bodies of fellow WAAFs following an air raid.

war, prompting Eleanor to briefly overcome her objections to a more intimate relationship. Such sequences emphasize the presence of the military woman in a combat zone; though she is a noncombatant, her role places her in danger. Scenes of military women under aerial attack, without the romantic or erotic overtones, also occur in *Flight Nurse* (1953), set in Korea, and in the epic *Battle of Britain* (1969), which goes so far as to display the bodies of WAAFs killed in a German attack (figure 13). Though excluded from the combat portions of war-romance narratives, scenes of military women endangered by enemy action speak to the instability of attempts to secure their distinctiveness through noncombatant status.

In the context of a home front under aerial attack and women's entry into spheres of work—the services, industry—traditionally understood as both male and masculine, Lant observes a process by which wartime British cinema reinscribes gendered space through an opposition between land and air. This distinction, she argues, is literalized through the use of point of view, such that an "aerial gaze," contemplating the landscape from above, is "fictionalized as male, in contrast to the land-bound female look, which in so many ways supports the skies as a male preserve." Lant points to an additional and complementary set of images "of home front women looking toward the sky from the land," going on to argue that women's war work is presented as rooted to the earth and the nation, supporting the efforts of military men whether in the air above or overseas.[65]

In *Airwoman* an image of a WAAF gazing at the planes flying above her accompanies the male voice-over's final salute to her vital but grounded

14. "You can take it. So can I": Ellen looks aloft in the final sequence of *Marine Raiders* (1944), her grounded state contrasted to the planes above.

work. A comparable image closes *Marine Raiders* as Ellen contemplates the planes taking off from the base where she works. We see her in medium close-up listening to a radio report of the action in which Dan has been centrally involved, anxiety evident on her face. She moves out onto the steps of the Operations Building and onto the airfield, swelling music accompanying the image of her solitary figure watching the planes take off. Her short walk from the building to the strip takes her through shadow and into bright sunlight, from anxiety to hope. She speaks out loud to her distant lover, of her hopes for their reunion and the work that will be required, her words ("You can take it. So can I") suggesting an equivalence between their separate labors (figure 14). In these movies images of the couple under aerial attack serve as an admission that both the male soldier and the military woman are playing an official part in the war. They come together in the context of danger, although the greater danger the male soldier faces is repeatedly underlined by grueling and spectacular combat sequences.

In the context of her comprehensive survey of the combat films of the Second World War, Jeanine Basinger finds *Marine Raiders* to be, in genre terms, "truly a problematic case." She writes that "the combat film is used as a kind of parentheses around a traditional and detailed romantic love story," but since the film begins and ends with combat and since "discussion of war and combat is ever-present," *Marine Raiders* demands to be included within the parameters of her study.[66] This classificatory dilemma points to the ways the figure of the military woman disrupts genre; she is consistently associated with generic hybridity, whether in the war-romance hybrids considered here, the comedies analyzed in chapters 4 and 5, the boot camp conventions explored in chapter 7, or the thrillers and investigative fictions discussed in chapter 8. Romance in these films is both immediate, defined by the passionate connections of the present, and forward-looking, requiring the possibility of a postwar existence, an end to the circumstances that bring the couple together. Films of war and romance tend to involve two key sources of dramatic tension: How will the couple come together despite the war and their personal histories? And once the couple is established, will the male protagonist survive his return to combat? Love brings both humanity and heightened vulnerability. Thus in *Force of Arms*, having fallen in love Joe is reluctant to take risks back on the line. When his buddy is killed and he himself is injured, Joe clearly blames himself for his hesitation under fire, his fear brought on by contact with the disruptive presence of the military woman. Though assigned to noncombat duties and free to marry Eleanor, he is plagued by nightmares and insists on returning to his unit to prove himself. Injured once more, he is listed as missing and presumed dead. In the final part of the film Eleanor (who is about to be discharged since she is pregnant),[67] refuses to accept that Joe is dead and searches for him across the country. The two are ultimately reunited in Rome, after Joe is released from a POW camp.

In *Marine Raiders*, too, Dan evades the safety of a desk job to return to combat, although since this takes him back to Australia it means a reunion with Ellen. His return to action is also thus a return to romance rather than a departure from the woman at home. Exclusion from combat is represented as *unmanning* the heroes of these films, a process that is linked directly to the presence of the military woman. As will become increasingly clear in the debates concerning women's combat role in the postwar period, the military woman poses a symbolic threat to the masculinity of military men. This sense of an erosion of tradition will be implicitly linked to an emergent feminism in later films such as *Battle of Britain*, which evokes the military woman as an (uncaring) independent woman in a fashion suggestive of contemporary (that is, late 1960s) discourses and debates. Here WAAF Maggie Harvey (Susannah York) tells her pilot husband, Colin (Christopher Plummer), that she is "just not cut out to wave a wet hankie on sooty stations." Produced long after the context of war, with its negotiations and accommodations, *Battle of Britain* is open in its misogyny, with the military woman signifying an unwarranted disruption to gender norms. Colin describes Maggie as a "parade ground suffragette," his anger at her reluctance to seek a posting near his new station expressed in terms of frustration with (implicitly masculine) military women more generally. His bitter assertion that he "never could stand marching women" couples his anger at a personal rejection to a disruptive female independence embodied by his career-focused military wife.

The incorporation of women into the British and U.S. military during the Second World War brought with it questions of women's status as citizens as well as soldiers, concerns which are also present in the romance narratives explored here. A schoolteacher in civilian life, Eleanor McKay in *Force of Arms* explains her decision to enlist in terms of a desire to play a part in the fight for freedom, for a better future. She wants to return to her small New Hampshire town with the feeling that she has played a part in keeping her world "free and safe." Since it is never questioned, Ellen does not explain her enlistment as such in *Marine Raiders*. She does, however, speak of her two younger brothers, stationed in Africa; we learn that Ellen raised them herself following the death of their parents and that she has not heard from them in five months, a poignant reminder of wartime loss.

Though Ellen is not called upon to explain herself, the film nonetheless stages a debate on the role of women in war and modern life. When the conversation turns to earlier times, Ellen extols the simple pleasures of the turn of the century, while Dan opts for the here and now. He tells Ellen that she is "too real" for that earlier time, that she "is meant for now when they need fighters," a compliment that clearly moves her. When Dan is reluctant to marry, as this might be unfair to Ellen, she turns the compliment back on him: "I have my rights, Dan. This isn't 1900. It's today. . . . I have a say in my life and I'm going to say it." It is perhaps ironic that her assertiveness is expressed in pursuit of the traditional goal of marriage, but Ellen's speech is nonetheless a plea for social inclusion as an equal, in the war and in their relationship, effectively echoing the recruitment slogans which insisted on women's place in the war effort. Later, in San Diego, Dan will counsel a fellow soldier also reluctant to marry, "You might remember that the girls are in this war too." Though he employs a rhetoric of "sides," emphasizing the differences between men and women, he also makes reference here to Ellen's words. And though the soldier he counsels is romancing a civilian, the words that Dan uses are those spoken by a military woman, one who lays claim to the citizenship that a military role bestows. Women's stake in the war is effectively fused here with more traditional entitlements, such as home, marriage, and family.

In line with the themes of female labor as newly necessary so characteristic of official discourse during the Second World War, both *Force of Arms* and *Marine Raiders* suggest that women's military service is generated by, and feeds, a changing society. Both films also clearly register the gender trouble associated with the military woman, the disruption to social hierarchies and conventional formulations of male and female, soldier and civilian. In *Marine Raiders* Ellen displays a passion for speed, initiating an extravagant (in the context of wartime restrictions) expedition by car, a directionless expression of action and energy that leads the couple first to a liaison on the shore (a physical intimacy that is subsequently legitimized by the decision to marry) and then into danger (the attack in which Dan is injured). Following the couple's marriage there is a moment of comic disquiet as Ellen tells Dan that he looks "beautiful" in his uniform. Bashful, Dan reminds her, "A Marine can't look beautiful," the point being of course that Marines are men. (The introduction of female Marines, in a comic vignette discussed in the introduction, comes somewhat later in the film and goes unremarked by Dan.) Later Ellen must leave Dan's bedside to go on duty, another instance of her association with work as much as with waiting.

We might contrast the film's attempts to convey a modern military woman as a figure of movement and vitality with the first part of *Marine Raiders*, set in Guadalcanal at the beginning of the Japanese campaign. Here the conventions of jungle combat are fully on display. Dan expresses his distaste for night fighting and for the waiting involved in this kind of warfare: he is a man of action and waiting is associated with women. He briefly talks to another soldier, who speculates on life as a process of waiting, whether for Japanese attack, for manhood, or for marriage. Uncomfortable with waiting and repelled by an enemy constructed as entirely other, Dan is a "restless soul," requiring a partner who can match as well as complement him. Ellen's toughness, so explicitly marked as necessary in the "here and now" of wartime, does not make her any less female; yet many of the films discussed in this chapter show traces of an anxiety that such toughness might erode the critical, newly precarious difference between women and men. *Force of Arms* takes the theme of women's usurping male authority somewhat further through overt jokes (and evident male discomfort) about female manliness. In this context its release in 1951 is perhaps significant; the "battle of the sexes" rhetoric increasingly central to postwar comedies (including those featuring military women) is now firmly in evidence. Equally the postwar future of the couple forms a more significant concern of this film as it draws out potential tensions as male citizen soldiers and newly mobile women accommodate themselves to each other.

At their first meeting Eleanor rejects Joe's offer of a drink, which he interprets as a judgment about rank (she is a lieutenant, he a sergeant). The following day Joe is promoted to lieutenant as a result of his heroism on the battlefield, eliminating this potential obstacle to romance and the threat to male authority posed by a woman who outranks her male partner. Yet Joe's antipathy (and attraction) to Eleanor as a female soldier remains. He disdainfully comments in Eleanor's presence, "WACs ain't women. They're officers and gentlemen—Congress says so." His aggressive insistence that a military woman is a contradiction in terms, and the implication that her very existence results from the meddling of politicians, registers the heated debates of the war period. Opponents regarded the establishment of the WAC as an unacceptable challenge to American womanhood. Thus "women's military service was at best inappropriate and at worst marked the abandonment of more fitting responsibilities."[68] In this view WACs potentially relinquished their femaleness when they enlisted, an anxiety that informs both official and popular discourse of the period.

Immediately after his bitter dismissal, Joe overhears Eleanor brushing off a colonel's invitation to the ballet, pleading the pressure of work and with a joke about her disinterest in "grown-up men in tights chasing muscular women across the stage." The exchange intrigues Joe, who had read Eleanor as preoccupied only with rank and status. If the remark suggests her desire for traditional gender relations (rather than a world of muscular women and men in tights), in the date that follows the two are once more caught within troubled gender hierarchies. Thus when Eleanor speaks of the independence that the Army has given her, Joe testily responds by asking if she means independence from men. A little later he asks her directly whether she hates men, underscoring the perception of military women as antagonistic toward men and conventional feminine submissiveness. This first date almost comes to an abrupt end when Eleanor first asks Joe to the ballet and then pays for their drinks. When he recalls her earlier distaste, she responds suggestively, speculating, "Maybe the women will chase the men tonight." Although much of the early tension in their relationship stems from Eleanor's *refusal* of physical intimacy, here she seems almost predatory. When she pays the bill for their drinks Joe seethes, commenting bitterly, "That's what I like about you. You're such a perfect gentleman." He expresses his resentment of female independence by suggesting more or less explicitly that the military woman has usurped a male position, becoming mannish in the process. More generally, however, *Force of Arms* locates the distinctiveness of the military woman in both her noncombatant status and her sexual respectability, even as it plays with the suggestion that she is either mannish or occupies a position of inappropriate authority (over men).

In the context of the contested respectability of the female soldier in the war period, as Meyer astutely notes, "bad women were those who acted like male soldiers."[69] The morality of sexual encounters during wartime forms a key subject of tension between Joe and Eleanor in *Force of Arms*. Although Eleanor makes it clear that she is not offering sex, Joe repeatedly attempts to initiate physical intimacy, whether through verbal insinuation or direct approach (putting his arm around her, kissing her). His frustration is evident. When Eleanor continues to resist his advances, Joe expresses resentment at being made to feel "like some kind of creep." The film's relative frankness about sexual activity outside marriage reflects its later date of production, but is also surely a response to contemporary perspectives on women in the military. On their first meeting Joe suggestively invites Eleanor for a drink, and she refuses. In subsequent meetings she explains her reluctance to begin a romantic or sexual commitment in relation to an idea of decency and the loss of her former lover—whose grave she was visiting on the first meeting in the cemetery—but also in terms of disgust at the exploitation of civilian women. She expresses her anger that local girls and women are forced to exchange sex for goods (exchanges strongly implied in earlier scenes showing GIS on liberty), characterizing American troops, or perhaps war more generally, as corrupting. While Joe's commanding officer encourages him to have sex with local women, Eleanor's sexual propriety is clearly regulated. In these ways the film highlights the very different expectations associated with the sexuality of male and female soldiers, underscoring Eleanor's status as good woman and respectable WAC.

If the war-romance hybrids tend to foreground differences between men and women, other films of the Second World War foreground differences such as class, region, and nationality more explicitly. The MGM drama *This Above All* (1942), which centers on the developing romance between the aristocratic WAAF Prudence Cathaway (Joan Fontaine) and the working-class Army deserter Clive Briggs (Tyrone Power), exemplifies the extent to which the dynamic figure of the military woman could serve as a sign of modernity and national continuity. The couple's relationship is shaped by their different class backgrounds and their attitudes to nation and duty: Clive is intensely bitter at the British class system and the folly of military leaders appointed on the basis of family connections rather than soldiering ability. An example of what Mark Glancy terms "the British film," placing the term in quotation marks to signal the status of movies set in Britain but produced in Hollywood, the film was adapted soon after Eric Knight's novel was published.[70] The explicit dialogue on class, nation, and equality in *This Above All* is informed by a number of different factors: contemporary debates concerning potential U.S. involvement in the war, American perspectives on Britain, the recent commercial success of gothic romance, the predilections of the production team, and the previous roles of its stars, Fontaine and Power. As Clayton Koppes and Gregory Black detail, in the difficult moment of a developing alliance with a colonial power the British Office of War Information was concerned that Hollywood films resist the temptation to draw on either the British Empire as a glamorous setting for adventure or stereotypes of British aristocracy: "For propaganda purposes British society had to be democratized and its empire written out." In this context they judge *This Above All* as the most overt attempt to deal with the "theme of England as a class-ridden society."[71] As Glancy suggests, the movie adaptation centered attention on the love story and the character of Prudence; with her forthright views on class (absent from the novel), she becomes "the moderator between the old and the new England," a figure who stands for necessary change.[72] Neither Koppes and Black nor Glancy have much to say on the role played by a *military* woman in this drama of class, democracy, and war. Yet her enlistment is surely significant, functioning as it does to tie the themes of female mobility to class mobility and social change.

This Above All begins in 1940, the setting an affluent English home. In the sitting room an assembled group, dressed formally for dinner, listen to the radio and news that France has signed an armistice with Germany. Life for this family is both leisurely and luxurious: they have space and servants at their disposal. In this privileged space of comfort preens the complacent Iris, an image suggestive of inappropriate self-involvement. The events in Europe seem both terrible and unreal, the threat to Britain denied by some in the party and confronted squarely by others (clearly "right" in the film's terms), who point to the need for preparedness. The opposing attitudes within the group are summed up in emotional terms as excitement and restraint, which also clearly reference stereotypical constructions of Englishness. Subtly these terms are transferred onto an issue of appropriate class and gendered behavior when Iris cautions her brother Roger that his daughter Prudence "is not behaving in a manner befitting her position." Iris is concerned that Prudence is fraternizing with lower-class men; Roger responds with egalitarian rhetoric, addressing the class transgression though not the implicit criticism of Prudence's morality. The rationality of Roger's perspective is set against Iris's rather comical, airy insistence that she is "not against equality." "I'm perfectly prepared to be equal with anybody," she remarks, adding, "providing they don't start being equal with me." Having set up an opposition between decorum and equality, the film introduces Prudence, played by Fontaine in breathless fashion. In the discussion that follows she is revealed as the new aristocratic woman of Britain, initially seemingly preoccupied by the trivial and pointedly feminine prewar pursuits of shopping, beauty, and leisure but shyly and almost in passing revealing that she has enlisted: "I did some shopping, and er, I had my hair done, and er, then I joined the WAAFS."

That concerns about class underpin the opposition of respectability and responsibility mobilized in these establishing scenes quickly becomes apparent when the assembled family object not so much to the fact that Prudence has joined the WAAF, as to the fact that she has joined the *ranks*. Her uncle Wilfred points out that he could have secured her a commission, a suggestion to which Prudence responds decisively, "I don't want to be an officer until I've learned to be a private." To Wilfred, becoming a private means setting aside a traditional entitlement to lead, while to Iris it represents a rebellion typical of young girls of the time who "think it clever to be different," a word she enunciates with all the scathing contempt of her small-minded, upper-class position. Prudence recoils at her family's complaisance, proclaiming her modernity against their traditionalism, her presence in the here and now: "I'm in 1940 and you're in 1880." Once again the modern woman of today is compared to the restrictions (and here inappropriate, class-bound assumptions) of the nineteenth century. In *This Above All* discourses of the modern woman and of the need for an egalitarian society reinforce each other. Indeed there is an insistent process of displacement, as both the romance plot and the question that underpins Clive's desertion (is Britain really a country worth fighting for?) develop over the course of the narrative.[73] There is a clear suggestion that Prudence has transgressed more than class boundaries here, and that the erosion of class boundaries brings with it the threat (or promise) of sexual opportunity. Indeed such presumptions lay the ground for the romantic liaison that forms the center of the film.

The second scene shifts decisively from the affluent home to the WAAF camp, in which women from diverse class and regional backgrounds mix together. The new recruits feature in a generically familiar montage of transformation: first seen assembled in civilian clothes, then being given their uniforms and equipment, in their barracks, on the parade ground, drilling, undertaking physical exercise, gas mask drill, and marching behind a band. The friendliness of the comical working-class Violet Worthing, who promises Prudence she will fix them both up with boys, confirms the potentially compromising consequences of social mixing. Prudence is at first true to her name, rejecting Violet's offer of a date. (Violet's response, "You ain't a bluestocking?," is a telling condensation of classed and gendered norms of behavior.) Caught off-guard Prudence later agrees to assist Violet in her plan to get her boyfriend, Joe, alone so that he can propose. Brought along as a decoy, Prudence is left in the dark with the mysterious Clive; her observation that she doesn't usually "come out like this" prompts him to describe her as a "very superior sort of WAAF," a comment that registers both class status (of which he is acutely aware) and an inappropriate sexual distance.

In her study of British wartime culture, Antonia Lant deftly analyzes the complex symbolism and pervasiveness of the blackout: "Living through the wartime dark was experienced by everyone, regardless of class, age, sex, race, or regional abode. Universal in nature, the image of the blackout became a synecdoche for war in cultural life." In narratives of chance encounters "the wartime night" is revealed "as an eroticised, hypnotic space."[74] *This Above All* rehearses its chance encounter exactly thus, in the night. The sexualized charge of the meeting and of the relationship that subsequently develops between Prudence and Clive is less overt than in the source novel but is nonetheless apparent.[75] Attempting to escape from the rain, the couple are expelled from a hotel, the owner clearly assuming that they wish to use the premises for sex. Later, following an alcohol-fueled encounter in a haystack, Prudence rashly agrees to go away with Clive for a week during her first leave. Their illicit passion is sanctioned by the ticket inspector, who, recalling his own experience in the First World War, conspiratorially allows them a carriage to themselves. Their trip to the coast seems romantic and exciting at first, but then becomes rather sordid. (A chance encounter with the prurient Iris flusters Prudence.)[76] Clive's military buddy Monty overtly treats Prudence as a sexually available woman in these scenes, despite Clive's assurances as to her character. Thus *This Above All* clearly exploits the erotic opportunities, here heightened by interclass mixing, associated with military service during the war (figure 15). Even so, Prudence's class and gender status serve to reassure (we know that the working-class Monty and the aristocratic Iris are both incorrect in their presumptions), allowing her character to signal both continuity and a society in transition.

The military woman is evidently a democratizing figure in *This Above All*. Yet the meanings of the military woman in wartime cinema involve more than a simple statement of patriotism or modernity. Prudence's private's uniform signals her defiance of tradition and class entitlement, but it also poses a question about shifting gender norms and sexual morality. In the seclusion of their train carriage, Clive asks her to change out of her uniform, to appear for him in the guise of a civilian woman. Yet when she does so, in an erotically charged scene, it is not only her conventional feminine beauty that is revealed, but her decidedly upper-class status. That status had been temporarily masked by the very anonymity of the uniform. Darkness (the blackout) and the uniform both serve to ease sexual and social difference in the film, differences that are all too apparent here. Presumably Clive had hoped to see Prudence as a woman rather than a WAAF, but even out of uniform she remains a disruptive, troubling figure, one that needs to be contained.

This Above All differs from the war-romance hybrids discussed earlier

15. The erotic and romantic possibilities of cross-class mixing in
This Above All (1942).

to the extent that scenes of combat are excluded from the drama (ex-
cepting Clive's spoken recollections). The movie plays instead with the
conventions of romance, courting gothic overtones in the later scenes, in
which Clive emerges as a traumatized figure (by both combat and class
inequities). As Glancy makes clear, this evocation of the gothic was a
deliberate production decision to emphasize Prudence's point of view and
effectively exploit "Joan Fontaine's most recent films, *Rebecca* (1940) and
Suspicion (1941), in which her character is in love with a man she does not
understand or trust."[77] *This Above All* certainly owes much to the gothic
melodramas with which Fontaine had been recently associated (and indeed, as Glancy notes, to Power's converted skeptic in *A Yank in the RAF*).
Moreover the fact that Prudence spends a significant portion of the film
out of uniform, notably during her coastal holiday with Clive, suggests a
shift to romance. Yet when Prudence and Clive are finally reunited, she is
in uniform once more, emphasizing her status as a military woman over
her aristocratic social position. This last part of the film also casts Prudence as a figure who waits: at the railway station for an appointment
Clive cannot make (since he is incarcerated), while her surgeon father
operates on the injured Clive, and finally by Clive's bedside during an air
raid. Her assertion of her own modernity (inscribed through her military
service in the ranks and her relative sexual freedom) is distinct from the
frail femininity of Fontaine's gothic heroines; in this context her inscrip-

tion as a woman who waits functions as a reassuring sign of the military woman's commitment to a submissive femininity.

Representations of the Second World War, both popular and official, centralize the military woman while insisting on her auxiliary status. Her service is typically taken as a sign of modernity, rhetorically contrasted to previous generations of women constrained by a femininity understood as inappropriate to the needs of the present. To this end, tropes of personal transformation are a recurrent feature of the images and narratives discussed above. Though women's military service is valorized and celebrated, it is construed as temporary, inextricable from the immediate context of total war. Representations of the war certainly acknowledge the culturally disruptive aspects of the military woman (the extent to which the female soldier is felt to be a contradiction in terms), seeking to reassure traditionalist sentiment while mobilizing a rhetoric of national necessity. Both recruitment materials and feature films also speak to contemporary concerns that military service might trouble gender norms, rendering women masculine or mannish or facilitating inappropriate sexual possibilities (promiscuity or lesbianism). Thus the transformative training camp films considered in this chapter underline the effectiveness and respectability (i.e., femininity) of military women. The films of war and romance equally speak to contemporary discourses, exploiting military women's proximity to men within the reassuring format of romance. Romance also features prominently in the next chapter, which focuses on military nursing narratives. Here, however, the presumption that nurses are not really soldiers allows a different iteration of the military woman, as a dedicated professional rather than a temporary necessity.

It is as a nurse that the military woman has most often been represented in film and television fictions. Nurses are often supporting characters in such fictions, routinely used to provide romantic interest for male protagonists. Yet nurses are also portrayed as tough soldiers who do a difficult job in dangerous circumstances. The geographic location of the nurse as a noncombatant who nonetheless may work near or at the front underscores that she is simultaneously a military and a nonmilitary presence. Connie L. Reeves describes nurses as both "invisible soldiers" and "the forerunners of today's women in the military."[1] The cultural anxieties that attend military women are played out in distinct ways when it comes to nursing, no doubt as a consequence of the sort of invisibility that Reeves points to. Popular fictions often emphasize nurses' military identity, depicting them in basic training, wearing khaki or fatigues rather than the traditional whites, and traveling with the military overseas, where they are witness to death and the severe physical traumas of war. Equally, however, film and television fictions routinely foreground romance and a selfless duty of care as the defining, and appropriately feminine, characteristics of military nurses.

The exploration of auxiliary military women in the previous chapter suggests that military women are defined by a gendered opposition of combatant and noncombatant personnel. The requirement for nurses' labor at the scene of combat is at odds with that opposition. Although gaining military recognition relatively recently, nurses have long served in and near combat zones.[2] Indeed the history of the professionalization of nursing, and of women in the profession, is intimately connected to war and to military institutions. The extensive involvement of American and British women in nursing during the First World War laid the ground for their formal incorporation into the military. At moments of crisis military necessity has produced enhanced opportunities for training and education, expanding the numbers of women serving as nurses and the opportunities available to them. Enloe identifies such a moment of necessity in the Second World War, which, coupled with the efforts of black nursing leaders, led to the removal of restrictions preventing black women from attending nursing schools or joining the Army and Navy Nurse Corps.[3] By the commencement of the Second World War, nursing had become an established and more or less respectable profession for young women. There is nonetheless a pronounced sense of what Enloe terms "risk" associated with the presence in the field of female military nurses. As she suggests, a "woman who was nursing soldiers, even a woman of respectable class background, even a woman officered by a woman superior of rigid moral outlook, remained a woman among men."[4] Postwar films and fictions, as the chapters in part 2 explore, routinely use military women's proximity to men and male bodies as a source of comedy and sexual innuendo. Wartime narratives typically eschew such humor, however, providing reassurance with an emphasis on duty and chaste intimacy.

Even if the profession involved a level of cultural risk, by the time of the Second World War the concept of the *female nurse* did not carry the shocking connotations of modernity that the *female soldier* seemed to so readily mobilize. This is largely because the role of nurse secured a traditional conception of femininity, such that female presence and intimate proximity to male military bodies seems less overtly troubling than in other narratives featuring military women. The presence of the military nurse is effectively normalized. The female military nurse does not escape the contradiction between the categories *woman* and *soldier* explored in chapter 1, however. Rather she embodies them in a particular manner. Indeed many of the narratives explored in this chapter precisely suggest that the military nurse is not *really* a soldier at all. By definition a noncombatant, the nurse is associated with healing and nurturing and also with sacrifice. Her selfless devotion to her patients provides a mirror for men's selfless sacrifice in combat; the nobility of war and care are thus twinned while being divided into separate, gendered spheres of action.[5]

A particularly explicit instance of such gendered assumptions occurs in an episode of the television series *M*A*S*H* ("Stars and Stripe," 17 December 1979) in which Maj. Margaret Houlihan's lover Sergeant Scully dismisses her (superior) rank in comparison to his own. "That's not the same," he tells her. "You're a nurse—that's an honorary thing—so you can boss around a bunch of nurses, but not men. Not real soldiers." Scully's dismissal clearly relates to Houlihan on two connected levels, as a woman and as a nurse. Thus when she asserts the importance of her rank, insisting that she has "earned" her officer status, Scully becomes angry; accepting Houlihan's military identity, he rejects her sexually and romantically. Gesturing to her wardrobe he dismissively remarks, "No wonder it's all khaki in there." In acknowledging that Houlihan is a soldier after all, Scully scornfully suggests that she is not a woman. The terms remain incompatible, conceived as distinct though complementary areas of male and female service.

The particular ways in which nursing narratives suggest that military nurses are not really soldiers betray some continuity with the discourses explored in chapter 1, which conceive women's service as auxiliary and supportive of male endeavor. But these film and television fictions are just as forcibly shaped by long-established nursing stereotypes. Julia Hallam identifies the prevalent "public images of the nurse" as "the white angel, the doctor's handmaiden, the battleaxe and the sexy nurse."[6] All these types are evident in the narratives explored in this chapter, inflecting images of military women as dutiful but nonetheless provocative.

The toughness of military nurses is repeatedly evoked in cinema and on television, yet it is staged in a manner perfectly compatible with these stereotypes. Thus a perception that women are simply too feminine to cope with the necessities of war or the orderly character of military life does not typically extend to the military nurse. Although *M*A*S*H* treats its chief nurse, Margaret Houlihan, as a figure of fun and mocks her investment in military life, her professional abilities are repeatedly displayed, suggesting that both her femininity and her toughness are required in wartime. As Hallam suggests, the popular image of the nursing pioneer Florence Nightingale (and her approach to the profession she sought to regularize) encompassed both the Victorian feminine ideals of care and service and a tougher dimension, a "military image of authoritarian female power" which underpins the nurse as battleaxe. For Hallam this authoritarian dimension of the nursing image is coupled to social hierarchies, the moral superiority manifesting "an explicitly colonialist aim of reforming and recreating the home of the sick poor into a facsimile of the female, middle-class home."[7] The nurse thus enters inappropriate spaces (male, diseased, disreputable) for redemptive purposes.

The seeming contradiction of the military nurse, a figure who cares and heals in support of killing and conquest, echoes the doubleness of nursing itself. As nursing historians such as Hallam and Anne Summers note, despite sustained attempts to construct nursing as a suitable profession for young, middle-class women, the job itself is far from genteel. Nursing brings women into proximity with illness, death, and the bodies of the sick. For Hallam the "starched white aprons, high white collars and stiff white hats" of the nurse's uniform aim to suggest an "untouchable purity," a negation of the physical intimacy involved in nursing. Such strategies emerge from and are embedded within social hierarchies (it is the task of the working or serving classes to clean up dirt), which in turn produce the contradictory public image of the nurse as both angelic and a "sexualised, worldly-wise female."[8] For military nurses, associated so immediately with death and bodily destruction, the contradiction is heightened in its intensity.[9]

As nurse and soldier the military woman signifies "working woman" in overdetermined fashion; after all, she has not one but two professions. The rhetoric of vocation, acutely involved with images of nursing, serves to qualify this sense of career-oriented (and thus implicitly selfish rather than selfless) womanhood. Nonetheless the construction of military nursing as a recognizably female professional identity impacts in numerous ways on the fictions considered here. The movies of the Second World War explored in chapter 1 repeatedly emphasize the *temporary* character of women's military service. While all the fictions explored in this chapter are set in time of war, an articulation of the exceptional character of this particular form of wartime work is not so insistent. In narratives produced after the Second World War, including *Flight Nurse* and M*A*S*H (both set in Korea) and *China Beach*, set in Vietnam, the idea that the female military nurse has "chosen" to serve (in contrast to the conscripted men she cares for) underscores nursing as both career and vocation. The pilot episode of *China Beach* ends with McMurphy opting for another tour, framing the series in terms of her commitment to the soldiers for whom she cares and the sense that, for her, Vietnam is "home."[10] Many other narratives involving military nurses stage the relationship between career and romance in terms of conflict and choice. The presentation of work and romance (or family) as incompatible for women (though not for men) becomes an increasingly marked feature of postwar culture, with the choice to opt out of the public domain serving as the hallmark of more recent postfeminist fictions centering on affluent white women.

Put crudely, military nursing would seem to allow an atypical articulation of female agency and independence. Popular associations between nursing and the glamour of travel, adventure, and escape from routinized femininity are certainly a factor here. Writing on late nineteenth-century Britain, Summers notes the powerful imagery already acquired by military nursing, even while the numbers of women engaged in such work was relatively small: "To be a nurse in war was to be abroad, free of domestic ties and comforts, ready to surmount hardship and encounter danger. It could bring a woman to the heart of the action on a world stage. It also meant being where the men were. The prosaic realities of most Army Nursing Sisters' working lives could not diminish the power of these images of freedom and agency."[11] Such imagery has remained resonant.[12]

Wartime campaigns aimed at recruiting women into the nursing profession (both civilian and military) draw on themes of duty and opportunity in a manner comparable to the other services. Recruitment materials directed at boosting the numbers of military nurses typically foregrounded the smart uniform, the officer status of nurses, wounded soldiers in need, and a quasi-religious sense of vocation. A poster from 1943 evokes the nurse as an angelic figure of purity (there is no evidence of the patient's bodily trauma; he has been both saved and cleansed) alongside an invitation to personal development ("Save his life . . . and find your own"; figure 16). The figuring of work as transformative emerges as a central theme of military nursing narratives. Where women occupy the periphery of the narrative, the emphasis falls on the ways military men are transformed through their encounter with the nurse, a process that reinforces the supportive, supplementary character of female service. In *To the Shores of Tripoli* (1942) Navy nurse Mary Carter (Maureen O'Hara) in her crisp whites offers playboy Chris Winters a glimpse of a better life. She is, in effect, a reward for good behavior, once Winters finally learns to subject himself to military discipline.[13] Recuperating military men meet

16. Campaigns to recruit nurses in wartime figured both angelic purity and self-interest.

and romance military nurses in numerous fictions and films; Hemingway's *A Farewell to Arms* is one well-know literary progenitor. In *Operation Pacific* the divorced couple played by Patricia Neal and John Wayne (she a Navy nurse, he a submariner) are reunited by the end of the narrative. As Lt. Maggie Haynes, Neal is once again ready to both nurse and romance Wayne in the epic film *In Harm's Way* (1965). The convention of an attraction between nurse and recovering patient, otherwise strangers, is evoked in a number of films; typically, as in *Perfect Strangers* (1945), *The Hasty Heart* (1949), and *They Were Expendable* (1945), the couple's meeting occurs away from home, suggesting possibilities out of the ordinary.

In fictions centered on military nurses—and there are far fewer of these—it is *female* transformation through labor that is foregrounded.

The romance of self-discovery and independence associated with nursing in general, and military nursing in particular, permeates the narratives explored in this chapter and indeed many other narratives. Consider for instance how Nellie Forbush's status as Navy nurse has transported the Little Rock native to the exotic island surroundings of *South Pacific* (1958). Nellie may be preoccupied with romance rather than nursing (indeed we don't see her nursing at all), but the narrative choice she makes to overcome her small-town prejudice and continue in her romance with Emile de Becque suggests that escape from Little Rock (and from her mother, whose injunctions Nellie relays at various points) has (in a rather circumscribed way) liberated her.[14]

For Enloe romance is an explanatory device, one which serves to diffuse the troubling aspects of the military nurse as a woman in combat. She writes that perceptions of women's nature allowed the portrayal of military nurses as "experiencing not warfare, the preserve of manly men, but romance, the natural arena of feminine women. In the life of the female military nurse, war thereby became adventure; care was converted into romantic love."[15] The recurrence of themes of romance—and the ways they emphasize the distinctiveness, the difference of the military woman—forms a central focus of this chapter. In particular I am concerned with the ways the transformative character of both work and romance inform, contradict, and occasionally complement each other in military nursing narratives.

This chapter is divided into four sections and is organized in broadly chronological terms, moving from narratives of the Second World War to those set in Korea and later Vietnam. I explore the representation of military nursing, arguing that it is their very constitution as "invisible soldiers" that seems to have allowed the visibility of female military nurses within a number of popular genres. I examine the portrayal of military nursing as closely coupled with combat, exploring how a desire to visualize the realities of military nursing is frequently in tension with not only Hollywood glamour but conventional constructions of femininity. More generally I am concerned here with the particular ways that film and televisual fictions tend to portray military nurses as not really soldiers and, as such, an inappropriate presence so close to the combat zone, or alternatively, as not really women, casting them as "one of the guys," unavailable for romance or physical intimacy.

Two films released in 1943, *So Proudly We Hail* and *Cry Havoc*, demonstrate the remarkable visibility accorded military nursing in wartime Hollywood cinema. Thomas Doherty describes them as the period's "two big-budget female-centred combat films," while Jeanine Basinger reads them as instances of the merger between the woman's film and the developing form of the World War II combat film.[16] Both films portray the work of military nurses and auxiliaries on Bataan in the period leading up to its fall in April 1942. The high profile of these two films reflects the visibility of the fight for Bataan and of women's role in it. The events of 1942 were far-reaching for military nurses, prompting changes in basic training that sought to recognize the danger in which their role potentially placed them. In all, eighty-three American military nurses were taken prisoner in the Pacific during the Second World War, the majority in the surrender of Bataan and Corregidor.[17] A small group escaped to Australia on an airplane, others on a submarine. On their return to the U.S., the bravery of these women was publicly celebrated: they were decorated and employed by an intensive recruiting drive to enlist more nurses. Newspapers and magazines printed stories testifying to the heroism of the nurses, characterizing them as, in Elizabeth Norman's words, "selfless, calm, courageous." Yet, according to Norman, many of the stories embarrassed the women, a response she attributes to the stories' status as "pure fiction or rank, degrading melodrama."[18] This tension between recognition and exploitation can readily be mapped onto an opposition between realism and melodrama, with Hollywood's attempt to celebrate (and cash in on) the currency of military nurses seen as degrading. Both *Cry Havoc* and *So Proudly We Hail* enact narratives of female transformation through the conventions of the woman's picture, blending work, duty, and romance in the attempt to visualize the military woman as a figure of agency while securing her femininity.

As narratives that purported to tell the stories of Bataan nurses, *Cry Havoc* and *So Proudly We Hail* shared the challenging task of appealing to a domestic female audience, while constructing a positive spin on a significant and very recent military setback. *So Proudly We Hail* has the more upbeat ending of the two, with the majority of the group returning home. The film centers on three women, and although one, Olivia (Veronica Lake), is lost in the hasty evacuation from Bataan, in the closing moments of the film Lt. Janet "Davy" Davidson (Claudette Colbert) is aroused from the catatonic state into which she has lapsed by the words of hope in a letter from the husband she had presumed dead. In contrast to this sentimental conclusion, *Cry Havoc* ends with what remains of its female group surrendering as Bataan falls. Of the original group of thirteen, one has been killed, one has been driven insane by her experiences, one is badly injured, and another is dying of malignant malaria. Despite this, the film does what it can to construct the last stand on Bataan as a heroic holding action rather than a futile loss. The presence of women in these films reinforces the very extremity of the situation, affirming the Second World War as a total war, a conflict requiring the absolute commitment of all members of society.

The female group in *Cry Havoc* are primarily civilian rather than military women. As the opening male voice-over puts it, they are women who, "until that fateful day in December, knew no more of war than did you or your neighbor." The construction of ordinary women caught up in a total war (you, your neighbor) is a familiar feature of wartime filmmaking. Here the device functions to address the domestic female spectator in a narrative of mobilization. Viewers are asked to question their attitudes, to set aside complaisance by *witnessing* the hardships and sacrifices of both civilian and American military women in the Philippines. Crucially this address frames and explains the transformation of the women in the film, most particularly their willingness to set aside a femininity which is portrayed as inappropriate in wartime.

Cry Havoc opens with Smitty (Margaret Sullivan) treating a patient in a Bataan field hospital. To the injured men she exudes care and confidence, but to Captain Marsh her exhaustion is evident. The desperate and deteriorating character of the situation is clear, underlining what the audience already knows will be the outcome of this campaign. Smitty's illness and her determination to remain serves as a metaphor for the more general strategic position. Her refusal to leave represents an affirmation of her commitment to her patients and to what we know will be a lost cause, but also, as we will later learn, a desire to stay near the commanding officer of a nearby message center to whom she is secretly married. Staying in danger is thus an expression of Smitty's wifely as well as her military duty, a strategy which neatly secures her femininity in conventional terms. Assistance for these military nurses and their patients comes from a group of civilian women whose transformation is played out through the course of the film. The film exemplifies the incorporation of nonmilitary women into a supportive or auxiliary role, the militarization of women in the sense suggested by Enloe's work. Such unofficial participation was a defining feature of nursing in the First World War.[19]

The civilian clothes of the volunteers foreground their femininity, in contrast to Smitty's and Marsh's uniforms and the fatigues worn by Flo as the more experienced aide. Initially the civilians seem unlikely to supply the sort of labor that is required. "You're all so young and pretty," Smitty tells them, clearly disappointed. However, the women's disheveled appearance (we see them dirty and sweaty, pushing a defunct Army truck along a dirt road) indicates that they are already changing into useful and productive (rather than consuming) bodies. Though not military women, they are rapidly militarized; issued with work clothes, they take on an auxiliary function as nurses' aides, governed by orders and the regulations of military life. As the action progresses, the women come to look, dress, and behave more like a team and, crucially, more like soldiers. One will even participate directly in combat, helping to shoot down a Japanese plane (events that take place offscreen).

Personal transformation is a familiar trope of the woman's film, a process typically signified through costume and other elements of appearance.[20] The women in *Cry Havoc* adopt fatigues and learn to work together, overcoming differences of class, region, ethnicity, and military status. *Cry Havoc* thus combines the themes of personal transformation so characteristic of the woman's film, with the movement toward group cohesion that Basinger traces as a key feature of the emergent genre of the World War II combat film. That the women's civilian occupations (dependent, student, waitress, burlesque performer, fashion journalist, switchboard operator, factory supervisor) do not obviously equip them for their new situation underlines the radical nature of the shifts in women's public role that the war will require. The militarization of these ordinary women in the extreme context of the American position on Bataan serves as a wider metaphor of the transformation of women's roles during wartime. In this spirit the women pitch in and do what they can, demonstrating commitment and bravery. They set aside the supposed triviality of femininity in favor of the masculine world of military endeavor. When given the chance of evacuation they stay on to tend the wounded; in all this, they become visually coded as military women, remaining identifiably female but distanced from civilian femininity.

17. Davy (Claudette Colbert) is first seen in *So Proudly We Hail* (1943) in a state of shock, a contrast to the vigor and efficiency which characterizes her for most of the film.

So Proudly We Hail focuses on a group of military women rather than militarized women. The movie's marketing campaign declaimed that its military nurses "shared a soldier's life . . . a soldier's love . . . a soldier's glory," suggesting the possibilities of romance and equality under fire. Like *Cry Havoc*, *So Proudly We Hail* is clearly indebted to the conventions of the woman's picture. The film's three female stars—Claudette Colbert, Paulette Goddard, and Veronica Lake—were all firmly associated with Hollywood glamour. In the film all three are subject to narratives of transformation that remove them from glamour and femininity and situate them firmly as soldiers. The action, framed as a flashback, tells the story of a small group of nurses who served on Bataan. The film opens with their arrival by plane in Australia, trumpeted in the opening titles as a sign of hope in dark days. Davy (Colbert) is in a state of mental and physical collapse (figure 17). On the transport home a benevolent Army doctor encourages the other women to confide in him so that he might understand Davy's condition and assist her.[21] Thus the women begin to recount and reflect on their experiences. In this way contemporary audiences were explicitly invited to understand the film as voicing the stories of those nurses who had so recently been in the public eye.

That story is one of transformation; thus we are taken first not to Bataan but to San Francisco and the excitement of boarding ship. Immediately prior to the Japanese attack on the U.S. naval base at Pearl Harbor a group of military nurses are bound for Honolulu. Young Rosemary Larson's mother entrusts her to Davy's care; we learn that it is her first time away from home. (She will die when Japanese planes strafe a Bataan field hospital.) Meanwhile Joan O'Doul (Goddard) enlists Davy's help in managing the two fiancés who have come to see her off, thus firmly establishing her flirtatiousness.[22] The journey is presented as an enjoyable, leisurely experience on which the events of history only later begin to intrude. As they deal with their first casualties aboard ship, the nurses (unlike the audience) still hardly realize the seriousness of the situation. The preoccupations of femininity are mobilized to underline this fact, as one nurse expresses her hope that Bataan has "a decent beauty parlor."[23] But from the moment of their arrival, their proximity to the front—and to danger—is apparent. When they report to Capt. "Ma" McGregor at the field hospital they are already badly needed; the nurses stationed there are exhausted and casualties are mounting. Once again transformation is signaled through costume. Although they spend their first night working in nurses' whites (and even carry lamps), they have already been told that their uniforms are impractical; the next day they are issued ill-fitting fatigues.[24] Generic imagery of civilian women being handed uniforms and equipment is reprised as the military women take on a more explicitly "masculine" or "militarized" role at the front. They are now visualized primarily as soldiers, as military women, as noncombatants who are directly involved in combat.[25] Consider in this context two instances of official discourse relating to the nurses serving in the Pacific. The first is a propaganda image which depicts nurses from Corregidor clustered behind barbed wire in their whites and guarded by a menacing, caricatured Japanese guard (figure 18). Against the increasingly familiar wartime image of the nurse in khaki, the poster employs the visual rhetoric of the nurse as a "white angel," juxtaposing the implicit purity of the white American nurses with the implied savagery of the Japanese soldier. The second is a recruitment poster for the Army Nurse Corps in which an exhausted nurse in fatigues looks out at us; in the background a rifle is used to suspend a medical drip while the text informs us, "*More* nurses are needed!" (figure 19). Both images depict women in peril, yet the iconographic shift from whites to olive drab speaks to the contemporary visibility of nurses as a part of the military.

An imagery of embattled yet heroic womanhood is effectively employed in these posters and in *So Proudly We Hail* as a strategy for making

18. Nurses from Corregidor are pictured in traditional whites, juxtaposed with a racial caricature in the Japanese soldier who guards them.

19. In contrast to figure 18, here the military nurse appears in khaki, an image which emphasizes her involvement in combat.

sense of the position of military nurses in the Philippines. In cinematic terms romance and realism were central to the selling of *So Proudly We Hail* to domestic audiences, presenting the film as novel, modern in its focus on military nurses, and generically familiar. Thus on the one hand we have the harrowing scenes of the chaotic departure from Bataan and the last days on Corregidor, and on the other the image of a "honeymoon in a foxhole" and the posters maintaining that the film's women "Love as Hard as They Fight" (figure 20).[26] We see nurses who are dirty, ill, and thin as supplies become scarce. We see the field hospital attacked and nurses killed or injured. The numbers of the wounded and the scale of the defeat are shocking, as are the crude conditions in the improvised field hospitals. The recent historical events portrayed are rendered both impersonal and personal, sentimental and brutal: Captain McGregor loses her pilot son but remains stoic in her grief (later a picture of her grandson brings hope); Davy badly burns her hands attempting to save a young nurse during a Japanese attack; Davy's husband undergoes an operation without anesthetic; a young soldier drowns as he attempts to escape, desperately holding onto the boat that Davy rows toward Corregidor (figure 21). In this brutal context, the romance narratives which *So Proudly We Hail* constructed around Bataan nurses not only provide a marketing hook, but give a personal dimension to the impersonal—and for the U.S. humiliating—historical events in which the characters are involved. But of course they also anchor the portrayal of military women to familiar gendered archetypes, confirming their "ordinariness" and typicality to domestic female audiences. One of the film's taglines proclaimed: "HEROINES FIRST . . . BUT WOMEN ALWAYS . . . even under fire!" It is telling how explicitly the audience is reassured here that the heroic military woman retains her female identity. Glamour provides a central term in that reassuring gender discourse. Thus promotional materials for *So Proudly We Hail* informed audiences, "You'll find them [the film's stars] even lovelier looking than ever, for nurses' uniforms add glamour to all," disregarding the fact that the stars spend most of their screen time in fatigues. Indeed this strategy was echoed in the recruitment materials produced by Paramount and directly associated with the film; exhibitors were advised to honor local Army and Navy nurses and to partner with their local Red Cross affiliate in an effort to boost recruitment to the Army and Navy Nurse Corps.[27]

Pulling in two different directions to tell the "Screen's First Great

20. *So Proudly We Hail* (1943) mobilizes contradictory discourses of romance and realism; here the "honeymoon in a foxhole" scene foregrounds romance.

21. In contrast to its romantic scenes, *So Proudly We Hail* (1943) depicts the withdrawal from Bataan in more realist, at times brutal fashion.

Woman's Story of Our Girls at the Fighting Front!," *So Proudly We Hail* employs contradictory discourses regarding women's competence and professionalism. The women are both capable and hardworking, and at the same time are motivated by intensely personal desires and forces. Although these forces—primarily love and revenge—are also associated with male characters in war movies,[28] their preeminence here serves to underscore (and secure) the femininity of the military women. The markers of femininity deployed in both *So Proudly We Hail* and *Cry Havoc* subtly suggest that military women, though their work is necessary and can even be celebrated, remain a fundamentally *inappropriate* presence. The linked anxieties, routinely expressed in American and British culture, that military women are either too masculine (and therefore sexually suspect) or too feminine (and therefore unreliable) for effective service return here in all their contradictory character. Both films' various attempts to reassure audiences that the military nurses and aides are still women— through an emphasis on heterosexual romance and feminine glamour— ironically also serve to undermine arguments for their effectiveness in a military context.

How, then, do narratives of romance and tropes of feminine glamour inform attempts to visualize the military woman in *Cry Havoc* and *So Proudly We Hail*? I've mentioned the role that costume plays in the transformation narratives at work in these films. Most obviously it is the move from nurse's whites or civilian clothes to fatigues, coded as both male and military, that underlines the toughness that the women in both films are developing. In *Cry Havoc* Captain Marsh cautions the volunteers that their work will be "distasteful" (because it will bring them close to dirt, bodies, and death), that they will be prone to disease, and that they will be subject to military regulations. Connie, the woman who is most obviously out of place, retains a bottle of perfume, keeping up a losing battle with the smells of labor and death. Such refined sensibilities, the film insists, need to be set aside in wartime. No surprise, then, that Connie is later killed when she is caught by a Japanese plane while swimming. Basinger reads such deaths as generic; pausing to contemplate nature is dangerous in time of war.[29] Connie's indulgence of the sensual pleasure of water (and her aspiration to cleanliness generally) marks her as out of place in wartime. In *So Proudly We Hail* Joan's black silk nightgown, the "morale booster" to which she is described as clinging desperately, signals the allure of prewar glamour. Onboard ship she uses the nightgown to improvise a stunning outfit for the Christmas party; later she persists in wearing it at night while the others sleep in their Army underwear. This gently comic attachment to an item of female clothing proves disastrous in the sequence where they must evacuate the field hospital. When Joan insists on going back for the gown, despite Davy's urgency (and her direct order), the group comes under attack and the three male soldiers who were to accompany the nurses are killed. The trapped women escape only after first Olivia and then Davy take decisive action. In one of the film's most notorious scenes Olivia sacrifices herself to save her fellow nurses. Letting down her long blonde hair (Lake's trademark), she tucks a grenade into the cleavage of her fatigues and walks toward oncoming Japanese troops, literalizing her image as a sex bomb and presumably taking her revenge for the death of her fiancé.

Davy shows both bravery and leadership in getting the truck started to effect a getaway, yet the necessity for her display (and Olivia's dramatic suicide) is triggered by Joan's foolish attachment to an item of feminine, female clothing. Over forty years later the television movie *Women of Valor* (1986) would fall back on this repertoire of inappropriate femininity in evoking the perils of Army nurses on Bataan: Helen delays the nurses' evacuation from their hospital to reclaim an item of black lingerie given to her by the other nurses to celebrate her imminent wedding. In both these instances, but more particularly in *So Proudly We Hail*, the bravery of military women is counterposed to signs of their frivolity, their inability to set aside a femininity which may get them (and others) killed. The awkward juxtaposition of frivolity and determination points to an evident tension within *So Proudly We Hail* between a desire to exploit the glamour of the female stars and an impulse to portray the nurses in a more down-to-earth fashion.

In both films the romance plot serves to secure conventional femininity. This too is expressed partly through costuming; when Davy announces her intention to marry she borrows one of McGregor's (military) skirts "just so the whole thing isn't too confusing." This attempt to reclaim female attire at the moment when Davy defines herself as a wife suggests that the nurses' masculinized identity is incompatible with the hierarchies of the heterosexual couple, but also that it is temporary and context-bound. *Cry Havoc*'s Smitty is introduced as a tough military presence, starkly setting out to the new aides their roles and responsibilities. An early phone call during which she sighs and smiles reveals a romantic involvement and works to soften her. The fact that her marriage must be kept a secret generates conflict when one of the aides sets her sights on Smitty's husband. It also places the audience in a position of superior knowledge, setting up a poignancy connected with how much Smitty must repress in the course of her duties. (When news of her husband's death is heard, *she* is not the one comforted.) Smitty's sense of duty and her desire to remain with her husband are closely entwined; valuing the lives of her patients above her own she displays a nurse's sense of vocation, a soldier's sense of duty, and a wifely loyalty to her husband, all mediated by the trope of triumph through sacrifice so characteristic of the woman's picture.

Like *Cry Havoc*'s Smitty, Davy in *So Proudly We Hail* does not willingly leave her station, and, again like Smitty, her motivation has to do with a man with whom she is romantically involved. While the centrality of men and romance to the lives of the Army nurses shown in these movies guarantees their humanity and their normalcy, even contemporary commentators observed the danger of perpetuating troubling stereotypes. Koppes and Black cite an official in the U.S. Office of War Information saying of *So Proudly We Hail*, "The worse feminine characteristics have been emphasized."[30] When Davy and her future husband, Summers (George Reeves), first meet, she is firmly in charge. Though he is a soldier, her role as nurse positions her in intimate proximity to (and gives her authority over) his body; she gives him a sponge bath despite his protestations (trade materials dubbed him "tall, dark and embarrassed"), a scene which flaunts the very physical intimacy that rendered nursing so problematic for contemporary gender norms (figure 22). Davy initially rejects any relationship, insisting that her job and responsibilities preclude love. Her resistance is short-lived, however, and the two declare their love for each other before they have even set foot on Bataan. While Smitty is secretly married, Davy marries Summers with the tacit approval of her commanding officer. Marriage may be against regulations, but under the twin forces of siege conditions and the narrative demand for romance, it seems inevitable. Joan too reminds Kansas (Sonny Tufts) that fraternization is against regulations, seeming to place military protocol over the possibility of a relationship. But she too ultimately succumbs to romance, reinforcing the film's implication that men and women who work side by side are inevitably caught up in relationships. That such romantic relationships are effectively required by Hollywood's gender norms and narrative conventions, while at the same time being illicit and inappropriate to com-

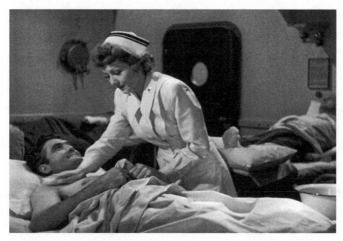

22. In *So Proudly We Hail* (1943) Davy's role as a nurse positions her in intimate proximity with male bodies.

bat, is a fundamental contradiction which *So Proudly We Hail* seemingly cannot escape. The contrast between the impassive figure of Davy as she is stretchered off the plane and the first scene of the flashback, in which she is a capable, caring, and authoritative career Army nurse, could not be more marked. The message seems clear: giving in to romance has literally weakened her, such that she physically collapses when forced to leave without her husband, who is missing in action.

Widely differing perspectives have been expressed on the significance of *So Proudly We Hail* in terms of its portrayal of Army nurses and nursing more generally. In her account of the American nurses on Bataan, Elizabeth M. Norman records that the nurses themselves hated the film: "It trivialized their experience, they said, their sacrifice, their ordeal."[31] Of course Norman rightly notes that it would serve neither the goals of propaganda (and indeed recruitment) nor those of entertainment to dwell on, or even substantially deal with, the more brutal aspects of the fall of Bataan. Yet the film aspired to celebrate the Bataan nurses, and there is clear evidence of attempts to provide accuracy in elements such as set design. Lt. Eunice Hatchitt, one of the ten nurses who escaped to Australia by plane, was assigned by the Army to provide technical assistance to the film. Norman records that Hatchitt, though initially enthusiastic, became increasingly disillusioned with the portrait of the Bataan nurses that began to emerge, and finally requested reassignment (her request was declined) in horror at the staging of Olivia's "erotic suicide."

In contrast to the responses of the nurses themselves, Hallam cites a survey of images of nursing in which *So Proudly We Hail* is described as "Hollywood's greatest tribute to the nursing profession," alongside James Agee's contemporary review, including the barbed assessment of the film as "probably the most deadly accurate picture ever made of what war looks like through the lenses of a housewives' magazine romance."[32] Agee's witticism draws on an implicit opposition between the hard-hitting verisimilitude of the war picture and the (supposedly) fantastic character of women's popular culture. That this is the culture of women far from the front and a form centered on romance seals the point, in the process reiterating the incompatibility of *woman* and *soldier*. By cinematic standards of course *So Proudly We Hail* was in many ways a landmark in its representation of military women at work. After all, it seeks to present the commitment of the nurses as heroic and celebrate their achievements. It attempts to maintain a precarious balance between military and love stories, as well as fulfilling contradictory expectations of both action and glamour. Yet it is clear that the celebration of military nurses' service ultimately conflicts with Hollywood's rigorously enforced gender norms, a conflict which produces the contradictory mix of patronage and patriotism which is so marked a feature of *So Proudly We Hail*.

ROMANCE AND TRANSFORMATION IN
NARRATIVES OF MILITARY NURSING

While romance serves to secure the femininity of the military woman in numerous popular films, both the ambiguity of the military woman's gender and the narrative drive toward romance and couple formation function in a variety of ways within narratives of military nursing. I explore some of these strategies in two very different nursing narratives from the Second World War: the B movie *Parachute Nurse* (1942) and *Homecoming* (1948), a postwar feature of romance and war pairing Clark Gable and Lana Turner. In the latter, romance is adulterous yet ennobling, while in the former it tends to feed into the simultaneously celebratory and trivializing treatment of the achievements and motivation of military nurses. Both films are instructive of the ways romance shapes Hollywood's characterization of military nursing during the 1940s.

Although *Parachute Nurse* opens with a respectful dedication, the temptation to trivialize is more than evident in the movie's tag line: "Sharp-Chutin' Lovelies . . . Doing Their Daring Bit for Uncle Sam!" The film does not locate the female group in combat; rather, in keeping with the conventions of the boot camp narrative, it stages the women's induction into military life, culminating in their successful graduation. The opening scenes present the movement from civilian to military nursing as a paranurse comes to the hospital to drum up recruits for the new force. The sequence plays up the women's delight at the prospect of enlistment; at its end they march around the hospital lounge in a show of high spirits. The nurses' talk centers on their irritation at the unreasonable demands made by fussy patients. The importance of this new nursing work—military nursing—is contrasted to the implicit triviality of civilian medicine as the paranurse declares, "I just got tired of those pampered pets who wanted their backs rubbed every fifteen minutes." Military service is thus explicitly presented as a route out of the mundanity of civilian nursing, the more degrading and servile aspects of which are emphasized. Both visibly girlish and seeking a flight from pampered femininity, these women see military nursing as an exciting opportunity and worthwhile work.

Processes of transformation through militarization are once again foregrounded. Already qualified and capable nurses, the women undergo basic training; they are beginners in military terms, aspiring to what is described as "the toughest service ever open to women." The film's release in August 1942, shortly after the fall of Bataan, would have ensured an initial reception framed by the sort of celebratory media context sketched above. Against the test (and the promise) of elite service, the women must physically challenge themselves. That this might involve a toughness coded as masculine is confirmed by their instructor, Lieutenant Woods, who tells them, "Parachuting takes muscles." The image of the nurse-soldier summoned up by the costume, mise-en-scène, and training sequences of a film like *Parachute Nurse* echoes the developing public image of the nurse as a figure in khaki rather than whites and the immediate historical context of events in the Philippines.

At a little over an hour the recruitment goals, group bonding, and romance narrative are all firmly compressed in *Parachute Nurse*. Three narrative strands are developed. The first centers on the antagonism between Cadet Glenda White and Cadet Helen "Kit" Ames. The second narrative strand concerns the developing romance between White and Woods. The third involves the exclusion and subsequent suicide of Cadet Gretchen Ernst, whose brother fights for the German Army. Although Ernst is, in the CO's words, "as much an American as the rest of us" and "a darned good soldier," she ultimately succumbs to bullying behavior; deliberately failing to open her parachute during a jump, Ernst falls to her death as the cadets watch horrified from the ground. These last two plot elements reinforce the first, pitting White against Ames. Indeed because Ames is also romantically interested in Woods, her conflict with White deepens throughout the film (reminding us that even military women compete for men). And while White and Cadet Morrison prove their patriotic integrity by attempting to include Ernst in the military group, Ames is quick to condemn on the basis of ethnicity alone. Ultimately it is Ames who will be excluded, forced to resign by the CO, who assures her, "We don't need girls like you around here, and we don't want 'em." Ames's jealousy and vindictiveness, depicted in actions such as sabotaging a parachute, manifest an excessive, capricious femininity, qualities ill-suited to the regulation and discipline of military life.

Boot camp movies typically culminate in a trial that tests soldiers' skills, teamwork, and individual strength of character. For the parachute nurses, the key test is their ability to jump from a plane, a task which the film presents as an unusual and physically challenging role for women. Ernst's (deliberate) failure in this task eliminates her from the action and underlines her weakness even as her role in the narrative is to feed into an argument for the ethnic diversity of the U.S. military. Her suicide also triggers an inappropriate hysterical response (one clearly coded as feminine) on the part of the hitherto capable (i.e., masculine, soldierly) White. As White recovers from her outburst, Woods is compassionate but cautions against any "excessive" display of emotion. Shifting from concerned lover to superior officer, he cautions her severely, "We're all entitled to a little personal and private hysteria, but the way you acted might well break down the morale of the whole corps." During their first jump White, the otherwise exemplary cadet, freezes; despite Woods's best attempts she is too terrified to jump. Thus the final narrative problem for the film to resolve is White's "irrational" (and implicitly womanly) fear.

In a hackneyed move that belies the film's focus on the courage and determination of military women, White's buddies and commanding officers work together to trick her into making the jump. Romance is the key: the group pretend that Woods's plane has been downed and that he is injured, in need of urgent medical attention. White's concern for her lover predictably overcomes her fear, and she jumps, then finds Woods hiding in an old plane wreck that is now used for target practice. The two embrace and the film concludes with a dissolve to images of the marching ranks of paranurses, picking out White and Morrison among their number. Ironically, at this precise moment of courage fueled by feminine solicitude, Woods explains that they came up with the scheme because she is "a swell guy." The characterization of military nurses, indeed military women more generally, as "one of the guys," even when they are romantically involved, even at such a deeply conventional narrative moment as this, indicates something of the ambiguously gendered nature of this figure. If romance narratives foreground femininity, the theme of fitting in, being one of the guys, involves a never quite complete attempt to alleviate military women's difference.

Centered on training and the transformation of civilian to military nurses, *Parachute Nurse* does not feature scenes of nursing in the field. *Homecoming*, by contrast, in which much of the action is set in a busy field hospital, is a rather different case. The last of the nursing narratives set in the Second World War considered in this chapter, the film, as its title suggests, offers a postwar perspective on the events portrayed. Romance plays a significant part in the movie, but the tropes of transformation through service are not enacted around the female characters. Instead the film focuses on the transformation of its initially self-centered male protagonist, Ulysses D. Johnson (Clark Gable), through his wartime experiences and his encounter with a tough army nurse, "Snapshot" McCall (Lana Turner). The military nurse is defined here not in contrast to other nurses but against the figure of the woman who waits at home, in the form of Johnson's wife, Penny, whose anxieties are allocated significant screen time. The film's flashback structure and its foregrounding of remembrance and loss, as well as personal change under dramatic circumstances, would likely have been strongly resonant for postwar audiences. *Homecoming* looks back to the war in order to think about the possibilities and character of a peacetime future. Crucially, although Snapshot is a figure of moral authority in the film, her death suggests that this new world is one in which the military woman (indeed any woman who ventures beyond the confines of the middle-class home) does not have a place or a voice.

Narratives of military women frequently concern themselves with the women's effect on men, whether they are regarded as disruptive, inspiring, desirable, or even repulsive. From the beginning Snapshot is introduced as a disruptive political voice, challenging the breezy optimism of Johnson's views. She not only argues for the need to get involved in domestic and international issues but casts judgment on his personal choices. (Praising the value of parenting, she tells the childless Johnson that he doesn't know what he has missed.) This encounter follows an extended picture of Johnson's prewar success—his position as head of surgery at a top hospital, the attentions of his female patients, his wealth and personal extravagance—clearly contrasting with Snapshot's forthright manner and sense of conviction. Johnson's self-centered prewar life returns to haunt him in his war work when a local boy in whom he has taken an interest dies as the result of untreated malaria (a health problem Johnson had previously known about but dismissed as of no interest). Snapshot's indignant rage at the indifference of Americans to illness and poverty at home reinforces the consequences of Johnson's previous affluent carelessness. Johnson has enlisted because it is the thing to do; Snapshot has a much clearer idea of why she is involved. Already widowed (her pilot husband was killed fighting in China six years previously) and mother to a six-year-old son she left behind to serve her country, her sense of passion and commitment, her disdain for Johnson (her nickname for him is "Useless"), and her articulation of forceful political opinions are striking. During their first meeting Johnson dismisses her on various counts, suggesting that she enlisted to seek excitement and that her proper place is with her child. He tells her, "When women talk world politics it makes me laugh." Ultimately Johnson realizes both his love for Snapshot and the shallowness of his previous existence; he will return to the U.S. (and to his wife) chastened. Through his encounter with a tough military woman, Johnson is effectively transformed into a "good doctor," a character who came to form a staple of popular medical romance in the postwar period.[33]

Posters and promotional images suggested a smoldering sexual charge between the couple, capitalizing on Gable's and Turner's star presence. Yet the pair do not kiss until late in the film, when Snapshot is about to depart from the unit. Brief moments of intimacy occur in fleeting fashion under enemy attack; even the pair's more promising meeting on leave in Paris is disrupted by news from the front. In general terms Snapshot facilitates Johnson's personal transformation in a comradely friendship, which only later develops into romance. Indeed when his wife writes revealing her jealousy, Johnson is indignant, describing Snapshot not as a woman, but "just a pal, a soldier." (A fellow officer observes that she is a

23. "Snapshot" McCall (Lana Turner) appears in military rather than glamorous guise in *Homecoming* (1948).

"darned pretty soldier.") Prohibitions against representing adultery clearly figure in the relatively chaste relationship between Johnson and Snapshot (and indeed the latter's death after her attempts to return to her unit). Yet a romance between soldiers, even of the conventional kind played out between doctor and nurse under fire, is not the basis for the postwar world of domestic femininity that the film ultimately endorses. A brief shot of the two embracing gives way to the image of the returning Johnson, his ship pulling into port through the mist to be met by his wife and butler.

As a pal, a soldier, and, albeit briefly, a lover, Snapshot looms large for Johnson. Yet *Homecoming* tells his story rather than hers. From her death-bed she sends him home with an Army saying—"When a soldier leaves his outfit, all debts and friendships are canceled"—that frames their relationship in particular terms, emphasizing both its temporary character and her defining identity as a soldier. It is perhaps significant in this context that Turner's glamour is downplayed in the film. She set aside gowns for a WAC uniform three years earlier in *Keep Your Powder Dry*, yet that film featured a signature scene in which she dresses for a date in her best uniform. In *Homecoming* Turner's character typically wears a shapeless cardigan over her functional khaki and a knitted hat or helmet over her blonde hair. Since the film is not concerned with *her* transformation, Snapshot's military garb is a constant, implicitly contrasted to the elegant femininity of Johnson's wife back in the United States (figure 23).

Snapshot as soldier and woman makes a claim for citizenship, for the right to hold and to voice her opinions. Though she has left her child to fight, the film does not code her as a bad or neglectful mother. Her very forthright character and strong opinions seem to make her death inevitable; though the postwar world will be shaped by her values, she will take no further part in this process. Instead the film ends with Ulysses and Penny Johnson reunited, the latter jubilant that she is needed once more. The disruptive but compelling figure of the military woman, who had "stood up under everything that even men couldn't take," remains only as a memory, albeit a powerful one. Snapshot stands for the temporary gender disruption of the war period, so thoroughly a soldier that she cannot, it seems, be refigured as a woman.

ROMANCE AND THE PROFESSIONALIZED MILITARY WOMAN: *FLIGHT NURSE*

Flight Nurse (1953), set during the Korean War, stages a transformation narrative around its female protagonist, Lt. Polly Davis (Joan Leslie), such that throughout the course of the film her character shifts her primary identification from romance to career. Davis transforms from a woman who sees herself as a wife-in-waiting to one who is defined by her professional identity as a flight nurse. The film's portrait of a fully professionalized military nurse is resonant of a period in which the U.S. military was coming to terms with the extent of its dependence on female personnel. (The production was supported by the Department of Defense and the U.S. Air Force.) Produced during the Korean War and released shortly after the armistice was signed,[34] *Flight Nurse* sets aside the total war discourses informing representations of the Second World War, foregrounding instead an opposition between Western democracy and the communist regimes of North Korea, China, and the Soviet Union.

While U.S. citizens in the 1950s were encouraged to understand themselves as part of (or at least aspiring to) a privatized domestic unit supported economically by men and emotionally by women, women continued to undertake paid work and the military continued to require their labor. Thus although the 1950s may be (rightly) associated with the emergence of domestic ideology and the rolling back of the limited economic and social inclusion offered to women during the Second World War, the postwar military continued to need women (just as the postwar economy more generally relied on women's low-wage labor). Indeed official efforts to recruit women on a voluntary basis did not succeed, so that Korea was the first conflict in U.S. history for which female reservists were recalled to service.[35] This provides a context for the shift from the framing of military women as a temporary necessity within the discourse of the Second World War to imagery of professionalized military women of the sort foregrounded in *Flight Nurse*. Moreover the film insists that this professionalized identity requires the ultimate refusal of romance, marriage, and domesticity.

The excitement of military nursing is effectively set against, even opposed to the rather more sedate pleasures of small-town domestic life in *Flight Nurse*. The film makes full use of the tropes of agency and freedom long associated with military nursing, coupling these with the novelty, glamour, and adventure of air travel. As discussed in chapter 1, the glamour of flight figured in recruitment for the Second World War and was featured prominently in fictions targeted at girls and young women. Published in 1945, *Cherry Ames, Flight Nurse*, the fifth in the popular series of books aimed at girls, also harnessed the appeal of airborne adventure, with trainee Ames expressing awe that "her new home was the sky." The excitement of the role is described in terms of freedom, movement, gleaming machines, and the men who work with them, as in this passage: "Everywhere, aloft and on the earth, were sunburned young men in khaki uniforms, or hard-working young men in green fatigues. Cherry's dark eyes shone. She put one hand on her blouse. She, too, like the young men, would wear silver wings there."[36] Her status equated with that of military men, the military woman as flight nurse is transported to the heart of the action, aiding in the treatment and evacuation of wounded soldiers. Both these texts foreground the mobility and professionalism of the flight nurse. The last-minute departures and snatched periods of sleep depicted in the film suggest the excitement and unpredictability of the flight nurses' work; their mobility as military women is literalized in a role that transports them with unaccustomed immediacy to the scene of action.

The proximity to "sunburned young men" remarked on in *Cherry Ames, Flight Nurse* recalls the erotic potential so often associated with nursing narratives. The opening scenes of the film feature the military nurse as a figure of sexual spectacle as well as alluding to more comradely relations between military men and women. En route to Korea, Polly Davis banters cheerily with two airmen, establishing herself as both friendly and authoritative before proceeding to dress herself in preparation for arrival. The image track provides ample opportunity for the viewer to contemplate her upper body, a provocative juxtaposition of bra and dog tags. The body of the military woman is displayed for the audience's pleasure in conventional terms, underlining her sexual desirability. The film's poster also foregrounds physical intimacy, dominated by the image of Davis and her lover embracing. Reproducing the image, Enloe observes Hollywood's routine romanticizing of military nursing.[37]

Even while the film's promotional materials foreground romance, the narrative trajectory of *Flight Nurse* is bound up in a professionalization that requires such connections be set aside. As Davis's body is on display in the opening scenes, her voice-over recalls this former self critically: "I had no thought of anything but my guy." As she works with the wounded and witnesses the war, the appeal of domesticity diminishes. Initially inspired by her love for Mike Barnes, Davis comes to realize not only the importance of her work but the extent to which her identity is bound up in it. The film's evocation of female comradeship underlines this point when the other flight nurses articulate a shared understanding that their mobile life is simply incompatible with romance. Lt. Ann Phillips cheerily tells Davis, who has carefully positioned her framed picture of Barnes on the bedside table, "Flight nurses never get their man." Lt. Kit Ramsey adds, "You catch onto a good one and he flies his way, and you fly another," a summary that underlines the mobility of both parties. Phillips's experiences provide a counterpoint to Davis's dreams of settling down with Barnes in Texas. She recalls a comparable moment in her own life when she visited a lover's family and of how oppressive she had found the prospect of small-town life. This tale (although later qualified to suggest that Phillips has been rejected rather than choosing not to marry) prefigures Davis's decision not to marry Barnes at the end of the film.

Flight Nurse features plenty of the generic staples that register the peculiarity of a woman's presence within the military and near the front. Male servicemen seem predisposed to dismiss the capabilities of military women; impressed, they wonder aloud at Davis's achievements. "She's got stuff," says Capt. Bill Eaton with admiration. A young technician stumbles in addressing Davis in suitable military terms: he misremembers her (superior) rank and calls her "Sir," a common trope that registers the military woman as a remarkable, and in some instances masculine-coded figure. Both her presence at the front and her noncombatant status are emphasized under fire, with Eaton protecting and restraining Davis during an aerial attack (figure 24). Yet she is also included in scenes of group bond-

24. Polly Davis (Joan Leslie) comes under fire during the Korean War in *Flight Nurse* (1954).

ing which, while common in Hollywood cinema, rarely include military women; the final image, for instance, sees Davis reunited with her flight team, gleefully anticipating the friendship and adventure of military camaraderie.

Davis is overwhelmed by and fully immersed in the nursing work that needs to be done, quickly realizing after her arrival in Korea that "no other thing mattered." She explicitly includes both Barnes and marriage in the list of things that no longer matter (although he will continue to matter to her for some time), recounting to herself here and at the film's end the "creed of the flight nurse," with its endorsement of care and glory. Thus the film concludes with her rejecting Barnes and the promise of cozy domesticity, opting instead to return to the field. Basinger regards Davis's choice of career as traditionally feminine, "actually a form of duty and sacrifice."[38] Certainly the construction of nursing as a vocation, a role to which selfless, angelic women are called, is a factor here. It is Polly Davis's identity as a military *nurse* that allows *Flight Nurse* to effectively construct her as both a soldier and a woman. In those scenes which show her working as a nurse, her femaleness is foregrounded rather than downplayed;

on the hospital plane she applies lipstick to reassure the frightened men, for instance. That the gesture is a performance—of femininity and courage—is made clear not only in her words ("They say this reassures the patients") but in a shot showing the men eagerly raising their heads to gaze at her.[39] When the plane's pilot, Eaton, comments on the looks she is getting ("Like they've never seen a girl before"), she confidently informs him that they are not seeing her but a more general idea of woman. In the sequence that follows, Eaton watches Davis interacting with the men and understands that this is true. His voice-over describes what he imagines the wounded soldiers to be seeing in the figure of the flight nurse. The film invites us to share his perception of these male fantasies in a series of dissolves that show the soldiers projecting loved ones or female archetypes onto her form (mother, girlfriend). These idealized images of femininity are juxtaposed with Davis's nursing skill and professional demeanor, as when, against all odds, her capable and decisive action saves the life of a man with a chest wound.

In their final meeting at the hospital where both are recuperating from their injuries, Davis tells Barnes with a genuine sense of loss, "It's not that I don't want a home with you. It's just that I'm not the girl for that kind of life. . . . This is where I belong." She rationalizes her choice as a rejection of safe domesticity ("I'd go crazy in a little town") and by affirming the value of her service. She no longer wants the domestic life she had so recently longed for; it seems wrong to her "just to sit on a porch in a house, when everything is happening *here*." The film in no way troubles the idea that, for women, romance, family, and career are fundamentally incompatible. At her insistence on duty Barnes sighs, "Polly, the lady warrior," as if naming her a soldier identifies the insurmountable obstacle he faces in making her his wife. In the film military life connotes—is premised on—mobility, while domesticity implies comfort, stasis, and potential boredom. Thus *Flight Nurse* negotiates the category of female soldier, making it manageable by enlisting the caring connotations of nursing and by insisting on the incompatibility of the professionalized military woman with conventional femininity.

TELEVISING THE MILITARY NURSE:
*M*A*S*H* AND *CHINA BEACH*

Whether depicting the Second World War or the Korean War, Hollywood movies featuring military nurses celebrate women's bravery, even acknowledge the need for their presence near the scene of combat. They also typically insinuate that military women are either not really women or not fully military. As Enloe writes, the popular image of military nursing "sustains a particular conventional notion of femininity; it doesn't upset it."[40] In such a context, this last section considers two television series, *M*A*S*H*, which ran on CBS from 1972 to 1983, and ABC's *China Beach*, which first aired in 1988 and ran until 1991. These shows not only feature—and in the case of *China Beach* centralize—military nursing; they also tackle questions of gendered military identity. Though *M*A*S*H* is a sitcom and *China Beach* a drama, the former featuring women as supporting characters, the latter centering on a female protagonist, they can be usefully considered together as shows that reveal much about the way female military nurses have become normalized, even unremarkable figures in American popular culture. Although there is much that can be said about both series—I return to *M*A*S*H* specifically as a comedy in chapter 5—the discussion here centers on questions of *visibility*, arguing that both shows form part of an evolving history of representation in which the female military nurse is seen to be present at or near the scene of combat even though she remains awkwardly incorporated into military hierarchies. Alongside this discussion of visibility, I also note how the military woman is figured in relation to conventional gender norms, whether these are affirmed or queried.

Both *M*A*S*H* and *China Beach* evoke nursing as a vocation and portray nurses in familiar terms as alternately tough, sexy, angelic, nurturing, womanly, and at times "one of the guys," a formulation that permits women's inclusion in the group by effectively downplaying difference. Chapter 1 detailed some of the ways popular culture assumes the categories of *woman* and *soldier* to be in tension with each other, or even completely incompatible. Another gendered opposition, one extensively employed in both *M*A*S*H* and *China Beach* and which features equally prominently in civilian medical dramas, is that between male doctors and female nurses. *M*A*S*H*'s pompous Major Winchester makes explicit an association between nursing, women, and menial work when he insists, "I'm a doctor, not a woman!" ("The Yalu Brick Road," 19 November 1979). If Winchester's function as a comic foil denies his views legitimacy, a gendered division of labor nonetheless structures the series and its hierarchy of nurses and doctors in which the latter are the central characters. The few exceptions tend to underline just how taken for granted this gendered

hierarchy is. When the Army refuses to recognize a male nurse's qualifica-
tions and forces him into a lower rank and menial work ("Your Retention
Please," 5 January 1981), the scenario foregrounds discrimination against
a man rather than speaking to the more prominent hierarchies of military
medicine in the camp. By contrast, "Nurse Doctor" (29 October 1979) has
Lt. Gail Harris (Alexandra Stoddart) preparing to take an aptitude test
for entrance to medical school. Harris is dubbed "nurse doctor" by the
other nurses, who, seemingly disquieted by her aspirations across the professional categories that structure the camp, ask to be assigned to alternate shifts. Harris's inappropriate sexual interest in the priest who tutors
her (a source of comedy in the episode) stands in for her more generally
transgressive behavior as she seeks to move from sanctioned female role
to an elite, male space. "Inga" (8 January 1979) stages the comic gender
consequences of a visit by a female Red Cross surgeon, Inga Helverson, to
the 4077th to observe combat surgery. Once again a high-status woman's
effect *on men* is centralized in this episode; Helverson's honesty in sexual
matters and her competence as a surgeon are simply too much for Capt.
"Hawkeye" Pierce (Alan Alda) and Winchester, both of whom attempt to
charm her and end up feeling foolish. The latter describes Helverson as a
"conceited, arrogant, pushy woman," extending his venom to an "under-
handed little nurse—naturally they stick together" in a manner that suggests a more generalized anger at women who step out of their place in
the medical hierarchy. Helverson's presence may threaten to temporarily
lay bare the sexual economy of doctor-nurse relations, but the episode is
atypical of the series in its explicit address to these concerns.

While in *M*A*S*H* we regularly see the traumatic impact of "meatball
surgery" on the male surgeons (indeed this is the chief mode through
which the central characters express their dismay at the human cost of
war), the nurses' responses are rarely voiced. Nurses are seen tending to
patients (and fending off sexual advances with good humor); occasionally their response becomes more significant, as when we see (through
Pierce's perspective) Lt. Kellye Yamato care for a young patient through
his final hours ("Hey, Look Me Over," 25 October 1982), or Houlihan recalling a young soldier's death ("Letters," 24 November 1980). More often
nurses look on silently as the dramatic themes of the episode are played
out through the principal characters. The telling title of one episode, "The
Nurses" (19 October 1976), suggests how rare it is for the series to devote
dramatic space or time to the experience of these women. Here the show

draws out the feelings of stress and trauma generated by nursing. One nurse defends her drunkenness in terms similar to the doctors, for whom alcohol is used habitually to alleviate boredom and to deal with emotion; she tells the reproachful Houlihan that she is "numb," drinking "to feel something." Such episodes are exceptional in hinting at a commonality of experience across the division between female nurses and male doctors.

The interaction of doctors and nurses in M*A*S*H is often as sexualized as it is professional. Given the primary focus of the series on the intense, stressful work of surgery interspersed by periods of boredom, sexual (and occasionally romantic) liaisons between the male doctors and female nurses of the 4077th function as a temporary distraction. Conventional sexual mores are effectively reversed in the early seasons of the show such that virtue is aligned with those characters who are sexually open, rather than those defined as repressed or uptight. In the early years the series frequently cast nurses as sexual sidekicks who dance, flirt with, and kiss male doctors. Such a sexualized atmosphere draws on long-standing stereotypes of the sexy nurse, a figure whose youth and availability make her an attractive diversion. Elana Levine describes the use that shows such as M*A*S*H made of "sexual openness" as a "symbol of the changing times, right alongside more forthright attitudes toward race relations, the generation gap, and women's liberation."[41] However, the coupling of women's liberation—of which their presence in the military is often taken as a sign—with sexual openness risks restating the sort of stigma played out extensively in cultural anxieties surrounding military women in the Second World War. Indeed for actual military women, assumptions about their sexual availability remain both pervasive and damaging.[42]

Although M*A*S*H is set in the Korean War, the show was produced during a period shaped not only by the Vietnam War but by high-profile feminist challenges to the legal and social position of women. The period was characterized by significant public and political debate on the educational and professional opportunities open to women, debates which impacted significantly on U.S. military policy. The military academies were opened up to women in 1976, and in 1978 the dissolution of the WAC resulted in the integration of women into a variety of units, some previously all-male. While such events increased the visibility of military women in American culture, military nurses effectively remained "invisible soldiers." That very invisibility provides an important context for the later

25. *China Beach* foregrounds the work of military nurses and their proximity to dirt and death.

China Beach, which explores the Vietnam War through the experiences of both military and civilian women working in the Ninety-fifth Evacuation Hospital and allied recreational facility. *China Beach* features a diverse group of American women involved in the war, not only nurses and enlisted personnel, but journalists, prostitutes, entertainers, and Red Cross volunteers. The show was first aired at a time when representations of the Vietnam War were achieving a new level of cultural visibility.[43] In revisiting that war and centering on women, *China Beach* consciously sought to imagine, to make visible military women and female veterans as part of that renewed attention. The subsequent dedication in 1993 of a memorial to female veterans in Washington, D.C. is described by Enloe as the "high point" of a "visibility campaign" in which *China Beach* had played a significant part.[44]

Though peripheral in *M*A*S*H*, the traumatic work and professional pressures associated with military nursing are central to *China Beach*. Informed by the conventions of both war and melodrama, the show explores the proximate relationship between its nurse protagonist and the dirt, bodies, and death that characterize war (figure 25). Lt. (later Capt.) Colleen McMurphy is the show's central protagonist and moral point of reference. The pilot episode stages her imminent departure (she has just one week of her tour remaining) and her decision to stay in Vietnam. This choice is rationalized in terms of a sense of belonging within the military unit ("I am home") and duty (her concern for "wounded, hurt, bleeding GIS"). Her decision to serve as an Army nurse (and her decision to stay in Vietnam) is explicitly presented in terms of McMurphy's reluctance to go home and an awareness of the limited options available to her in civilian life. At one point she tells K.C. (Marg Helgenberger) that she "couldn't wait to get away" from her home life and hometown ("You, Babe," 13 October 1990). In the pilot episode she confesses her love of the place, telling USO singer Laurette that she had never seen the ocean before arriving in Vietnam. On occasion *M*A*S*H* too featured this rhetoric of opportunity, as when Houlihan meets an older woman who contrasts the excitement of military nursing with the limited horizons of most women's lives, re-marking, "We see more of the world than most people dream of" ("Lil," 2 October 1978). Alongside the gruesome evocation of triage nursing and the themes of trauma and memory, *China Beach* draws fairly explicitly on associations between military nursing and freedom, travel, and adventure for women. McMurphy has joined the Army in part to escape the rou-tinized femininity of life in Kansas, a life she is unable to settle for on her return to the U.S. Thus *China Beach* sketches a military woman protago-nist who is not fully reconciled to conventional femininity, one who finds herself at home in a place where is she is needed but also resented.

M*A*S*H mediates sexual and racial antagonisms through comedy, with good doctor Pierce as an increasingly benevolent patriarch. Hos-tility toward military women is more overtly expressed in *China Beach*. Thus the season 4 opener ("The Big Bang," 29 September 1990) includes scenes of McMurphy's first weeks at China Beach and the hostility she encounters there; when she insists to Dr. Richard (Robert Picardo) that she is a "damned good nurse," he asks her to stand on a piece of paper on the floor, then remarks, "Now you're a good paperweight." The battle-hardened soldier Dodger tells her directly, "You don't belong here." In this episode McMurphy also expresses her frustration at the repeated sexual overtures she receives from GIS. When she protests, "I just need a friend," the response from a fellow nurse is a not particularly reassuring "Good luck," suggesting that for women, comradeship is not part of military life. Indeed the series describes relationships between military and militarized women, and, in turn, between these women and military men. Yet it is striking how rarely *China Beach* brings *military* women together and how rarely this connotes comradeship. Instead McMurphy develops complex and evolving relationships with a prostitute, a USO performer, and a jour-nalist. Such patterns of relationships perhaps prefigure those more recent tropes in which military women are represented as overwhelmingly iso-lated figures within a masculine military, a development addressed in the third part of this book.

Michael Saenz characterizes McMurphy as "a feminized, Irish Catho-lic version of M*A*S*H's Hawkeye Pierce."[45] While the analogy makes sense in terms of McMurphy's function as principal observer of the cha-otic events of war, it overlooks the strength of her self-identification as a *military* woman as well as a medical professional. Like M*A*S*H's Mar-garet Houlihan, McMurphy is defined by her military identity, a process that relates to the show's intent to make meaningful the military nurse as a soldier and as a veteran. While Pierce conceives of himself as an irri-tant to military life and culture, McMurphy is a conservative figure who struggles to come to grips with her complexly changing world. Her self-identification as a military woman conflicts with the male characters' understanding of combat as an experience that, in Carolyn Reed Var-tanian's words, "they, unlike the women, did not choose to be a part of," but which only they can understand.[46] Nurses are part of the war, but they are also removed from it; they are focused on caring, but their work sup-ports killing. *China Beach* emphasizes that making war relies on nurs-ing; despite the military nurse's conformity with a feminine vocation of nurturance and care, she is inextricably part of the war. McMurphy is shocked to discover that another nurse is advising a patient on the symp-toms he should report to ensure discharge and a ride home; later she will hand the same patient a gun so that he can wound himself, a change of heart which suggests her complex, deeply ambivalent relationship to the war and her work.

China Beach's hybrid of war and melodrama, as well as its focus on female characters, provides a generic space to address the cultur-ally contradictory figure of the female soldier. McMurphy is clearly an idealized figure, a woman with a sense of vocation; the emphasis on her Catholicism and her commitment to nursing are mutually reinforcing here, and quite in line with traditional images of the nurse as asexual minister to the sick. Yet the series also undercuts, even questions these associations, drawing McMurphy as a passionate, desiring woman who develops intense relationships with a series of male characters. In this and in the uneasy designation of McMurphy as "one of the guys," the show recognizes the tension between gendered and military identities. Indeed by the season 4 episode "I Could Have Danced All Night . . . But Didn't" (4 June 1991) McMurphy angrily rejects the terms of her incorporation into the military group. In this episode the tension between romance and camaraderie comes to the surface, McMurphy feeling, it seems, unsettled by her masculine, military identity. Addressing the group she asserts, "Sorry to disappoint you, but I'm *not* one of the guys. I'm not your buddy. And I'm sick of taking care of you." In her attempt to insist on her humanity, her identity as a woman (implicitly an identity at odds with the military) is brought to the fore. Thus she tells Dr. Richard, "This place, this uniform, these boots that are two sizes two big that I've been wearing for two years. This is not me." Moreover, in making a distinction between her personal and military identity, between "Colleen" and "McMurphy," she makes clear that both identities are important to her, but that they are in some way irreconcilable.

As a series *China Beach* elaborates a similar point with respect to the female veteran, attempting to make her visible and recognizable. Amanda Howell suggests it is an attempt to render the specificity of a female veteran's sense of disjuncture: "She [McMurphy] is a woman without options. Moving through the stifling silence of a hospital nursery at night, through the empty shell of her mother's house, across the desert, and on the verge of suicide in a hotel room, she becomes the feminist version of Travis Bickle, lost between stereotypes of family and military—the roles of daughter, nurse, lover, wife, and mother."[47] To the extent that marriage and motherhood are synonymous in popular narrative with moving on and coming to terms with the past, the final episode's imagery suggests the completion of *China Beach*'s therapeutic narrative of remembrance. Now part of a couple, McMurphy holds her young daughter as she stands at the famous wall of the Vietnam Memorial in Washington; here she recalls (and locates) the name of a young soldier who died during her final day in Vietnam, a soldier who had insisted that she would remember him ("Hello, Goodbye Part 2," 22 July 1991).

A memorializing function permeates the show; the final episode, which culminates in the characters driving through the night to visit the Vietnam Memorial following a reunion in 1988, features the dedication "To the Vietnam veterans, especially the women, who served and who inspired our show." Vartanian argues that William Broyles Jr., the producer of *China Beach* and a Vietnam veteran, chose "to position women as sympathetic and supportive observers of combat" as part of a wider strategy to emphasize the individual soldier rather than the compromised war as a whole; she cites his comments on the women involved in Vietnam: "No matter how involved you get with the tangled purposes of the war and its moral confusion and its unhappy end, what they did was purely heroic."[48] It is *China Beach*'s inscription of the female veteran that remains one of the show's most striking features. Pvt. Frankie Bunsen, whose return to civilian life in Chicago in 1969 brings her up against the trial of the Chicago Seven ("The Call," 8 December 1990), is seen attempting to establish a stand-up act, to insist in effect on her presence. Breaking off her routine, she addresses the audience thus: "I'm black. I'm a black woman. I'm a black woman Vietnam vet. I'm a black woman Vietnam vet. Isn't that scary?" Her self-designation here is an assertion of visibility and trauma from which the episode segues back to China Beach and McMurphy's construction of a memorial to the soldiers who believed in "all this—the lies." McMurphy, whose complicity with the war by virtue of her presence is so regularly highlighted, spray-paints the names of dead soldiers on a building in an evident allusion to the Vietnam Memorial.[49]

While the women's memorial in Washington would clearly represent both white and African American nurses, most popular fictions marginalize black women's military service. The nurses in *M*A*S*H* come from a range of ethnic backgrounds, yet the show tends to foreground white nurses, often through their involvement in romantic plots with the white doctors.[50] Lt. Ginger Bayliss, who features in seasons 1 to 3, is the series' most prominent African American nurse, although the specificity of her experience is, as with the white nurses, largely mediated through the perspective of the male doctors. Thus in the season 2 episode "Dear Dad . . . Three" (10 November 1973) Pierce and "Trapper" John McIntyre educate a racist white patient on the folly of his prejudice. (He expresses anxiety about the color of the blood he will receive in a transfusion.)[51] While Bayliss certainly plays a part in this scenario and has the chance to insist on her rank as an officer (ultimately the chastened patient will salute her), this pedagogical scenario is effectively an affair conducted between (white) men. The white surgeon heroes demonstrate their egalitarianism by taking a stand against racism. The episode's final image of Pierce's lecherous delight at being introduced to a blonde Swedish nurse is indicative of the show's rapid reinstatement of the desirability of white womanhood.

Although other stories are told, McMurphy remains the central character in *China Beach*, struggling to come to terms with civilian life and with alcoholism and ultimately confronting her Posttraumatic Stress Disorder (PTSD). The final series' elaboration on her experience as a veteran is mapped across a series of episodes through which she encounters figures from China Beach, culminating in the reunion theme of the final double episode. "Through and Through" (16 July 1991), in which McMurphy confronts her PTSD, is set in 1985 and is perhaps the most explicit working-through of these questions. Now married and working as a hospital administrator, McMurphy is troubled; although she is experiencing distressing flashbacks she does not initially understand her difficulties in terms of her wartime experiences. Just as Vietnam represented a perverse scene of opportunity, McMurphy's civilian life is equated with trauma and loss. This is partly about recognizing that her experiences in Vietnam, though dreadful, were also extremely intense and thus a source of ambivalent feelings. When she encounters Dr. Richard in 1972 McMurphy, at this point working in a manual job, speaks of the war regretfully: "I was valuable. I loved it there. . . . But it's over. It's gone" ("Juice," 10 November 1990).

When McMurphy does seek help from a Veterans Center, she struggles to define herself as a female veteran. Indeed she is misrecognized on her first visit, when the counselor assumes that she is *married* to a veteran. The failure to see her veteran or military identity suggests the show's didactic function in relation to women's participation in the war in Vietnam. Realizing his mistake the counselor chases after her, offering the words "Welcome home" in a scenario of redemption and return. Yet home is clearly an unsatisfactory space for McMurphy, and the scene showing her participation in a support group in which she is the only woman underlines her lack of fit. The men in the support group are uncomfortable with her presence, her troublesome difference. McMurphy's assertion that in Vietnam she was "just one of the guys" produces dissent; this is a fiction they don't wish to go along with. McMurphy responds angrily, "If I wasn't, it was because you wouldn't let me be." Her words suggest that for McMurphy as a female veteran, coming to terms with the past involves acknowledging both her service and her awareness that her presence as a military woman was (and remains) unwelcome. In response to the question "What did we [i.e., male soldiers] do?," McMurphy's explanatory, confessional comments lead to fragmented memories of the past, of the cost of chivalric behavior, of sexual harassment and male resentment, of the emotional cost of serving as the screen that stands in for feminine ideals as mother, girlfriend, sister, angel. In effect the show names and problematizes the spectacular function of the military nurse as a representation of idealized femininity, insisting on acknowledging the woman who inhabits that body. Against a context of cultural invisibility *China Beach* aims to make visible the military nurse as military woman, drawing on and contesting the lengthy history of representations which have refused the viability of that category.

China Beach champions military women and military nurses, self-consciously aiming to gain new visibility for women's contributions to and involvement in the Vietnam War. Across the film and television shows explored in this chapter, narratives of military nursing dramatize the anxieties attendant on military woman's presence in and near combat. As with all military women, concerns about respectability and appropriate gender behavior are pervasive. Themes of transformation, opportunity, and romance so central to the dramatic characterizations of military women explored in chapter 1 are also prominent in nursing narratives. The military nurse's proximity to the male body and to death challenges gender norms, while her commitment to healing is typically pictured in conventionally feminine terms. Tough by necessity and caring by vocation, military nurses do not typically constitute a provocative presence within the film and television shows in which they appear; neither are they figured as soldiers, however. Rather their visibility restates as much as it troubles the cultural contradiction of the "woman soldier."

PART TWO

During and after the Second World War, Hollywood cinema showcased the military woman as much in light entertainment genres such as musicals and comedies as in drama. The chapters that follow focus on these typically comedic uses of the military woman. A few of the narratives feature military women in the sorts of supporting or subsidiary roles framed as "auxiliary" in chapter 1. More often these musicals and comedies feature military women as protagonists. They certainly occupy more screen time than the romantic interest roles familiar from wartime drama. While reiterating the themes of transformation through service deployed in the dramatic and melodramatic movies and shows explored in chapters 1 and 2, almost all center on a romance plot of one kind or another. These narratives often exploit the comic potential of role-reversal that the military woman is taken to represent. Her presence in uniform or in a position of authority, sometimes directly over the male lead, is represented as a challenge, albeit a gentle one, to the established gender hierarchies of romantic and professional relationships. A cartoon of the Second World War on display at the Women in Military Service for America Memorial at Arlington sums up these concerns. A uniformed woman is seen on bended knee in front of a timid-seeming man in civilian dress who sits on a park bench. She holds a bunch of flowers, the iconography suggesting a proposal of marriage. The caption has her telling the man that she now has something to fight for and come home to. The cartoon achieves its comic effect by reversing the familiar imagery of a forceful (military) man in abeyance before a meek (civilian) woman to whom he is proposing. The meaning of this and numerous other, similarly themed comic strips, postcards, and comic vignettes of the era is clear. By virtue of her position the military woman gains in authority, a shift in her typically subordinate social position that is employed in the service of comedy.

The authority of the military woman is frequently portrayed as troubling for men in the films and television shows discussed in these chapters, most particularly the comedies which pick up on screwball traditions in which men are routinely disconcerted and confounded by either women's power or their "feminine" irrationality (or, perversely, both). The humor derived from the image of military women takes two broad forms. The first casts her as "masculine." This may involve an unexpected assertiveness and independence (as in the cartoon of a woman proposing) or a suggestion that she is mannish. In the latter case comedy comes from the mannish military woman's physical strength, butch appearance, and commitment to discipline. The threat to masculinity posed by an independent, professional (military) woman produces narrative dilemmas for the male protagonists of the late 1940s and mid-1950s in, among others, *I Was a Male War Bride* (1949) and *The Lieutenant Wore Skirts* (1956).

A second broad strand of comic representation exploits the supposed mismatch of the categories *woman* and *soldier* rather differently. Here, instead of suggesting that the military woman is inappropriately forward and assertive (masculine), humor comes from the juxtaposition of her femininity and the discipline required by military life. The comedy produced by an evocation of the military woman's excessive and inappropriate femininity is exploited in such films as *Operation Petticoat* (1959) and *Private Benjamin* (1980). Whether it is women's authority or their femininity that is played for comedy, both musicals and comedies mine the military woman's gender identity for laughs even as they celebrate such women's patriotism.

The regimented and spectacular aspects of military life make it a subject well suited to the musical. Indeed all four musicals considered in this chapter delight in the overlap between drill and the musical number. *Tars and Spars* (1946) features a parade ground number in which Chuck (Sid Caesar) sings surrounded by a throng of Guardsmen.[1] A number in *Up in Arms* (1944) features male soldiers and Army nurses embarking in formation. Both *Here Come the WAVES* (1944) and *Skirts Ahoy!* (1952) feature drill as part of the entertainment offered to servicemen and servicewomen. Indeed the trailer for the former promised, alongside its star attractions of Bing Crosby, Sonny Tufts, and Betty Hutton, "hundreds of those glorious gals of the U.S. Navy!," making clear the spectacular function of these military women. Drill is elaborately integrated into the film's final number, which employs WAVES (Women Appointed for Voluntary Emergency Service) as chorus members. In *Skirts Ahoy!* drill serves as part of the fare of an evening's entertainment provided by the USO. Here the WAVES and the cinema audience are treated to a marching number in which the women's drill is explicitly presented as analogous to a stage performance.

Drill is a prominent feature of military musicals, dramas, and recruitment films. It is perhaps inevitable that the elaborately choreographed numbers designed by Busby Berkeley spring to mind when it comes to the precision of drill and the rendition of woman as spectacle within the musical. In this context we might consider Lucy Fischer's observation of Berkeley's numbers: "The women lose their individuation in a more profound sense than through the similarity of their physical appearance. Their identities are completely consumed in the creation of an overall abstract design."[2] These comments clearly apply to both the chorus and the ranks. Carol Burke's analysis of the transformative metaphors and practices of basic training foregrounds the military necessity at stake in the spectacle. She writes, "Without uniformity, the highly choreographed dance of the military parade would dissolve into chaos. Drill effectively teaches recruits that each must keep every step, every line of the body, even every gaze in sync with the group. Close-order drill is important figuratively—to train individual soldiers under the orchestration of their leader to configure an army collectively."[3]

The musical's presentation of parading military woman as spectacular entertainment places servicewomen in a familiar generic setting. As performers military women display the conventional attributes of femininity. The significance of uniform as costume provides another link between the parade ground and the musical number. As Nadine Wills has explored, the tradition of using "women- in-uniform" in the Hollywood musical is a long-standing one. These are not actual uniforms of course but a variety of glitzy and revealing costumes that allude to uniforms of one kind or another for erotic effect.[4] Exploring the prevalence of such costumes in the Hollywood musical of the 1930s, Wills argues that the convention signals gender trouble. The costumes she looks at—sailor suits, Army uniforms, and cross-dressed outfits—are all variants of male military uniforms. Equally they all clearly reveal rather than mask the femaleness of the wearer. Wills believes the significance of the women-in-uniform costume lies in its *disassociation* from the military, "its very obvious lack of connection to any kind of combat or service," rendering it a safely patriotic sign for war-weary audiences.[5]

This is not to say that the culturally disruptive associations of the military woman, as explored in part 1, are not registered in the musical. Indeed such concerns are evident in, for example, the sexual role-reversals that routinely contrast strong, independent military women with ineffective, comical, or in some way diminished men. An assumption that (some) military women are also sexually active or even sexually predatory also features in these musicals, though it emerges most insistently in the more recent of the examples considered here. Of course musicals featuring military women also celebrate their achievements, patriotism, and bravery; in wartime they echo and positively reinforce the themes of recruitment drives. But, like the dramas and romances explored in chapters 1 and 2, they also, and often simultaneously, work to contain the potential unruliness of military women, their implicit challenge to male authority and hierarchies.

Military movies are characterized by a structuring tension between exceptional individuals, who are clearly the focus of screen and narrative attention, and the group they represent. At its most basic, military order revolves around a lack of individuation (in Fischer's terms) even as it relies on exceptional but disciplined individuals. Military narratives frequently emphasize the need for individual personnel to put the needs of the service before their own desires. This is an important point of commonality between the genres: both musicals and military narratives depict individuals working together for the good of the show or the service. Given stereotypical associations between femininity and disorder—associations routinely reiterated in the rhetoric of those opposed to women's military service—an evocation of the discipline required in group performance arguably works to affirm the military woman's capabilities.

Both the convention of adapting the male military uniform as an eroticized costume for female performers and that displaying the massed ranks of a precisely choreographed female chorus are employed in the concluding number of *Pin-up Girl* (Fox, 1944), starring Betty Grable. Grable transforms from a Merry Widow in black lace to a glamorous drill sergeant, replete with ceremonial sword and powder-blue uniform, drilling her female chorus (equipped with rifles) in a protracted fantasy display of martial order. The sequence conspicuously marshals glamour for the war effort, self-consciously drawing on Grable's status as pin-up while alluding to the contemporary visibility of military women. What distinguishes the musicals considered in this chapter from such a spectacle is that the female performers wear the uniforms of military women and not costumes fashioned after male attire; they thus reference a controversial and newly charged public status. These films demonstrate that the musical was more than capable of responding to such developments by incorporating them into its exuberant spectacle.

The four musicals considered here all foreground military life, but in keeping with the utopian quality of the Hollywood musical, combat (and death) is quite explicitly elsewhere.[6] To the extent that the combat experiences of military men overseas are represented at all, which is very

26. Musicals featuring military women foreground romance, spectacle, and entertainment rather than the dangers of wartime (*Tars and Spars*, 1946).

little, it is mediated through comedy, as in *Up in Arms*, or presented indirectly through verbal recollection. Even here it is typically disrupted or mediated. For instance, when we are first introduced to Johnny Cabot (Bing Crosby) in *Here Come the WAVES* he bemoans the physical restrictions that prevent him from enlisting, demanding that his buddy Windy (Sunny Tufts) recount details of an action at sea. Yet Windy's attentions are focused on women's bodies, and Cabot is repeatedly distracted by his female fans' requests for autographs, ensuring that an account of combat is perpetually deferred. In *Tars and Spars* Howie's (Alfred Drake) heroism in combat is recounted deadpan by Sid Caesar in a rare serious moment, but the assumption that he has perished is quickly corrected by his reappearance and enthusiastic participation in the show's closing number. Life and the vibrancy of performance thus replace the wartime threats of danger, loss, and death (figure 26).

As combat is effaced, other kinds of work are brought to the fore, although we see relatively little of the specifically military work of either men or women. Virginia and Mary are nurses in *Up in Arms*, as is Ensign Nellie Forbush in the later *South Pacific*, but we see little of their duties. *Here Come the WAVES* shows Rosemary communicating with aircraft from a tower, but her main work, together with her sister Susie's, centers on a spectacular show designed to boost WAVES recruitment. SPAR Christine Bradley is seen in an office setting in *Tars and Spars*, but she also performs in the service show, and *Skirts Ahoy!*, which features WAVES in training, also sees them putting on and attending shows. Thus, as we might expect of the musical, entertainment emerges as the most important form of labor. Typically the actual work that both military men and women do daily is sidelined in favor of an emphasis on musical performance and the plot twists of romantic attraction, misunderstanding, and reconciliation.

Employing the established conventions of the integrated musical, three of the films explicitly feature shows within shows, providing a setting for star turns. *Up in Arms* is the only one of the four not to feature an elaborately choreographed show within a show, but even here there are set-piece performances for the stars: Danny Weens (Danny Kaye) performs for the crowds waiting outside a cinema; Lt. Virginia Merill (Dinah Shore) makes a record of her voice before departure; and both Kaye and Shore perform onboard ship to entertain fellow soldiers. Howie too makes a record as a way to serenade the SPAR he loves in *Tars and Spars*, singing "I'm Glad I Waited for You," a number that the two will perform together later in the film.[7] While the war-romance hybrids explored in chapter 1 combine scenes of combat (focused on military men) and romance against the context of war (the military couple), the musicals discussed here portray entertainment as a site of shared labor for military men and women. Their patriotic endeavors serve to entertain the forces and boost recruitment.

The construction of entertainment as work is most central to *Here Come the WAVES*, a film concerned with recruitment. The film was directed and produced by Mark Sandrich, who had previously worked with Bing Crosby (on *Holiday Inn*) as well as with Fred Astaire and Ginger Rogers. The previous year Sandrich had also directed and produced *So Proudly We Hail* (a melodramatic celebration of the bravery of military nurses discussed in chapter 2), establishing an association with upbeat portrayals of women's military service in line with official recruitment goals. Much of the narrative action of *Here Come the WAVES* centers on Cabot's production of a theatrical show to recruit WAVES. A reluctant impresario, he lands the job when Susie (Betty Hutton), a member of the WAVES and an avid fan, who fears for his fate should he be sent to sea, proposes the idea in his name. Involvement in the show represents a literal displacement or delay of active service for Cabot, as it does for Howie in *Tars and Spars*. Entertainment work is opposed to combat in gendered terms. Cabot resolves his dilemma by putting together an elaborate and successful show incorporating filmed footage of himself and Windy. He is thus able to return to duty at sea and retain a presence in the show. The film's final number features massed ranks of WAVES onstage waving farewell to a vast projected image featuring Cabot and Windy, among other sailors, boarding their vessel. The scenario spectacularly literalizes the "Free a man to fight" rhetoric of recruitment campaigns. The WAVES are not only assembled as spectacle here; in bidding farewell to the pictured sailors, military women are both working *and* waiting.

All four musicals acknowledge or directly incorporate the themes centered in recruitment drives directed at women during the Second World War. These themes include patriotism, self-confidence, a healthy lifestyle, and the novel personal and professional opportunities offered to women by military service. The theme of freeing a man to fight, and thus the distinct roles of military men and women as combatant and noncombatant, is also mobilized; thus *Here Come the WAVES* has Susie speak passionately of the value of the WAVES, enthusing, "Even *I* replaced a man." Given the recruitment focus of its narrative, it is not surprising that *Here Come the WAVES* is the most explicit of the four films in its use of the themes and rhetoric associated with contemporary recruitment materials (themes outlined in chapter 1). The close relationship is illustrated by the opening sequence. The film's first shot portrays a WAVES recruitment poster on the side of a trolley car which serves as a mobile recruiting station. Six WAVES backed by four sailors sing to the assembled crowd:

Join the Navy
It's the place to be
Join the Navy
Be a W-A-V-E.

Civilian women queue to find out more amid the hustle and bustle of the city street. As the song continues on the soundtrack, we cut to a wide shot of a woman seated at a desk in a spacious office. Clearly visible through the picture window is a billboard with another WAVES recruiting poster set off by the city skyline. The woman peruses a series of mocked-up advertisements, screwing up her face at the image she is looking at; a cut reveals the offending item: "Chew your way to Victory. Use Pemeco the Patriotic gum." When the woman turns to look out of the window, the camera tracks far enough for us to see what she is seeing: the WAVES poster. When the camera swings back it shows her smile with delight, throw the posters aside, grab her purse, and exit, presumably to enlist. A second vignette shows a young woman bidding farewell to her family, kissing her mother and father and saluting her little brother. This image explicitly echoes a poster from 1943 which showed a WAVES recruit about to embark on her training. A third scenario features a couple kissing at the train station, the man in naval uniform. Clearly emotional following her lover's departure, she turns, sees a Navy recruiting booth, and smiles, walking toward it purposefully. Once again there is a direct link with contemporary recruiting materials, specifically a poster from September 1944 depicting a woman in civilian clothes embracing a sailor at a train station with text that advises prospective WAVES, "Bring him home sooner." A line from the movie's opening song drives the point home: "Join the boyfriend / Across the foam / Help to bring him back home." These women are exemplary recruits in terms of their motivation and enthusiasm. Songs and images encapsulate different but equally valid motives for enlistment, whether it is patriotism, personal development (boredom with a superficial job in advertising), or personal ties (loved ones in the Navy).

Diverse motives for enlistment are comically represented by the two military women at the center of *Here Come the WAVES*, Rosemary and Susie Allison, a twin nightclub act, both played by Betty Hutton. Rosemary is a down-to-earth redhead, Susie a "ditzy" blonde obsessed (from afar) by the crooner Johnny Cabot. Rosemary's decision to enlist is expressed in explicitly patriotic terms. Following the opening sequence, the twins burst onto the stage to deliver an up-tempo version of the "Join the Navy" number. In long sequined skirts and midriff-revealing tops, they entreat the audience, "Do your doo-doo-duty today," their act projecting eroticized patriotism. Back in the dressing room Susie is shocked that Rosemary plans to follow the lyrics of their song and enlist. Susie's reluctance emphasizes her disorganized femininity. While as Rosemary, Betty Hutton is moderate, patriotic, and disciplined, in her role as Susie she embodies feminine excess. Susie stumbles, trips, faints, shouts, gets her clothes muddled, desires aggressively (her fandom intimidates Cabot), impersonates her sister, falls in the water, and so on; in short she is out of control, a "destroyer" in Cabot's nautical metaphor. Hutton's star persona was marked by intense energy; Alan Dale characterizes her as "an artist of mania."[8] But, as Dale notes, for women slapstick and romance don't easily mix. Thus *Here Come the WAVES* employs the twin device, allowing the demure Hutton to secure mature romance, and the raucous, slapstick Hutton an energetic freedom which culminates in the raunchy "A Fella Waitin' in Poughkeepsie" number.

In its brief training montage the film focuses on the inexpert Susie rather than the proficient Rosemary. Susie trips during drill and is inept at the ordered aspects of military life, from saluting to bed-making. Yet by the end of the sequence she beams at the coordination of her own feet with a smile that suggests a combination of astonishment, pleasure, and pride. If it is hard to swallow an experienced dancer's pride in newly acquired physical coordination, we can perhaps frame Susie's expression in terms of drill as pleasurable group activity. Indeed this brief sequence provides an interesting and highly compressed enactment of what were most often presented as the attractions of military life for women as well as an address to the kind of public concerns that framed recruitment efforts. There are repeated shots of drill, some picking out Susie as an individual and others taken from a distance or from above, in a demonstration of the group's developing precision. Civilian clothes are gradually replaced by military uniforms. We see the WAVES recruits receiving instruction, but rather more screen time is given to scenes of sport and leisure. We see the WAVES bowing their heads in prayer as a service is conducted, then eating in the mess and back to drill to mark the end of the sequence. These images endorse the official response to concerns about the inclusion of women in the military. Recall the WAVES recruitment handbook discussed in chapter 1, which emphasized the importance of religion and the value of a healthy active life. *Here Come the WAVES* visualizes the reassuring words recruiters were encouraged to pass on to their prospects: on military discipline ("Discipline emphasizes the satisfaction of knowing you have an important position on this team"), drill ("a toning-up process"), religious belief ("Life in the Navy will deepen your religious faith"), and the pleasures of camaraderie ("Living in barracks is sort of like a college dorm or sorority house"). The film's scenes of liberty, friendship, benevolent authority, and of course romance echo official reassurances that the new recruit "will have time and opportunity for fun, dates, and leave for a visit home."[9] At the end of boot camp Rosemary announces to her roommates, "I never felt so good in all my life," affirming military life as positive and healthy for women.

Clearly *Here Come the WAVES* echoes the reassuring aspects of recruitment drives when it comes to maintaining contemporary gender norms. Yet the twin device allows the film to also exploit some of the more salacious associations of women's military service. As with the other musicals discussed in this chapter, the film responds to perceptions that male and female roles are rendered less rigid in wartime. Indeed Allen L. Woll suggests that wartime musicals more generally showcased a "new woman" who is portrayed as "stronger and more self-assured than ever before."[10] The fearful fantasy of the military woman as sexually predatory—so prevalent in wartime discourse—finds comic expression in all four films, revealing contemporary anxieties relating to women's shifting public and private identities. In *Tars and Spars* Christine's initial pursuit of Howie is mirrored by the comedy coupling of Chuck and Penny. In *Up in Arms* Virginia aims to help Danny get out of trouble by presenting herself as the aggressor, a strategy which gets Danny out of the brig (temporarily) but which makes him a figure of fun with his fellow soldiers. *Here Come the WAVES* most explicitly showcases the fantasy of a sexually predatory military woman in Susie's lengthy number "A Fella Waitin' in Poughkeepsie," introduced on the program as a sketch titled "If WAVES Acted Like Sailors." As this framing suggests, the number's narrative and mise-en-scène explicitly mine the comic potential of role-reversal, with the WAVES crowding into a cartoon bar replete with mannish bartender and male pin-ups on the walls (figure 27).

The sexuality of male military personnel was regulated in an entirely different way from that of female personnel, with a guiding assumption that male heterosexual activity was healthy and normal. By contrast, even the perception that military service might provide women with opportunities for sexual expression was a source of considerable controversy during the Second World War. The playful working-out of this possibility in the "Fella Waitin' in Poughkeepsie" number provides quite a spectacle. Sexy twin Susie (rather than demure Rosemary) sings the lead with gusto, revealing her little red book of addresses, a tattoo of a man on her arm, and an ebullient attitude toward the search for male company. She struts

27. WAVES recruit Susie (Betty Hutton) enacts a lascivious scenario of sexual bravado in *Here Come the WAVES* (1944).

around the stage winking at her fellow WAVES and at the audience, singing loudly of her sexual availability: "There's a fella waiting in Poughkeepsie, but I'm strictly on my own tonight." Extending the logic of role-reversal, Cabot and Windy (Sonny Tufts) camp it up as two civilian men ashore who are at the beck and call of military women on leave. Acting the part of comically feminized men, they carp over who wears what, are rowed around the lake, and ultimately ditch the WAVES played by Susie and Tex for a couple of Marines, in a gesture to themes of interservice rivalry. With its broad humor, energetic performance, and role-reversal the number frames the independent, sexually predatory military woman as an appealing comic fantasy, a fantasy safely contained within the show.

The contrast with Rosemary's big duet with Cabot is noteworthy. "I Promise You" casts her as a civilian destined to wait at home while her military lover leaves to serve his country. The set involves an elaborate field of flowers, arranged to fashion a slope, at the top of which we discover the couple in each other's arms. A homely cottage, lit from within, occupies the left of the stage. In the course of the number, the pair make their leisurely way from the floral side of the stage to the door of the cottage; here Cabot drops his bag for a final embrace, leaving Rosemary to feebly lift her hand in farewell. While Cabot wears a naval uniform in this scene, Rosemary wears a long, full gown and has flowers in her hair. As if to reiterate her feminine compliance further, at one point in the number she even sits at the crooning Cabot's feet (figure 28). He sings of a faith-

28. In contrast to twin sister Susie, WAVES recruit Rosemary (also Betty Hutton) adopts the more conventional position of the woman who waits (*Here Come the WAVES*, 1944).

ful heart; this is, in effect, a song of goodbye, and although the number precedes the final reconciliation between the couple it testifies to the intensity of their love. Thus while Susie embodies many contemporary fears concerning the sexual morality of military women, Rosemary allays these fears through her performance as a feminine woman who waits.

In the narrative world of the musical the military woman represents generalized gender trouble; she disturbs hierarchies in an exhilarating and often comic manner. A sequence from *Up in Arms* illustrates this comic disruption nicely. Having been called up, Danny and Joe (Dana Andrews) are told to report to the gate to carry the bags of two lieutenants, who turn out to be Virginia and Mary (Constance Dowling), the two nurses with whom they had been romantically linked in civilian life. Danny is delighted, effusing, "I don't know whether to salute you or kiss you!," but a sergeant warns them sternly against fraternization. In the trolley car scene that follows, the couples, aware of a watching MP, address their friends with sentiments intended for their lovers. Thus the two same-sex couples address each other in loud tones with comments clearly meant for the other party but interpreted by the civilians around them as a shocking display of queer sexuality. This brief scene plays on the confusion of the film's already tangled love plot: Virginia loves Danny, who in turn loves Mary, who loves (and is loved by) Joe. The camera and editing patterns do little to clarify, withholding the establishing shot that would allow us to see the spatial relations on the trolley car. Instead the shots are framed fairly tightly so that we are invited to delight in the implications of scandalous desire and the shocked responses of the other passengers, safe in the knowledge of the heterosexuality of the couples.

The point of course is that the military woman stands for a world comically awry. As military women and as officers, the female lieutenants usurp male authority, setting into motion a comedy of disreputable queerness and role-reversal, which was to become a staple of those narratives in the 1950s that centered on the military woman. Required to salute the women, Danny is disoriented, addressing Virginia as "Sir" and the sergeant as "Ma'am." Gags involving incorrectly addressing military women as "Sir" have persisted for decades; at the most basic level they signal comic anxiety about the implications of the category *female soldier*. In the film's terms it is simply *funny* that Virginia and Mary should have this new authority over their former dates; as women and nurses they occupy a subordinate position within the hierarchies of civilian life, but in the military they have an enhanced status, providing a perverse source of pleasure. The assertive or authoritative military woman is routinely counterposed in these films to deficient male characters. That is, the military men who romance, or are pursued by, the military women in these films are not the strong, heroic figures showcased in *Marine Raiders* or *Force of Arms*, films of war and romance. Instead they are presented as lacking, whether in experience, maturity, or physical strength. This juxtaposition of powerful women and deficient men underlines the way military women are figured in terms of their impact on military men.

The narrative of *Tars and Spars*, for instance, centers on a grounded Guardsman, the hapless Howie Young. Desperate to go to sea, he remains stuck in an office. Pinning his hopes on the arrival of SPARS, Howie is delighted to find SPARS recruit Christine Bradley (Janet Blair) at his desk and embraces her with enthusiasm (and consequent misunderstanding). Chuck misleads Chris into believing that Howie's disheveled appearance results from combat action, building his buddy up as a hero. On their subsequent date the deception brings turmoil and embarrassment as rumor talks up Howie's supposed achievement beyond all recognition. Appropriately enough, Chris discovers that she has been deceived when she hears a musical number entitled "He's a Hero," which Chuck sings while Howie and the company mascot (a dog) are carried aloft by the massed ranks of Guardsmen. Chris appears on the scene just in time to hear the following damning verse:

> Behind each one of our fighting men
> you'll find not one but maybe ten
> *men* who stay on shore
> but that's the war.
> The paperwork to be done's immense
> it takes a lot of intelligence.
> Hence, a guy like he
> don't get to sea.

This contrary state of affairs underlines the familiar recruitment slogans extolling women to free a man to fight or, in the terms of one recruitment poster for the SPARS, "Your duty ashore . . . his afloat." This sense of a world gone awry in gendered terms—the sailor who can't get to sea—is also displayed in a jibe directed at Windy by one of his shipmates in *Here Come the WAVES*: "You're the man behind the woman behind the man behind the gun." Only laughter can result from such a degraded position.

Although Howie's actual bravery in combat resolves the confusion and misunderstanding that have kept the couple apart, it is staged off-screen. It is tempting to read the comic approach taken to heroism in *Tars and Spars* in terms of its release immediately after the war; in this way its lighthearted approach might be seen to result from a moment of relief and release. Yet the wartime hit *Up in Arms* has similar fun with the status of its male protagonist's heroism, tracing Danny's development from hypochondriac city elevator operator to Pacific War hero. The opening sequence has a beaming Danny in tattered uniform, held aloft by his fellow soldiers and surrounded by nurses and Islanders. When we finally see his heroic action it is played out as a slapstick sequence in which he tricks a Japanese officer during interrogation. Taking on the officer's uniform and persona, Danny's only Japanese phrase, which seems to mean "Follow me," allows him to lead the group of enemy soldiers down holes, through the mud, and ultimately to capture. Clearly it is Danny's zany antics that save the day rather than traditional military masculinity. Throughout the film Kaye's talent for comedy, impersonation, and gleeful performance across gender and nationality is given free rein. (He acts out, or is positioned as, male and female, human and animal, Scottish, Irish, and Japanese during the course of the movie.) The theme of female strength coupled with diminished masculinity continues in *Here Come the WAVES*, in which Cabot's color-blindness initially excludes him from military service. Cabot wants to follow in his dead father's footsteps and to serve aboard the USS *Douglas*, yet he can get into the Navy only when the physical thresholds are lowered. His physical inadequacy is comically underlined by his vulnerability in the face of his female fans, who repeatedly attack him en masse. Such contrasts seem to suggest that when women gain a position of authority, men must correspondingly lose status; though this dynamic involves a play with the social meanings of gender, equality cannot be visualized or narrativized.

In none of the musicals considered here does the limited freedom of gendered hierarchies extend to race. There are generic, industrial, and historical factors at work here: in the war period both the U.S. military and the Hollywood musical operated as segregated institutions, whether officially or not.[11] In his study of black performance, blackface, and the musical film, Arthur Knight notes that the emergence of the "integrated" musical eschews the evident lack of racial integration in the genre. Thus "the creation of the ultimate utopian feeling in the integrated musical relied on an explicit social-racial segregation, and no quantity of formal invention could hide that."[12] African American performers feature regularly in musicals of the 1940s, but they are typically cast in walk-on rather than character parts. The musicals considered here are no exception; none of the three films of or about the Second World War features black performers or military personnel. Even the later *Skirts Ahoy!*, though it features African American and white servicewomen together in its dance-drill number, restricts the black Billy Eckstine to a number performed as the white couple, Young (Esther Williams) and Elcott (Barry Sullivan), dine together at a supper club.[13] The absence of African American men and women from military musicals, and military movies of this period in general, is telling. Though a rhetoric of national unity across ethnic and sometimes racial groups was a recurrent feature of American propaganda, Hollywood cinema did little or nothing to reinforce the message.[14]

It is not perhaps coincidental that the first number performed in the patriotic show designed to boost WAVES recruitment in *Here Come the WAVES* features Cabot and Windy in blackface. In the same year that would end with Roosevelt insisting that African American women be admitted to the WAVES, the staging in blackface of "Ac-Cent-Tchu-Ate the

Positive," one of the film's hit songs (which would have a long life as a nightclub standard), starkly poses the limits of the Hollywood musical's ability to acknowledge blacks as citizens. Staged aboard the USS *Traverse Bay* for troops recently returned from the Pacific, the pair perform in oversized uniform-style costumes. These are not military uniforms, however: Cabot is cast as a postman and Windy as a doorman. The chorus cautions against a lack of commitment or sense of purpose, advising us not to "mess with mister-in-between." The stylized, cartoon-style set features two recruiting booths, one for the Navy and one for the WAVES. The chorus is made up of one WAVES recruit, one sailor, and a group of young white men and women, variously costumed in either civilian clothes or civilian uniform costumes (milkman, bellhop, usher) that echo the outfits worn by Cabot and Windy. At the climax of the number the chorus troops into the booths, emerging in military uniform to dance in formation while Cabot and Windy reappear to underline their message of helping the war effort. The number thus stages a militarization of the citizenry of one city street, replacing the (relative) diversity of civilian dress and movement with the discipline of military uniform and drill-inflected dance routines.

More than a historical anomaly, in 1944 blackface—a feature of other Crosby films[15]—summons up a "folk" tradition in which, Michael Rogin argues, America is figured in terms of assimilation and national unity. Writes Rogin, "In insisting on the blackface roots of American entertainment, the blackface musical wanted to create a seamless tie to the past."[16] This configuration is particularly significant given the tendency to erase or silence the figure of the African American military woman from not just the musical set in the Second World War but most of the film and television texts explored in this book. The whiteness of the WAVES seemed to accord with the effective segregation and exclusion in operation in Hollywood too. Though he does not write about *Here Come the WAVES*, Knight comments on Crosby's other blackface performances that while the crooner was "often affiliated with black performers in his films . . . the blackface numbers and numbers performed with blacks . . . stand not as the climaxes of the story but as incidents in it; in Crosby films, the climaxes are reserved, in usual musical form, for white, heterosexual couple formation."[17] Cabot's and Windy's blackface replaces and erases the contribution of African Americans to the musical and the war. Their blackface injunction supervises the recruitment effort in which white women are militarized on stage as part of the spectacle. Absent from the patriotic show, black Americans are not included—even as entertainers—in the putative citizenship projected by the film as associated with military service. Instead the song's lyrics imply the attitude of accommodation that blacks were encouraged to adopt with respect to domestic racism in the war period.

The blackface performance of "Ac-Cent-Tchu-Ate the Positive" might also be framed in terms of the instability that characterizes the masculinity of the white male hero and the comically expressed fears of an assertive female sexuality (whether that of fans or of fantasized military women), which are both enacted in *Here Come the WAVES*. In this context blackface functions as an eruption of reassuring tradition within a film that attempts to incorporate and even neutralize the disruptive potential of the military woman. We can further situate this performance alongside the other racial and ethnic crossings apparent in Crosby's role in the film. As Cabot he is first introduced in white pants and jacket, topped by a nautical cap, an outfit associated with affluent leisure rather than military service and clearly contrasted with Windy's naval uniform. This summarizes his status as an entertainer (and an entertainer of women in particular); Susie delightedly and Rosemary skeptically watches while young girls scream and faint in the auditorium around them. Cabot, "discovered" and seemingly awakened by scantily clad chorus girls in "native" costume, gives a rendition of "Black Magic" against a fiery "exotic" South Seas set.[18] We see Cabot adopt a rather different garb to evade his female fans: a Semitic disguise consisting of moustache, long beard, and dark glasses. His second public number (in between he privately serenades Rosemary with "Lets Take the Long Way Home") is the blackface "Ac-Cent-Tchu-Ate the Positive." His third public performance is as a feminized man at the beck and call of the military woman played by Susie in "A Fella Waitin' in Poughkeepsie." Only in the penultimate number, "I Promise You," is Cabot returned to a position of racial and gender authority, singing of his plans to be faithful to the woman who waits. This reinscription of the departing warrior prefigures the final number as he and Windy are shipped off, waving goodbye to us, and to the WAVES on stage, on the movie screen (figure 29). That in a musical comedy about white military women Cabot is repeatedly associated with exaggerated racial and ethnic signifiers of otherness is telling. Though foregrounding

29. In *Here Come the* WAVES (1944) performing WAVES bid farewell to the departing sailors and male stars of their show. The scenario effectively suggests the appropriate place for male and female endeavors in wartime.

the service and value of military women, a sign of modernity in 1944, the film insistently worked through what this means for patriarchal authority, ultimately putting the besieged white guy back in charge.

WOMEN IN UNIFORM, MARRIAGE, AND MEN: *SKIRTS AHOY!*

In terms of Hollywood's patriotic portrayal of white military women *Skirts Ahoy!* is an intriguing endeavor, one which suggests how the contradictions played out in the films of the 1940s continued to register in the shifting context of the 1950s. Released in 1952 the film is not framed by the discourses of total war that were so pervasive in the Second World War. The ongoing Korean War is never mentioned in the film. The film's press book comments, albeit briefly, on the training its stars undertook at the Great Lakes Naval Training Station in Illinois, attributing the following sentiments to Esther Williams: "I saw at first hand what an important part of the Navy they have become. They are not all just secretaries. At Great Lakes they were filling in at jobs as medical technicians, accountants and a dozen other occupations. Some of them even worked as mechanics in the transportation pool." Here the film's promotion uses the former athlete to endorse the work of military women, underlining their participation in nontraditional roles and the seriousness of their patriotic labor: "They are a serious-minded, hard-working group," Williams is

30. Foregrounding military women as sexual spectacle: the stars of *Skirts Ahoy!* (1952) on the cover of *Picturegoer.*

quoted as saying. Such assurances indicate the continuation of wartime themes into the postwar period, clearly acknowledging the continuing need for women's service in the U.S. military.

Such high-mindedness does not evidently inform promotional images for the film, which instead strongly played on the sexual connotations of the title and the scenario of women in uniform. Posters either featured Williams in a swimsuit and nautical (but clearly nonmilitary) cap or the three female leads in their WAVES uniforms, skirts blown up to reveal their legs in pin-up style, as on the *Picturegoer* cover in figure 30. At the most basic level such imagery reassures audiences of the sexual desirability and gender conformity of these military women. Basinger describes *Skirts Ahoy!* as "glamorous entertainment," adding that the film "takes place during peacetime, and the women's problems are all with men."[19] Promotional materials certainly played to the idea that men are the women's primary concern: they are described as joining the Navy "either to *get* or to *forget* a man." The trailer too spins the narrative in this way, pronouncing, "They all joined the Navy and became three girls with one idea: men."

Though the WAVES stay firmly ashore (in line with policy at the time), the Navy seems the natural service for the aquatic star Esther Williams. Casting her as the wealthy, independent, and sexually assertive Whitney Young, *Skirts Ahoy!* makes effective use of the at times awkward fit between Williams's star image as a strong, athletic woman and Hollywood's preferred version of submissive femininity. As Catherine Williamson writes in her analysis of the emergence of Williams's celebrity, "Those traits which competitive sports supposedly foster—strength, independence, competitiveness—directly contradict traditional gender roles assigned to women—weakness, dependence, passivity—making the female athlete a problematic and potentially disruptive social subject."[20] The film delights in the potential or actual unruliness of its WAVES, generating comedy through gendered role-reversal. The film also centrally concerns itself with transformation, female agency, independence, and camaraderie, themes handled with the combination of sentiment and exuberance so characteristic of the musical.

The opening scenes of *Skirts Ahoy!* introduce the three female protagonists in turn. Each is defined by a distinct regional and class milieu, but all are situated explicitly in relation to heterosexuality at the moment of its celebration and institutionalization: marriage. In Ohio Mary Kate Yarborough (Joan Evans) has been jilted by her fiancé, Dick, who, it seems, wants to travel and "live a little." Her desire to escape small-town gossip and to forget Dick prompts her kid brother to suggest the Foreign Legion. Cut to Long Island, where we see Whitney Young (Williams) walk away from an elaborate society wedding to a rather hapless-looking man who isn't even named. (Later we learn that she has had no fewer than twelve engagements but has never been married.) Finally we see Vivian Blane as Una Yancy working as a wedding dress saleswoman in New York. Yancy is comically figured as a garishly sentimental New Yorker who has endured a two-year engagement to a man with whom she has had only one date. When Yancy's guy happens to march past the window in naval uniform we cut to WAVES marching and the arrival of new recruits at the training camp, Yarborough and Yancy among their number. Thus the film situates Yarborough's, Young's, and Yancy's enlistment in terms of their relationship to men; as the narrative unfolds it seems clear that the film envisages military service as offering opportunities for romance while functioning as an alternative institution to marriage. The film ends with the three women setting off for a posting in Paris via Washington. Their sailor boyfriends bid them farewell at the train station. (A little vignette in which they reject the attentions of three glamorous WACs suggests that they will be faithful.) The film thus concludes with a reiteration of its defining role-reversal in which the WAVES depart for duty and the Navy men are left behind.

The idea that military women are preoccupied with men is addressed directly in one of the film's numbers, provocatively titled "What Good Is a Gal without a Guy?" Performed by the three women during their first liberty in Chicago, the number puts into play the double standards relating to sex and romance for servicemen and servicewomen. While the movie's trailer celebrates links to *Anchors Aweigh* (1945) and the liberty sequence explicitly evokes *On the Town* (1949), the sexual freedom associated with narratives of male sailors on leave works very differently for the WAVES. The three split up to enjoy the city but subsequently meet again in a sedate café where civilian women sit, clearly bounded by codes of appropriate feminine behavior. It is the sight of male sailors and their dates enjoying their freedom on the street outside that triggers the women's alternately assertive and lamenting rendition of "What Good Is a Gal without a Guy?"

Skirts Ahoy! takes the figure of the WAVES recruit as lascivious sailor further than *Here Come the WAVES*, making this one of the central themes of the film. Thus rather than simply lamenting women's relative lack of sexual freedom, Yancy proceeds to act on her provocative idea that "sailors can do anything." With evident sexual suggestiveness she asks the café's manager to recommend a cocktail bar "where women are admitted, but grudgingly." Leaving the inexperienced Yarborough behind, Yancy and Young head to a former men's bar, where both attempt to seduce the base doctor, Lt. Cmdr. Paul Elcott. Young's subsequent pursuit of Elcott forms one of the central storylines of the film, finding comedy in the latter's evident discomfort in his role as the object of female desire. (At one point he instructs Young to "stop looking" at him.) Just as it seems that Elcott may be gaining ground during their first date, managing to discomfort Young, their meal is interrupted by the wolf whistles of three WACs at a neighboring table and their invitation to him to "come over to the Army." Once again he becomes subject to the comically lustful gaze of women in uniform. Having gone into town to seek "a little unfeminine fresh air," Elcott finds himself both the subject of and witness to a brawl between Young and the three WACs (a fight the film keeps offscreen). Subsequently he lectures Young on how her behavior—getting involved in a fight, making advances to a man—might compromise the Navy, reminding her, "People are still prejudiced about women in the services." Entering spaces in which women's very presence is considered provocative (the military, men's clubs) positions these women as culturally, and more specifically, sexually risky figures. Yet Young is unrepentant about her behavior. Even at the end of the film (the point at which Hollywood movies usually insist on the reappearance of an appropriate femininity) Young apologizes to Elcott for making him feel uncomfortable, but adds, "I still believe in asking for what I want." Elcott is clearly attracted to Young but is troubled by her assertiveness. As he puts it, "You're the kind of a girl who can't be sent for." Young persists in her pursuit of Elcott, insisting that she likes him. When he mentions her previous fiancés she counters that they were different: "They liked me." Here, by contrast, she is following her own desires, something Elcott finds deeply unsettling. Spelling it out for her, Elcott angrily insists on his right as a male to pursue women and not to be pursued.

The distinctiveness of the musical lies in part in its ability to resolve narrative dilemmas through song and dance; numbers stage the conflicts, attractions, and concerns of the film, bringing them to spectacular resolution. *Skirts Ahoy!* employs just such a strategy in resolving its role-reversal romance. When Elcott rejects her with a predatory and military metaphor ("I just want to do my own hunting"), Young admits defeat and takes solace in a nighttime swimming pool solo. The number has her dancing with, caressing, romancing, strangling, and ultimately bursting (with an overly enthusiastic embrace) a sort of inflatable sailor that she designates as Elcott's stand-in. The number ludicrously enacts the themes of the film—aggressively desiring woman, man as passive object of affection—while displaying Williams's body and swimming talents. Narratively speaking, Elcott's bubble is indeed burst. Having dismissed Young, he immediately has second thoughts; realizing that he does love her after all, he applies for a transfer to be near her in Paris. Thus the issue of the gendered terms of power between men and women, central to the film's comedy, is more or less magically resolved.

Williams's athleticism and independence make her character an exemplary military woman. Young's assertiveness is also in part a function of her wealth and social status. When she first arrives at the camp (draped in a fur coat) there have been calls from admirals and members of the Navy Department on her behalf. Asked by the lieutenant commander why she hasn't applied for a commission, she asserts that she "didn't want it made easy." Asked why she has joined the WAVES, she replies, "I wanted to feel useful—I never have." These exchanges allude to the common narrative conceit whereby military service provides character-forming discipline for wealthy women, a device seen in *Keep Your Powder Dry*, in the Korean War–era *Never Wave at a WAC*, and as recently as 1980 in *Private Benjamin*. These are all transformation narratives, whereby boot camp provides the structure and sense of purpose these women lacked in civilian life. *Skirts Ahoy!* works out its most explicit narrative of transformation not through Young, however, but through the frail, homesick Yarborough, who declares herself ill-suited to naval life and "not much of a person." Agreeing to help her get out of the Navy, Young and Yancy encourage Yarborough to make a spectacle of her inability to cope, her feminine dependence. Just as this performance is about to pay off, Yarborough is confronted by her now penitent fiancé, who pronounces her enlistment "ridiculous." He insists that she "can't be a sailor" since that would require her to be "independent and tough, and maybe go to strange cities and live by [her]self and work hard." This description of her feminine ineptitude pushes Yarborough into an angry assertion of her independence, and she becomes a woman who plans on enjoying her own mobility and the opportunities offered by the Navy. Of course in terms of the romance plot, she isn't "much of a person." Dick falls in love with the newly assertive woman she has become; as if to reinforce his conviction, he follows her example and joins the Navy himself. It is significant in a comedy of role-reversal that Yarborough's feminine passivity is so thoroughly ridiculed and that female self-reliance and strength are so overtly celebrated. While the military woman may remain the source of comedy, the joke here has to do with the overcoming of a frail model of femininity and the protective masculinity on which it depends.

Musicals featuring military women take gender disruption as a comic premise, typically expressing this theme through the juxtaposition of capable, assertive women and deficient military men. Her provocative presence provides a spectacle for audiences while the consequences of her presence for military men generate narrative twists and comedy. Indeed it is telling that the military woman's attractiveness and her capacity to disorient men are as prominent as her professional capability. In foregrounding the spectacle of drill and in displacing military tasks into the labor of entertainment—putting on a show—these films also draw on reassuringly conventional models of femininity. With respect to the evolving discourses discussed in part 1, the films considered in this chapter span the construction of women's service as a temporary necessity during the war period to the ongoing, if supportive and auxiliary role of military women in the 1950s. The sort of gendered role-reversal scenario played out in *Skirts Ahoy!* would become a staple of comedies in the 1950s featuring military women, films explored in the next chapter.

Alan Dale borrows a phrase from Jerry Lewis for the title of his study of slapstick, *Comedy Is a Man in Trouble*. If this is true, then the military woman who underlines that comedy also is a woman on top. This is the purchase and the analytical strength of Kathleen Rowe's evocation of the "unruly woman" in her book of that title exploring women in comedy. Of her project Rowe writes, "I consider how the figure of the unruly woman—too fat, too funny, too noisy, too old, too rebellious—unsettles social hierarchies."[1] Comedies centered on military women feature a distinctive combination of female authority and male deficiency, that is, men in trouble and women on top. The disruptive or provocative presence of the military woman has consistently been played for laughs in popular movies. In the first part of this chapter I explore a number of films from the 1950s (and one from the late 1940s), each characterized by a formulation of men in trouble and women on top: *I Was a Male War Bride* (1949), *The Lieutenant Wore Skirts* (1956), and *Francis Joins the WAC* (1954). All exploit the comic implications of shifts in conventional gender roles for which the military woman serves as a potent symbol. *Never Wave at a WAC* (1952) is rather different in its use of the screwball star Rosalind Russell and its central (generically atypical) proposition of a *woman* in trouble. It is also the only one of the four to focus on female friendship, and the only one which does not end straightforwardly in the formation (or reunion) of a heterosexual romantic couple. These films demonstrate the ways postwar cinema thematized the military woman as auxiliary and as disruptive, even as they assume her capability and the necessity of her service.

The second part of the chapter turns to the military woman as she appears in a number of sex comedies, focusing in particular on *Operation Petticoat* (1959), *Operation Bullshine* (U.K., 1959), and *Petticoat Pirates* (U.K., 1961). These films combine the voyeuristic pleasures of barrack-room scenes with cheeky innuendo about the sexual possibilities of men and women living and working in close proximity. They also demonstrate a more explicit sexual humor emerging as British and American filmmakers alike push at the edges of censorship regimes. In all three the disruptive presence of military women generates comedy as military men (aboard a submarine, staffing a mixed battery, and onboard ship) struggle to accommodate the "opposite" sex. That they also ultimately work to keep military women in their place, subordinated in professional terms (auxiliary, ashore) and with respect to their narrative function as romantic foil or sexualized object of display, demonstrates the ideological conservatism of some, though not all, comic perspectives on gender as a "battle of the sexes."

A PROVOCATIVE (COMIC) PRESENCE:
MILITARY WOMEN IN COMEDY

Comedies involving military women routinely play out humorous scenarios centered on role-reversal and gender confusion. Comedy is typically built not so much on the figure of the military woman herself (by the late 1940s she is not funny per se) as on the challenge she poses to civilian and military men. The centrality of a "crisis" of masculinity in some of the movies analyzed here threatens to eclipse the military woman. Of the films discussed in this section, this is perhaps most evident in *The Lieutenant Wore Skirts*, in which Sheree North's Katy plays the straight (military) woman to her husband's comedic enactment of a midlife crisis. It is not surprising, then, that when the films explored here have been discussed critically it has typically been with respect to men and masculinity. To some extent this emphasis relates to the awkward position of women in comedy, whether as a genre or a performance style. The "unspoken rules" that Dale identifies in film comedy—broadly that physical comedy cannot be reconciled with the conventional femininity of the romantic lead—are clearly in evidence in the films considered here. Only *Never Wave at a WAC* allows the female protagonist, Rosalind Russell's Jo, to take the pratfalls of physical comedy, perhaps significantly pairing her with a very different comedienne in Marie Wilson (at the time most frequently cast as a "dumb blonde"). As Dale writes, it seems as though physical comedy staged by female characters "is seen as a form of impurity, as if pratfalls . . . imply that the heroine is altogether too physically available."[2]

The comedy played out around the military woman derives from either a conventionally masculine independence (sometimes explicitly coded as mannishness) or an exaggerated femininity. In both instances the military woman is comically out of place. In this context it is worth considering the purchase of feminist scholarship on film comedy. Rowe's formulation of the comic, carnivalesque "unruly woman" is at first sight problematic, given the emphasis on discipline and regularity that we have seen celebrated in musical comedy (notably in drill). And yet the conventions of service comedy are very much concerned with the sort of managed unruliness associated with the carnivalesque, challenging authority and poking fun at often unwieldy military regulations. More generally the terms of service comedy and sex comedy have much in common, deriving humor from the inversion of social hierarchies (men and women, officers and enlisted personnel). In this sense Jo in *Never Wave at a WAC*, like Judy Benjamin in the more recent *Private Benjamin*, is quite literally unruly; she does not respect and does not follow Army rules and regulations (not at first, that is). Jo's unruliness spells trouble for herself and for the military. It is willful (required to practice drill, she blithely sits against a tree and smokes), disorganized (expressed in slapstick scenes of the wealthy senator's daughter ineptly performing menial and military tasks), and very funny.

Lori Landay's work on the female trickster offers a different perspective on comedies featuring military women. Landay constructs a chronology that shifts from "the possibility of equality between men and women," evident in comedies of the 1930s, to the temporary equality in pursuit of national service characterizing the war years, and the "domestic ideology" of the postwar period. She characterizes film's female tricksters thus: "As fantasy figures of strong women who assert their individual will (rather than submit to men's) and who participate equally on the slippery terrain of comic pratfalls and humiliations, the screwball heroines cross the boundaries between 'good' and 'bad' femininity, elite and common class, and honest and deceptive behavior with their female trickery." Once again the fit is not an exact one; the cinematic military woman is, on the whole, associated with honesty and directness rather than disguise and duplicity. The seductive properties of the trickster's clothing are undercut by the regularity and conformity of the uniform. Even so, in *Never Wave at a WAC* Clara Schneiderman (Wilson) employs conventionally feminine trickery to secure a proposal of marriage from the hapless Sergeant Jackson. WAC Sgt. Joan Hogan, rival to Sergeant Bilko in *The Phil Silvers Show* (1955–59), was also cast as a trickster from her first appearance. Landay's characterization of the female trickster as a figure who feigns submission while covertly exercising power is in many ways opposed to that of the military woman who openly stakes a claim to traditionally male territory. Yet her attention to "the discomfort of social change," a discomfort expressed through comedy, is clearly pertinent.[3] Indeed the trickster suggests that submission to the regularity of military life also seems to constitute a form of provocation.

Such a provocative commitment to rules characterizes WAC Lt. Catherine Gates (Ann Sheridan) in *I Was a Male War Bride*. Her ease, proficiency, and military status place her in a position of authority in which she evidently takes great pleasure; her satisfaction at Henri Rochard's (Cary Grant) numerous mishaps is raucously and repeatedly expressed in her laughter. *I Was a Male War Bride* is emblematic of the "man in trouble" and has been regularly discussed in these terms.[4] Rochard is a French captain assigned to work with Gates in postwar Germany. Though he outranks her, Gates's confidence and even insubordination (presumably coupled with her status as an American soldier) means that Rochard has little authority over her. Gates regards Rochard as a sexual predator. For his part, Rochard declares Gates "repulsive," attempting to show her up in front of her colleagues. (Significantly, he does so with a display of her intimate laundry, which he produces from his briefcase, implying a sexual liaison that has not in fact taken place.) Their sparky relationship, developed over a bizarre journey in which misunderstandings and physical obstacles (roadblock, waterfall, haystack) are put in their path, ultimately leads to romance and marriage. The comedy in the first part of the film relates to the various mishaps encountered by Rochard in pursuit of his mission. Although not all of these are directly provoked by Gates (some are), Rochard blames her for his misfortunes. At the same time Gates is consistently placed in a superior position, openly laughing at Rochard's misadventures to the extent that Rebecca Bell-Metereau describes her as "unsympathetic, almost sadistic."[5] Gates's enjoyment of Rochard's discomfort, her laughter and physical confidence, mark her as an unruly woman in Rowe's terms.

Once the couple's antipathy turns to romance and the two agree to marry, Rochard's mishaps continue, but the film's comedy shifts its primary focus from their sparring to the absurdities of military bureaucracy. To satisfy regulations and religious obligations, the couple must marry not once, but three times, in a German civil ceremony, an American military ceremony, and a French ceremony conducted by Rochard's pastor. "It's the Army's way of finding out if you really want to get married," Gates tells Rochard when he balks at the amount of forms that must be completed. Since the procedures of the U.S. military are designed for the brides of male soldiers, Rochard must accept the designation *bride* (just as in *The Lieutenant Wore Skirts* Gregory Whitcomb serves as Katy's "wife" on the base) and endure the "humiliation" of being treated like a woman.[6] The Army's inability to recognize a "war groom" echoes, indeed is a product of the supposedly contradictory figure of the military woman.[7] Even as Gates's confidence and assurance forcibly underline her efficiency and military status, the Army cannot deal with the implications of her, in effect, taking a bride. This bureaucratic process of exclusion, and the comedy of humiliation it generates, culminates in Rochard's dressing as an Army nurse to get aboard the ship taking his wife back to the U.S. Here, as with numerous other films explored in this book, the figure of the military woman is framed primarily in terms of her impact on male characters, military or otherwise.

For Bell-Metereau, *I Was a Male War Bride* exemplifies a grim comic vision in which "the man dressed as a woman is the central object of ridicule." She writes that the film can be regarded as "the supreme representative of the anxiety-ridden, paranoid rendering of the theme of sexual role reversal." Emphasizing Rochard's repeated mishaps and Gates's laughter, Bell-Metereau treats the film as an exemplar of the disillusionment experienced by returning male soldiers during the postwar period. She has little to say on the repeated insults (and indeed laughter) that Rochard directs toward Gates, or the evident pleasure he takes from their embattled relationship. For her, Gates's character comes to stand for the repression and order of the military and the state. Thus *War Bride* "exemplifies the feelings of masculine powerlessness and chaotic reversals by presenting a woman who behaves like a man and a man who is forced to behave like a woman."[8] From this perspective the military woman is a nightmarish rendition of the woman on top, taking sadistic pleasure in the fate of the man in trouble. Certainly the cross-dressing in which the film culminates seems to literalize the relationship between Rochard and Gates as reversal. That Rochard's female disguise makes him ridiculous (in part because he portrays such a mannish Army nurse) is also undeniable. And yet the film does not consistently portray Gates as mannish or Rochard as feminized. Rather their sparring, like that of earlier screwball couples, stages a battle of the sexes in which the stakes are the establishment of a romantic or sexual relationship founded on equity.

These dynamics are played out in an early scene at the motor pool. Since Rochard's mission has a low priority, the only transportation available is a motorcycle and sidecar. And since only Gates has been approved by the motor pool, only she can drive. Rochard responds to the loss of dignity consequent on becoming a low-priority passenger by casting aspersions on Gates's technical proficiency; she responds by loudly asserting her credentials. Specifically responding to his taunts about whether she intends to ride sidesaddle, Gates produces a pair of trousers from her bag and heads off to change. Bell-Metereau draws attention to her garb, describing Gates as a "mannish, threatening figure," yet, and this is surely important, Gates does not wear *male* clothes in these scenes, but her own, military clothes (figure 31).[9] When the sidecar and motorcycle become uncoupled and Rochard is left gripping tightly to a stationary vehicle, we are led to understand that the military woman's ability and agency leave men comically stalled. This encounter prefigures a later and more serious rupture between the two when Gates makes use of her (male) military contacts to complete Rochard's mission for him. Having ignored his wish that she not get involved, Gates belatedly steps back and thus allows Rochard to be arrested by German MPs. As with her evident pleasure in their "sex antagonism," Gates proves herself something of a trickster here. That is, she exploits her submissive respect for Rochard's orders—and indeed her adherence to Army regulations—to once more unsettle his authority.

In all this comedy of female authority and male distress, Gates's military woman is never rendered mannish. Although a male American major reassures Rochard of Gates's suitability for the mission with the words "She's your man," Gates is quite clearly a woman. Her desire to secure her reputation, as against Rochard's sexual interest in her, generates a series of comic mishaps for him during their night at the inn. Just as explic-

31. Gates's (Ann Sheridan) assumption of authority—here she is in the driver's seat—disconcerts Rochard (Cary Grant) in *I Was a Male War Bride* (1949).

itly Gates's request that he retrieve her lipstick—which ends with him stranded on a rail-crossing barrier—is a comedic moment that stems from her desire to fix her makeup and their shared allegiance to gendered codes of behavior. If anything, this suggests, or perhaps archly refers to, the inappropriate femininity that characterizes so many cinematic versions of the military woman. Though Gates is certainly independent, to read her as mannish is simply to insist on the same cultural logic which tells us that *woman* and *soldier* are contradictory terms. Despite the fun it has with gender roles, *I Was a Male War Bride* does not present the military woman as a contradiction. Conventionally attractive, professionally capable, dealing effectively with the sexual interest of military men, Gates is at ease with her fellow soldiers, male and female. She is also a desiring woman, and like Rochard she is frustrated, to the point of tears, at their repeatedly interrupted wedding night. This is not a liberatory vision, but it does use comedy to articulate the military woman as a disruptive and energetic presence in the postwar world.

In chapter 2 I touched on the ways nursing narratives, including *Homecoming* and *Flight Nurse*, could be contextualized by both military necessity and postwar conceptualizations of appropriate femininity. These same tensions are played out in comedy of the 1950s, albeit in different terms. Both *The Lieutenant Wore Skirts* and *Never Wave at a WAC* overtly acknowledge the domestic ideology of the 1950s, though they situate their military women characters differently in relation to marriage and military service. *The Lieutenant Wore Skirts* fits a particular strand of cinema of the 1950s that exploited the comic potential of a man in trouble. The star, Tom Ewell, had recently played the archetypal figure of a white male enduring a midlife crisis in *The Seven Year Itch* (1955) and *The Girl Can't Help It* (1956). In *The Lieutenant Wore Skirts* Katy Whitcomb is the straight woman, and her husband, Greg (Ewell), comically enacts anguish, self-doubt, and self-deception. While Katy's military career is a source of consternation for Greg, she is either unaware of his discomfort or desires to reassure him of her continued affections. She certainly does not laugh openly, as Gates does in *War Bride*. At the film's outset the couple are ensconced in the routines of civilian domestic life. Now a writer for television, in the Second World War Greg was a hero, and wrote a best-selling book about his experiences as a pilot. Katy herself, much younger than Greg (her relative youth is the source of her husband's chief anxiety), is a veteran of the Korean War. The framed photo that shows them on the day they met has Katy in her uniform whites, Greg in formal civilian clothes; the pose accentuates her youthful, curvaceous body and firmly points to her prior identity as a military woman. The film opens on the day of the couple's planned anniversary party, when Greg is recalled to duty and the routines of domesticity are sharply disrupted. When other means fail, Katy reenlists in order to stay with her husband. The narrative's comedy twists begin when Greg is then rejected on medical grounds but Katy must remain in the service.

The comedy initially centers on Greg's attempts to deal with his new position, first sharing an apartment with his bachelor agent, then setting up in a Hawaiian hut, and finally living with Katy on base. Unable to reconcile himself to the shift in Katy's relationship to him and the public world, Greg suggests that she secure a dishonorable discharge (an idea she indignantly rejects), then ultimately concocts a harebrained *Gaslight* scenario designed to convince her that she is insane. Ultimately the "problem" of Katy's military status is resolved through her pregnancy, a state which requires her to leave the service and ensures the reunion of the couple in a scene of civilian domesticity.

Despite the suggestiveness of her role as working wife, Katy is by no means a woman on top in the fashion of *I Was a Male War Bride*'s Lieutenant Gates. This is largely because, though she typically facilitates the gags, she is not in on them and has little cause for laughter. Neither is this a comedy of feminine incompetence since Katy proves herself more than capable in her return to military life. And much as she loves Greg, she acquires a renewed self-worth in the Air Force, echoing tropes of transformative service familiar from the Second World War. Though Katy is genuinely torn and distraught, Greg remains confused, self-centered, and scathing about her sense of duty: "Do you have some wild idea the Air Force would miss you if you left?" Just as Dick's doubts in the Navy musical *Skirts Ahoy!* ensure that Mary Kate Yarborough stays in the WAVES, Katy responds emotionally to Greg's disdain: "I do know I feel I'm important to them." The presentation of this discourse of self-worth through military service is here brought into comic conflict with contemporary discourses of domestic femininity, suggesting an unmanageable tension between public and wifely duties.

It is of course crucial to the narrative that Katy is a *married* woman. The film certainly plays up the opportunities for sexual indiscretion that her posting to Hawaii offers, even while indicating clearly that she does not intend to make use of them. Thus although Greg's doubts about her fidelity are clearly groundless, his anxiety about her public role as a working military woman ("Your job is to be with me") and his reluctance to allow her a measure of independence ultimately, if temporarily, wreck their relationship. Katy's exhaustion and anger prompt Greg's ultimately short-lived resolution to support her, expressed as a determination to be "the best darn wife [she] ever had." Implicitly of course Greg's new role as "wife" casts Katy as husband and provider. The comedy of role-reversal poses a question, largely rhetorical as far as the film is concerned, as to whether or not women "need" men (and, of course, a concomitant fear that they might not). Yet there is no suggestion of mannishness here (a misogynist stereotype the film clearly makes use of at other points). Rather the comedy of male domestic incompetence that ensues underlines Greg's failure as a "wife," simultaneously reinforcing the topsy-turvy character of his situation. Thus although Katy's military woman is not a disruptive presence in the fashion of Lieutenant Gates, she serves as an occasion for comedy and a sign of disrupted gender relations.

Katy's conflicted status as both devoted wife and military woman forms the very premise of the comedy in *The Lieutenant Wore Skirts*: these identities are simply incompatible. In particular there is a tension between the supposed sexual freedom of military life and appropriate wifely fidelity. A promotional image for the film features a cartoon sketch of

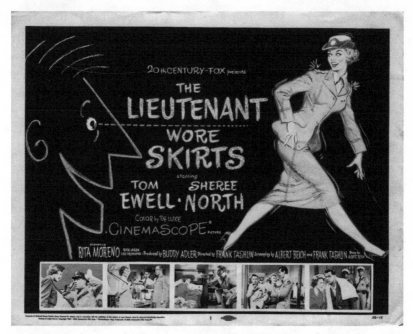

32. Promotional imagery for *The Lieutenant Wore Skirts* (1956) foregrounds comic sexual pursuit.

Katy in uniform; in flight she nonetheless looks backward with seeming delight (figure 32). The image she simultaneously flees and seems to invite is a crude line drawing of a male head in profile, smiling and eyes intent on her backside; a dotted line leads from the eye to her rear to graphically emphasize the point. The fear that his wife, a former military woman, might experience the potential for sexual freedom associated with male military service (even though this is expressed in an image of her being chased) becomes a source of comic anxiety for Greg, already insecure about his ability to retain the affections of his young wife. The film stages his midlife crisis through a fantasy about the sexualized military woman. Women's military service, while it serves as the source of comedy, is not questioned here. What is at issue is the comic impossibility of combining the roles of wife and working woman. Order is restored once Katy becomes pregnant; reinstated as wife, and newly inscribed as mother, she leaves military life for domesticity. The absurd comedy of Greg attempting to be a good wife (his failure to perform basic domestic tasks) is equally telling in terms of the film's temporary disruption of gendered hierarchies. As we'll see in later chapters, more recent narratives, both comic and dramatic, continue to suggest that married life (if not romance) is incompatible with women's military service. Within the context of the 1950s the young, white military woman clearly signals a troubling independence in need of taming; she represents the working woman writ large.

The theme of a military woman who discovers a new sense of self-worth, incidental to the main action of *The Lieutenant Wore Skirts*, is central to *Never Wave at a WAC*.[10] Jo McBain is the film's central comic protagonist, whose transformation in basic training provides the core narrative. Just as the musical *Skirts Ahoy!* introduces its three protagonists in relation to weddings that, for one reason or another, have not taken place, *Never Wave at a WAC* commences with a disrupted marriage. Jo, a Washington society hostess and senator's daughter, is extravagantly happily divorced from an Army scientist. Their sparring at a glittering cocktail party suggests a continuing liveliness in their relationship, albeit fueled by hostility. Her new beau, Lt. Col. "Sky" Fairchild, is about to depart for a NATO posting in Paris, as is the young, blonde, and newly enlisted Phyllis, whom Jo clearly perceives as a threat. In a moment of inspiration, Jo's father exploits his daughter's fantasies, proposing that she join the Army as the solution to her worries. In the exchange that follows the senator playfully suggests, "Nowadays many a man's head is turned by a pretty uniform," while Jo blithely assumes that her father will secure her a commission and a posting to Europe. The suggestion that a uniform might assist Jo in her romantic ambitions reiterates the sexual associations of the military woman, even though it is clear to the audience that the senator is hatching a quite different plan.

It is not Jo's age (jokingly acknowledged as thirty-five, though Russell was actually forty-five at the time), but her whimsy and arrogance, her general expectation of preferential treatment, that set her up for the indignities that follow during her basic training at Fort Lee. For her the WAC represents a trip to Paris, the chance to work alongside Fairchild, and, like rival Phyllis, to look "chic-ly patriotic." Jo gleefully instructs her assistant to fill out the enlistment papers on her behalf, gives the president as one of her character references, smokes through her physical, and orders her captain's bars from Tiffany. She is splendidly high-handed on her arrival at Fort Lee. Taken with the other recruits to see a parade, she breaks ranks and wanders over to introduce herself to the top brass, including the WAC's commanding officer. These scenes illustrating Jo's over-confidence set up the comic fall that follows: the senator insists that Jo remain a private, explaining to her superior that his daughter wishes to work her way up through the ranks. Like Val Parks in *Keep Your Powder Dry*, Jo's pampered woman has something to learn from Army life about status, duty, and the value of service. Having been tricked by her father into going through basic training (rather than getting the commission she had hoped for), she learns the positive value of teamwork and discipline. Like Parks she joins up for self-interested reasons but subsequently learns to value and take pride in Army life. These tricksters are transformed not by marriage, but by their allegiance to the Army.

The joke may be on Jo, but this is very much Russell's movie. Through the 1930s and 1940s Russell established herself as a high-profile comic performer, one who was regularly cast, in Basinger's words, "as a nightmare career woman." Her characters would usually relent in the final reel, yielding to domesticity in the appropriate feminine manner. Basinger cites Russell's own description of her roles as "Alice in Careerland": "My wardrobe had a set pattern: a tan suit, a gray suit, a beige suit, and then a negligee for the seventh reel, near the end, when I would admit to my best friend on the telephone what I really wanted was to become a dear little housewife."[11] Perhaps because she is too clearly middle-aged, *Never Wave at a wac* does not follow this route in straightforward fashion. Already economically independent, Jo learns self-worth in the wac through work and companionship, leaving behind high society—and ultimately her fiancé—in favor of Army life. In the final reel she discovers what she will be missing if she were to leave the Army for the "security" of marriage; as she drives away from Fort Lee, Fairchild droning on about his plans to work in advertising, she looks wistfully at the ceremonies and rituals of Army life. Having disdained drill, she is now moved by the sight of marching wacs; insisting that Fairchild stop the car, she chases after and climbs into a truck with a group of new arrivals, determined to re-enlist. "We're all going to be generals. What are you going to be?" ask the enthusiastic recruits. "Anything they'll let me be," responds Jo, delivering the film's final cheery, patriotic line: "Maybe I'll get a free ride to Korea." Submitting herself to the discipline of the Army (she will be all that they will let her be), Jo's disruptive presence is thus contained, though not by domesticity.

It makes sense to read *Never Wave at a wac* as screwball, not least due to Russell's star presence. But screwball in its most familiar sense belongs to a different era, that of the Depression, and while its legacy is evident in

33. Jo (Rosalind Russell) is subject to slapstick trials before emerging as an exemplary military woman in *Never Wave at a* WAC (1952).

the film, so is the rather different "battle of the sexes" format that came to predominate in the 1950s. In fact the film draws on both the verbal dexterity of screwball and the pratfalls of slapstick, leading us back to Hollywood's awkward inclusion of female performers in physical comedy. For Dale, Betty Hutton's slapstick performances are rare instances of a female presence in physical comedy. He offers a coda to this, however, which has to do with social status as much as gender, citing Charlie Chaplin's observation on the comic potential in "giving the rich what they deserve."[12] Jo's social status means that she has plenty of dignity to lose, and *Never Wave at a* WAC makes the most of this formula. As a middle-aged woman (inscribed not as wife and mother, but as troublesome daughter and ex-wife), Jo is cast as an overprivileged figure for whom Army life is both a slapstick trial and ultimately a character-forming experience (figure 33).

Unlike much male-oriented service comedy, military life is not ridiculed in *Never Wave at a* WAC. Instead the comedy of enlistment and basic training is derived from Jo's initial misunderstanding of, and then refusal to accept, her position as a private. While the sparring of Jo and her former husband forms a good part of the action, and a reunion of the couple is certainly implied, *Never Wave at a* WAC resolutely offers military (rather than married) life as the solution to the comic heroine's desires. To some extent this narrative trajectory is facilitated by the relationship between Jo and her younger sidekick, Clara Schneiderman. Jo's motivation, indifference to discipline, and laziness are counterposed to Clara, who unexpectedly excels not only at drill but at military life in general. This despite her initial, equally unrealistic expectations, played for comedy when she declares herself, in best dumb blonde mode, most suited to a career in "intelligence." The actress Marie Wilson specialized in comedy blondes and is given plenty of innuendo-laden dialogue (e.g., "I feel I'd like to give my country what I've got"). As Clara, Wilson plays a photographer's model (known professionally as "Danger O'Dowd") who joins the Army to get away from men and, implicitly, from a life of sexual exploitation. We are introduced to her disaffectedly posing for saucy, seasonal pin-ups before rejecting the man her sleazy agent brings to meet her. It just so happens that the WAC recruiting office is down the hall, and, as she passes, the posters catch her eye. In the WAC Clara determines to fashion a different life for herself, initially refusing the attentions of Sgt. "Noisy" Jackson, adopting glasses and a stern attitude, and focusing intently on her Army career. Though Jackson blackmails Clara into seeing him by threatening to reveal her former identity, she gets the better of him, "tricking" him into a proposal of marriage toward the conclusion of the film. While Jo's initial object is a man, she rejects him in favor of Army life; Clara, by contrast, who joins to escape men, is pursued by and then catches her man. Yet both women remain committed to the military, an institution which the film thus presents as entirely compatible with a range of feminine identities. Indeed in this film the Army effectively works to (comically) contain the socially disruptive civilian excesses of both the socialite and the sex worker.

It is not coincidental that *Never Wave at a WAC*, produced and released in the context of the Korean War, resists satirizing Army life and the place of military women within it. At a moment when women reservists were being called up for the first time in U.S. history, there were evident limits to the humor to be had from Army life, not least in a film made with the cooperation of the military and the Department of Defense.[13] Viewed in this context the similarities between the transformation of Jo's self-serving character and that of Val Parks in the earlier (Second World War–era) *Keep Your Powder Dry* are indicative. Both women learn to put the needs of the corps and the nation above their own personal concerns and rivalries. Many of the recruitment-oriented themes evident in earlier films also recur in *Never Wave at a WAC*. The posters glimpsed in the brief scene featuring Clara's decision to enlist set the tone. One shows a beaming female soldier flanked by parental figures, the text above proclaiming, "We're Proud." The second features a female soldier with the legend "Serve—Be Smart." While this may function as a play on the "dumb blonde," the value and appeal of military life is reiterated throughout the film. At the final dance her ex-husband tells the newly humbled Jo that her uniform is "one of the most becoming things [she's] ever worn." Thus while Jo's inappropriate expectations are played to full comic effect, Army life is introduced to us in overwhelmingly positive terms. A captain's welcoming speech presents a career in the Army as a source of personal fulfillment, a sentiment comically countered but never completely undercut by Jo's breezy (over)familiarity. Later a tracking shot presents us with snapshots of women from different backgrounds and regions of the U.S. who have come together for a new career and a new life. One tells of how she "got sick and tired of pounding a typewriter all day long in a stuffy office." Another explains, "I wanted to prove I could do something other than milk cows." These interviews, in which women talk about their ambitions, frame the comic business around Clara's and Jo's inappropriate aspirations, but they also reiterate key recruitment messages of opportunity, excitement, and mobility for military women.

By situating Jo as the figure of a "woman in trouble" and scripting a contrasting female sidekick, *Never Wave at a WAC* is the only comedy considered in this chapter not to rely on gendered role-reversal for its humor. Confusions of sex and gender identity continued to provide the premise for comedies featuring military women throughout the decade and well into the 1960s. Indeed such confusions structure *Francis Joins the WAC* (1954), the fifth in a series of Universal pictures centered on a talking mule (Francis) and his sidekick, Peter Stirling (Donald O'Connor).[14] Fundamentally the film enacts a comedy of the man in trouble when both Francis and the somewhat hapless Stirling are recalled to service and mistakenly assigned to the WAC. This glitch of Army paperwork provides the stage for raised eyebrows from male and female military personnel, scenes of female undress, cross-dressing (Stirling escapes in a nurse's costume), and the comedy of female bodies on parade (perplexed by a WAC's breasts, Stirling cannot tell whether she is standing at ease or attention). Stirling's arrival at the train station results in a series of slapstick encounters with the woman who will be his commanding officer, Captain Parker (Julia Adams). He bumps into her, knocks her on the head with his bag, and then douses her from the water tower, all before declaring her the "prettiest soldier [he's] ever seen." Ordered, "Think as we do and do as we do," Stirling joins the display of massed female bodies taking exercise on the parade ground.

Such physical comedy is familiar territory for the military woman in cinema. *Francis Joins the WAC* also includes an explicit (albeit comic) engagement with the contested category of the female soldier. (The film was made with the cooperation of the Women's Army Corps and even used WACS as extras.) On the one hand women soldiers are clearly the source of humor and sexual spectacle for the film. Charged with teaching camouflage techniques to the second platoon, Stirling simply cannot treat them in a military fashion. Neither are the women particularly committed to military modes: Stirling secures their devotion by buying them all perfume, earning a kiss from the glamorous Corporal Hilstrom (Mamie Van Doren). Against this trivializing treatment, a comic plot develops to do with the demonstration of the WAC recruits' military capabilities. Parker suspects that Stirling's transfer is the result of the interference of General Kaye (Chill Wills, also the voice of Francis), who, like Stirling, thinks that WACS are all very well, but in their place. An upcoming demonstration in camouflage, in which the WACS will attempt to evade the general's men, is seen by both parties as an opportunity to prove their case.

Kaye's open misogyny marks him as a stuffy Army bureaucrat ("a narrow-minded fuddy-duddy," as Francis puts it). Indeed Francis directly confronts Kaye on the subject of women in the Army: "Everyone knows women are here to stay. But you? You got the idea they're in the service just to keep your memos circulating." The result is an odd spectacle of comic splitting, the old-fashioned Kaye confronted by a jackass who uses his own voice to lecture him on the place of military women. Both Kaye and Stirling are in need of an education in the value of the female soldier. Part of Stirling's lesson comes in the "humiliation" of role-reversal, from his outrage at being designated a WAC, even temporarily, to his crossdressing turn, which reprises the wig fashioned from a horse's tail seen in *I Was a Male War Bride* (here courtesy of Francis). Stirling also receives more direct tuition in gender hierarchies from Parker, who lectures, "We prefer to think of women in uniform as a serious business."

The specter of military women as mannish is comically offset throughout *Francis Joins the WAC* in a repertoire of devices that underline their femininity and desirability. Although he ultimately comes to respect the WACS, Stirling's repeated gaffes and quips reiterate precisely this reassuring womanliness, linked to a nonthreatening auxiliary status. For instance, he digs himself yet deeper into a hole by suggesting that the WACs are "wonderful," but only in their place; he attempts to compliment Parker with the patronizing reassurance, "I thought you were as hard as nails. You're really very soft underneath," thus rehearsing a familiar gendered opposition. His unorthodox drill instructions (including the command "Lift those lovely, lovely legs") and disconcerted response to uniformed women's bodies all underline the disorienting spectacle of military women.

Francis, by contrast, is credited with an ability to see beyond the false assumptions of women's place in the military. Rejecting Stirling's comment that camouflage is a "man's job," the mule insists on the place of the WAC with a contradictory evocation of femininity as deception: "Every beauty parlor's a camouflage installation." Thus even as the film asserts the value of female soldiers, it comically undercuts its own premise, not only by having the sentiment voiced by a talking mule, but by mobilizing women's commitment to beauty culture as evidence of their suitability to perform within a conventionally masculine arena. Between them, Stirling and Francis use their combined male and horse sense to guide the women through the exercise triumphant, in the process demonstrating the inherent value of military women and their reliance on male authority. Comically articulating what would become increasingly pressing questions of the role of military women beyond supportive and clerical duties, *Francis Joins the WAC* explicitly reassures its audience, "Every WAC is a woman."

What seems clear from the comedies discussed above is that in films that acknowledge contemporary debates about the legitimacy of women's military service, the military woman herself rarely functions as a comic figure. Comedy emerges from the impact of her disruptive or unruly presence on men, whether soldiers or civilians, who, like the masculine institutions of the military itself, must learn to accommodate themselves to a changing situation. The military woman is routinely associated in these comedies with the comic confusion of gender roles, yet much of this confusion is worked out through male characters. The continuing resonance of the female trickster figure—a knowing figure rather than one who is the unwitting cause of confusion—is evident in *The Phil Silvers Show*, which first aired on CBS in 1955 (initially as *You'll Never Get Rich*) and ran until 1959. Built around the central character of the scheming master sergeant Ernest Bilko (Silvers) and based, far from the distractions of the city, at

Fort Baxter, Kansas, the show sends up peacetime Army life (and institutional life more generally). Bilko is a career soldier and con artist; constantly setting up elaborate schemes that almost come off, he is a gambler perpetually in search of funds. The comic situation played out in the show is essentially one of role-reversal with respect to rank; it is Bilko, rather than his colonel, who dominates Fort Baxter. For three of its four seasons, *The Phil Silvers Show* featured another master sergeant in WAC Joan Hogan (Elizabeth Fraser). Over its run the show also featured other WACs in supporting roles, but it is Hogan who is Fort Baxter's most significant military woman. Her characterization indicates not only how familiar a figure the military woman had become by the mid-1950s, but how comedy served to mediate the disruption represented by the auxiliary military woman.

Hogan is introduced in the show's third episode, "WAC" (4 October 1955) as both a rival and a romantic interest for Bilko.[15] They engage in a battle of wits, competing to take on a voluntary role that comes with a Jeep, a perk hidden in the small print that only Bilko and Hogan are aware of. Like Bilko, Hogan uses charm and deception to succeed; she employs her southern femininity to mask her intelligence and ability, underlining her status as trickster. The episode makes clear that she is effectively a female version of Bilko, a worthy opponent in what he dubs "the war of man against woman." Having failed to win over Hogan with the pleasures of a party designed with a male sergeant in mind, Bilko opts to bury her in paperwork. Hogan proves unflappable, countering Bilko's requisitions with paperwork of her own; indeed her knowledge of arcane Army regulations matches his, enabling her to play him at his own game. He next suggests cards, but backtracks when he sees her shuffling technique, deciding, as a last resort, on a strategy of seduction. In itself this scenario is comic, as Bilko is an unlikely but supremely confident lover. His two sidekicks rehearse what is clearly a familiar scene, demonstrating how Bilko will appeal to the isolation of his position as sergeant, seeking tenderness, tears, and sympathy from his female partner. As the scene is enacted by Bilko and Hogan, however, the object of the scheme reveals her own command of trickery. When Bilko delivers his killer line, "Six stripes, each a prison bar around my heart," Hogan effortlessly turns the situation around, simulating tears and appropriating Bilko's own rhetoric: "Prison bars around *your* heart? What do you think a woman soldier goes through? It's romantic for a man in uniform, but a woman in uniform?

That wall between her and every soft and tender feeling she's got." Bilko succumbs, holding Hogan close and comforting her. His offer to walk her back to the post triggers the episode's comic punch line, which signals his failure in the contest: "Why walk? I'll drive you there in my Jeep."

"wac" ends with Hogan turning away, leaving Bilko in bewilderment at having been so expertly outmaneuvered; from the doorway she calls in a tone of somewhat impatient rebuke, "Ernie!" His response, "Coming, dear, coming," sets up the relationship that will develop between the two in future episodes, that is, a relationship conducted within well-worn "battle of the sexes" territory, with Bilko desperate to hold onto Hogan but unwilling to commit to marriage. As a trickster in her own right, Hogan's military woman matches the show's male protagonist in playing military life and the battle of the sexes. Such a formulation of romantic connection linked to comic rivalry typifies a provisional acceptance of military women in American comedy, characterized not by equity but by a continuing insistence on both gendered conflict and the military woman's desirable femininity (that is, her specificity as a woman).

PETTICOATS AND PIRACY: SEX COMEDY
AND THE MILITARY WOMAN

The playful comic figuring of the military woman as disruptive or desirable gives way in the late 1950s and early 1960s to more explicit sex comedy. Here the military woman's presence in mixed-sex environments provides a cue for suggestive or salacious humor and scenes of sexual spectacle. This section explores the military woman's place within sex comedy through a discussion of three films: *Operation Petticoat* (Republic, 1959), *Operation Bullshine* (Associated British, 1959), and *Petticoat Pirates* (Associated British, 1961). All three were box-office successes (the last two in the British market), indicating the continuing popularity of service comedies. In all three military women are both central characters and the butt of the joke. Rather than foregrounding tropes of transformation as a strategy for managing the perceived distance between women and military life, these films exploit that distance as a *comic contradiction*. In keeping with the emerging conventions of sex comedy these films emphasize innuendo, sexual humor, and gags about the female body. Physical comedy is repeatedly played out around the body of the military woman and typically occurs at her expense; the physical presence of women, whether it is their "intrusive" breasts or their tendency to distract military men from their duties, results in their repeated inscription as a comic problem. In none of these films are the female characters in control of the comedy or even aware of their status as a running joke.

Operation Petticoat looks nostalgically back to the Second World War from the perspective of Cdr. Matt Sherman (Cary Grant). We see the newly commissioned *Sea Tiger* in 1941, damaged by Japanese bombers, followed by the efforts of Sherman and his crew to save their submarine from being scrapped before it has even seen battle. This sentimental attachment to the vessel, and the fear of obsolescence she seemingly signifies, is expressed in a series of metaphors to do with virginity, age, and experience, each playfully underscoring gendered naval language. Ships may be female, as this nautical language reminds us, but women remain an alien presence on board. Chief Mechanic Sam Tostin (Arthur O'Connell) is particularly clear on this point, protesting that women are bad luck when Lieutenant Holden (Tony Curtis) brings aboard five stranded army nurses.[16] The women's presence generates romance and provides a key source of the film's comedy.

That it is women's *bodies*, as well as their generally alien and unwelcome presence, that disconcert both captain and crew (and even the unflappable Holden) is evident. Though words finally fail him, Sherman attempts to explain to the nurses his concern, suggesting that "a submarine's not designed to be coeducational." Chief Tostin objects to the use of "his" engine room to dry laundry, commenting, "They're like snakes—when they shed their skin, look out!" Lt. Dolores Crandall causes particular consternation, her body providing a running gag throughout the film as sailors must press themselves against the walls to avoid brushing up against her breasts. (Sherman, who will later romance her, passes the word around that Crandall be given "clear passage"; figure 34). Crandall is the last to board ship, her physique the punch line to the gag that the women's arrival represents. As she is helped up, we cut to a side profile, emphasizing her chest. At the sight, one young sailor drops whatever it is he is holding. An older, somewhat grizzled sailor comments to his mate, who removes his cap in awe, "If anyone ever asks you what you're fighting for, there's your answer." *What* rather than *who* is the key term here, with women presented as either a symbol of home (a thing to be fought for) or, more cynically, as analogous to the various spare parts Holden has "scavenged" during the film. Later Sherman follows one of the nurse's discovery of a stolen pig with the wry comment "Yes, they're drafting every-

34. Lieutenant Crandall's (Joan O'Brien) intrusive body disrupts the male military space of the submarine in *Operation Petticoat* (1959).

body these days" that rather pointedly equates women with animals as well as with spare parts.[17]

The unmilitary, unmasculine result of women's presence onboard is most visibly signaled in the film's most striking image: the *Sea Tiger's* distinctive coat of pink paint. The women are not in any way responsible for the lack of gray paint which leads to the submarine's "feminine" appearance; nonetheless the sight of the ailing, pink submarine functions as a rich comic metaphor for their inappropriate presence. The nurses' status as *military* women is barely acknowledged in *Operation Petticoat*, although this clearly provides the rationale for their presence in the Pacific. Instead they function as the opposite sex in this "battle of the sexes" comedy; constructing the women as fundamentally different from the seamen with whom they are in such intimate proximity, the film resists any suggestion of commonality through military service of the kind seen in wartime features. They attend to no battle-wounded soldiers; indeed their only nursing tasks consist of dealing with the malingering seamen who invent illnesses to visit the women and delivering babies for the civilian women taken aboard later in the film.

The initially antagonistic relationship between Chief Tostin and Maj. Edna Heywood exemplifies the film's tendency to present military women as simply women rather than as comrades or peers. Tostin is the most vocal and insistent opponent of the women's presence. Outraged that Heywood has commandeered the engine room to dry the women's intimate laundry, he rejects her assertion of rank and military identity:

35. In *Operation Petticoat* (1959) Chief Tostin objects to women's presence onboard the *Sea Tiger*; the use of "his" engine room to dry their underwear fuels comic fury.

"Maybe Congress made you an officer, but God made you a woman, and a woman just shouldn't mess around with a man's machinery." Both the sexual innuendo of the reference to "a man's machinery" and the clearly defined gender roles that the chief insists on define the category of *military woman* as a politician's invention rather than a natural state, even as Tostin's discomfort is itself comic in effect (figure 35).[18]

Tostin is a comic curmudgeon, an old-fashioned figure who is subsequently won over by Heywood's knowledge of "a man's machinery," his visceral disgust at women overcome by her "masculine" knowledge. Their sparring is thematized in comic imagery that stages an invasion of masculine space with feminine frippery (the petticoats of the title and the film's insistence on women's underwear as a marker of their difference and desirability). Much to the chief's horror, for instance, the mechanically minded major fixes a defective pump with her girdle. Eventually a sort of mutual respect develops between the two, the chief confessing to Heywood that though he "has spent a lot of years disliking women," she is different: "You're not a woman. You're more than that. You're a mechanic." That Heywood seems genuinely pleased at this "compliment" exemplifies the taken-for-granted sexism of the period. However, in the film's terms, Heywood is perhaps "more than" a woman (i.e., not a woman at all) to the extent that she is a masculine, military woman. Her knowledge of how things work (as a nurse she presumably knows how bodies, as well as engines, function) is explained in terms of her family background, but her command is an achievement all her own.

If Chief Tostin represents a comically extreme misogyny, his refusal to recognize the nurses as military women is shared by the other crew members. For example, when Sherman concedes that he cannot leave the nurses with the embattled U.S. Army, which is retreating to fight a guerrilla war (in the process reminding us that women have no place in a combat zone), he formally invites the major and her "friends" to remain aboard. Unable to refer to the nurses as the major's "men," they simply become her "friends," clearly a civilian designation. Though Sherman is not as *vocally* opposed to women onboard as Tostin is, he is frequently lost for words. Cary Grant's familiar comedic performance style is put to good use here; as in *Bringing Up Baby* and *I Was a Male War Bride*, his sentences trail off as he seems powerless to resist the irrational force of female presence.

Lieutenant Crandall represents a particular assault on Sherman's person. As already mentioned, her large breasts are the focus of attention from the moment she steps onboard, "provoking" (in the film's terms) lust and consternation among the crew. Crandall is an unintentionally disruptive presence in the closed world of the submarine. Indeed she functions as an object lesson of the military woman as a provocative, inappropriate presence at sea, precipitating a catalogue of accidents: the heel of her shoe gets stuck on deck; she inadvertently hits the collision button, sounding the alarm; sprays water in Sherman's face; leaves her cigarette in his coffee cup; pesters him with vitamin pills; falls against him and mistakenly launches a torpedo; inadvertently knocks a seaman into the water; and positions her curling iron so that Sherman burns his rear. At one point Sherman confides in his log that for the first time in his life he has come "close to hitting a woman," and he wonders aloud whether Crandall might be a Japanese agent. That she has (inadvertently) interfered with the ship's guns extends the ongoing sexual innuendo which finds comic possibilities in the very presence of women among "men's machinery." That the possibility of violence toward the disruptive woman is replaced by romance and marriage speaks to the gendered hierarchies at work within the film. Characterized by metaphors of their animal nature (snakes, pigs), deception (Crandall as a Japanese spy), and ineptitude, women, it seems, are safe only once domesticated and removed from masculine public space.

Dale's comments on the extent to which women are off-limits for certain kinds of comedy perhaps explains why the physical comedy in which Crandall is involved is all inadvertent. She is an innocent abroad, unaware of the consequences of either her actions or her physical presence. Though an attraction develops between Crandall and Sherman, their relationship is the inverse of that between Tostin and the capable Heywood. Crandall is simply not designed for the world of the submarine, as the repeated shots of her progress down the narrow hallways, and even the quips of the other nurses about the need to cover her chest, testify. She is consistently coded as a feminine woman who is not cut out for military life. The horror of women's bodies and the comic associations of their underwear find their denouement toward the end of the film, when the submarine comes under attack from U.S. ships who regard its very conspicuousness (the pink paint) as an enemy ploy. Sherman sends up debris to simulate the submarine sinking, but to no avail. The resourceful Holden suggests an alternative, and shortly the nurses' bras are sent up as debris, comically expelled through the torpedo tube, the music underscoring the sexual connotations of this imagery of release. Intercepting Crandall's bra with a grappling hook, the Navy pronounces that it must belong to American bosoms ("Japanese have nothing like this") and cease fire. Crandall's breasts are once more both the source of humor and a representation of what the American troops are fighting for. As Heywood's girdle patches up the *Sea Tiger*'s engine, so Crandall's bra signals the sexualized character of the vessel that carries her. The military woman effectively sexualizes military space, space that previously served as a site of homosocial comradeship. The suggestive expulsion of the bra signals the need to purge the *Sea Tiger* of its female passengers.

Operation Petticoat's staging of the battle of the sexes mines the comic potential of men and women at sea together. The comedy of female presence within a symbolically male space prefigures more recent narratives and representations thematizing the disruptive and provocative role of military women. Indeed the remake of *Operation Petticoat* in 1977, a television movie serving as a prelude to the short-lived NBC sitcom, did not substantially revise the format of the original film although almost twenty years had elapsed.[19] Presumably relying on audience familiarity with the feature film, the television movie does not even pause to explain its co-ed crew or pink submarine. Since it functions as a pilot, narrative moves toward closure are sidestepped, yet the basic character dynamics and comic situations remain in place: the accident-prone Crandall; sexy female bodies on display in a masculine-coded space; Holden's schemes and his redemption through a combination of military service and his relationship with Lieutenant Duran. The animosity between Chief Tostin and Major Heywood (although not the romantic intrigue) also recurs. As played by Yvonne Wilder, Heywood frames her access to the masculine codes of mechanics in clichés of fiery ethnicity, her performance punctuated with loud protests in Spanish. The overarching comic theme of emasculated men seeking to prove themselves through action also remains in place, structuring the repeated failures of Sherman to off-load the group of nurses, and visualized in the *Sea Tiger*'s pink paint. Predictably the nurses are scantily clad, allowing for plenty of shots emphasizing legs and breasts. Gender confusion linked to the very presence of military women clearly underpins the comedy once more, demonstrating the longevity of these tropes from the 1950s.

Like *Operation Petticoat*, the British film *Operation Bullshine* looks back from 1959 to the Second World War. While the former builds its comedy on military men and women thrown together in a cramped submarine setting, *Operation Bullshine* uses a "mixed company" (the title of Anne Barnaby's original story) of gunners and ATS at a coastal battery. In doing so the film revisits for the purposes of comedy one of the most familiar, and revered, images of British military women during the war: the ATS spotters and predictors who served on such batteries and whose images were widely reproduced in both the British and American press of the period. Yet this is no high-minded celebration of military women's role; rather, in keeping with the traditions of service comedy, the emphasis falls not on combat but on sexual misunderstandings.

Female ineptitude is also strongly foregrounded in the film. The first response to an alarm reveals the unit's disorganization, a failure laid firmly at the door of the ATS personnel. Major Pym declares himself outraged at their performance: "I'd rather command a battery of one-eyed baboons than this, this hen party!" Although Pym is clearly a comic buffoon, the women's ineffectiveness and their general unsuitability for military life is one of the film's chief themes and a recurrent source of comedy. At the end of the film the battery actually manages to shoot down an enemy plane, but as John Hill observes, the event is "marked as serendipity." The playful presentation of women's participation in combat is reinforced in the film's final image, which pictures the fear replaced by delight on the face of the German pilot captured by the excited ATS recruits. While Hill is right to suggest that the film's comedy "derives from the incompetence of women to adapt to military circumstances,"[20] *Operation Bullshine*'s male characters seem equally inept. Where they excel is in playing the system to their own advantage. Indeed this assumption structures the scramble to prepare the battery for inspection, the need to put on a show for the brass (hence the film's title).

There are two narrative strands organizing the series of comic scenes and encounters in *Operation Bullshine*. One concerns the self-serving Pym's desire to keep the chain of command above him content. He sets the goal of winning the "smartest site" competition between units by being best prepared for an inspection; that the unit will stand or fall on *appearance* as much as performance is indicative of the film's comic perspective on military bureaucracy. The second narrative element concerns Lt. Gordon Brown's (Donald Sinden) attempt to manage the amorous attentions of Pvt. Marge White and to conceal the identity of a new private assigned to the unit, Betty Brown, who happens to be his wife. This comic treatment of military life and hierarchies is in keeping with the immediate historical context: the film was produced in peacetime during a period in which national service, for men at least, was still in force in Britain.[21]

Producer Frank Godwin described the film (then titled *Girls in Arms*) as "basically factual," pointing to the letters received "from ex-members of the Women's Service telling of incidents which make this picture look like a documentary." Even so, *Operation Bullshine* was promoted primarily in terms of glamour rather than realism. Indeed the same interview cites Godwin as follows: "There are no dressing-gowns in this picture, just flimsy nighties and we exploit or expose them to the full in a barrack-bedroom with the twelve most attractive starlets we could find in London."[22] The reference to dressing gowns alludes to Godwin's association with realist pictures, *Woman in a Dressing Gown* (1957) in particular. There is a nice play with this contrast in the film's opening sequence, as a montage of documentary images—wartime London, a lone soldier guarding the coast, men marching—and a serious newsreel voice give way to color footage of the marching ATS women (complete with regimental bulldog) and the rousing theme song "Girls in Arms." The earnest introduction associated with reverential wartime representation is punctured by the eruption onto the screen of *Operation Bullshine*'s "full scale comedy in colour about girls in khaki."[23] The credit sequence pictures the ATS in a series of cartoon figures, scantily clad and posed on either side of the frame, their jutting breasts directed toward the titles. These suggestively posed cartoon "girls" hold a variety of objects, including oversized bullets, rifles, binoculars, and musical instruments. The lyrics of the title song, meanwhile, celebrate the sexuality of military women, with lines such as "It's so exciting / to have glamour girls to do the fighting." Men and women serving alongside each other is presented as a source of comedy and confusion.

As the foregoing may suggest, films such as *Operation Bullshine* tend to present all military women in familiar comic or erotic terms. In this context it is useful to analyze the ways such comedies thematize gender and the military. *Operation Bullshine*, for instance, clearly distinguishes between conventionally attractive women, who are sexually or romantically available, and women deemed "masculine," who are aligned with the military as institution; excluded from flirtations and fun, these women enforce regulations and are either shocked by or get in the way of the other women's activities. Thus we have the stern sergeant who frowns at two women painting each other's toenails in the barracks ("That won't get you any promotions") or the gruff female commander who tells the curvaceous White, "Kindly take that uniform back to stores and get one that doesn't fit you quite so well." Clearly such types reproduce the twin phantoms of discourses surrounding military women from the Second World War: the sexually predatory, overly feminine military woman on the one hand, and the mannish, potentially lesbian woman on the other. Both function as sources of comedy in *Operation Bullshine*. The ATS women are presented as unduly preoccupied with romance and personal appearance. For instance, a sergeant instructs Brown how to proceed if the alarm sounds in the night: "We do not stop to put on our lipstick or comb our hair." Even as she speaks the words, White is holding out a compact and applying lipstick. Predictably, when the alarm does sound that night, Brown takes time to adjust her lipstick. The general impression in the barracks is of a sensuous rather than a military atmosphere. Indeed through costume we are offered an eroticized combination of the two, as when one ATS goes to leave the barracks, dressed in her uniform but having absentmindedly forgotten her slacks, giving the audience a view of her semiclad lower body, stockings and suspenders setting off the olive drab. Two women sit on a bed in nightdresses; one smokes as she polishes her boots, the other makes as if to do the same, before using the brush to add mascara to her lashes. A shower scene and various shots of the women exercising continue the visual spectacle. Sexual display, as these instances suggest, is both a source of visual pleasure and the key form of expression of the ATS women's rebellious attitude.

As the officer in charge, Major Pym is a doubly comic figure; his desire to protect the comfort of his own position signals his status as a stuffy representative of authority, while his hostility toward the ATS ("blasted women," as he refers to them) suggests the repressive, traditional function of his character. Indeed he instructs Brown to "keep the women in their place." That there is a sexual dimension to this need for control is made explicit in the exchange that follows this injunction, in which Brown informs Pym that one Private Partridge has been discharged "for the usual reasons" (i.e., pregnancy). As in more recent discourses that work to cast doubt on the capability of the military woman in terms of her capacity to reproduce, Partridge's pregnancy is presented as a solo achievement. Pym fumes, saying of the replacement (who turns out to be Brown's wife), "Let's hope we can get some work out of her before she starts having a baby." Pym's misogyny is comically deflated during the inspection, in which the brigadier is accompanied by "the whole of Fleet Street." A female reporter, pen poised, asks Pym a series of questions on his views on the women in the unit; each time, just as he is about to offer his actual opinion of the women, the brigadier intervenes with a positive evaluation. Ultimately Pym is left speechless with horror when the journalist expresses her delight with the words she has put into his mouth, trying out a line of copy: "The gentle touch of a woman's hand is helping to win the war." We do not see Pym's response, cutting instead to the far from gentle touch of Private Cox knocking over a vase as she furiously cleans in one of the huts.

That the inspection party features journalists and that the mixed company is an object of press speculation and interest is telling in terms of the war setting and of more contemporary debates relating to military women and the evident interest taken by the media in their training and work. White, whose performances of glamour and vulnerability mark her as the epitome of femininity throughout the film, is assigned special duties in the inspection. Her role (as instructed by the canny Gunner Slocum) is simply to walk around the camp, repeatedly coming across the visiting brass and journalists, dazzling them with her salute, smile, and looks. Her glamorous performance of military womanhood is snapped approvingly by a photographer, emphasizing once more that the military, like Slocum's "Operation Bull," has as much to do with appearance as with substance.

Operation Petticoat casts military women as a comic nuisance, while *Operation Bullshine* finds them delightful but inept. Neither film gives credence to the military status of the nurses and ATS personnel they feature; their role is rather to provide an opportunity for comedy and sexual innuendo. Made just two years later (with the full cooperation of the Royal Navy),[24] *Petticoat Pirates* directly addresses the limits placed on the service of British military women, although it once again falls back on comedy to contain the disruptive possibility of gender equality. When the female superintendent's plans for Navy women to serve at sea are rejected out of hand (the commander in chief refers to the idea as "feministic nonsense"), Anne Stephens (Anne Heywood) leads a group of some 150 Wrens on a mission to take over the HMS *Huntress*. Their objective: to prove women's capabilities "at all times and in all circumstances." An assault team of "frog girls" (clad in figure-hugging outfits) subdues the ship's skeleton crew. The senior officer on board, Lt. Michael Patterson, is confined to his quarters. That he is also Stephens's romantic interest in the film adds a personal dimension to her assumption of command.

Ultimately the *Huntress* returns triumphant, having seen off a frigate captained by the objectionable Jerome Robertson, who was sent to bring them back ("I know how to handle women"), and defeating the flag ship of the U.S. fleet in an exercise. (The American commander subsequently suffers a mental breakdown and, in a patriotic touch, the British win the day.) In the film's final sequence the commander in chief congratulations the WRNS on their success (for which he has taken full credit), promising to make further representations on their behalf.[25] The British trade magazine *Kine-Weekly* concludes its summary of the film with the rather telling observation, "The sea battle of the sexes ends even, and Anne and Michael presumably marry."[26] For this reviewer the battle of the sexes shifts from a contest between Navy men and women to the more personal "battle" between Stephens and Patterson; the addition of an assumed marriage provides a resolution through an implied domesticity that is not even present in the film. Certainly the film is unable to resolve that question of military policy, opting instead to play it safe and emphasizing the reconciliation between the central couple.

Though my interest in *Petticoat Pirates* has to do with its engagement with and use of military women, for British audiences at the time it would have been viewed primarily as a vehicle for the comedian Charlie Drake (his character is credited simply as Charlie).[27] The pratfalls and difficulties of Drake's comically ineffective sailor frame the film's narrative explorations of limits of active service for the WRNS. A sailor who hasn't been to sea, Charlie is short, scruffy, and prone to ungainly pratfalls. Not only does he spend part of the film disguised as a (comically unattractive) Wren, but he is introduced as a peeping tom; through a periscope he has constructed in the boiler room he ogles the Wrens as they exercise in the gym above him. Apprehended in his spying just as the women have agreed on their plan, he is captured and imprisoned. Although he temporarily escapes by dressing as a Wren, his female disguise ultimately ends up involving him in the boarding party.

As in *Operation Petticoat*, *Petticoat Pirates* offers a scenario in which military women are a disruptive presence in an all-male military environment. Chief Nixon aboard the *Huntress* confides that he is happy to forgo shore leave in precisely these terms: "At least you're safe from women here." A cut to the frog girls swimming toward the *Huntress* reveals his error as the women move to literally take over this "safe" male space. The Wrens are certainly formidable, yet their power and authority are repeatedly played off against their presentation as sexual spectacle. When an armed frog girl (one of the seamen thinks she's a mermaid) barks out "Hands up!" she is, initially at least, a threatening figure. When she follows up with the challenge "Who wants it first?" the delighted sailors grin and happily volunteer, playing on the sexual innuendo of "getting it" from a military woman. Nixon's response to the arrival of the frog girls is similarly contradictory. Surprise ("Blimey, the ship's crawling with bints!") gives way to delight (he opens his arms to welcome them) and then to distress as he is physically overpowered. Later Nixon will romance Charlie's fake Wren, underlining the confusions that women (even women's clothes) bring with them.

In relation to its presentation of women in the workplace, John Hill reads the film in positive terms, highlighting the contrast between the film's Wrens and the inept ATS women featured in *Operation Bullshine*. Thus he writes, "The women in *Petticoat Pirates* have successfully defied male expectations and proven their abilities in performing traditionally male roles."[28] In addition to the sequence in which the Wrens seize the ship, the film features two lengthy montage sequences showing the women performing their duties at sea efficiently and capably. The uplifting music that accompanies these scenes suggests a positive endorsement of the seafaring capabilities of the WRNS. Set against this imagery of capable military women getting a chance to show their mettle are scenes of saucy sexual spectacle in which Wrens wander about in decidedly non-regulation underwear (mediated by Charlie's presence as voyeur in drag). The "gently salacious humour" that Geoff King finds in the *Carry On* films is also clearly present here.[29] At a time when the boundaries of what could be shown and said in relation to the body and sexuality were being openly tested, the sexual display evident in *Petticoat Pirates* smacks of a rude liberality. The *Kine-Weekly* review draws attention to this aspect of the film's attractions: "The supporting Wrens, often seen in their undies, are nothing if not comely."[30]

These images exploit the humorous mismatch of femininity and a military setting. The association of women with an inappropriate femininity also frames the narratively inexplicable sequence in which the Wrens sunbathe on deck, sipping drinks and playing records. The association drawn here between women and an imagery of leisure—rather than women at work—recalls the fantasy construction of beautiful, sunbathing nurses lounging about the decks in the wartime musical *Up in Arms*. As with the scenes dwelling on Wrens in their underwear, the bathing suits in *Petticoat Pirates* are far from military, signaling to the audience that although these are military women, they are also desirable women. The scenes in which Charlie spies on the women suggest their covert availability as sexual spectacle; here the Wrens publicly present themselves as bathing beauties, colluding in their own objectification.

The confusing consequences (for men) of physical proximity between military men and women is a staple of service comedy. When, in *Operation Petticoat*, Sherman finds Lieutenants Duran and Holden kissing, he confines Holden to his quarters and remonstrates with Major Heywood: "If you can't control your women, lock them up." The evident chaos that follows from the presence of the group of nurses on the *Sea Tiger* offers a comic enactment of many of the issues that would be rehearsed in more recent debates. Most obvious among these is the contention that men and women cannot serve together since the presence of women is too provocative. *Petticoat Pirates* pursues this logic to the limit, so that when Patter-

36. Stephens and Patterson temporarily share command of the HMS *Huntress* in *Petticoat Pirates* (1961).

son and his crew are given the freedom of the ship they are torn between the impulse to attempt to regain command (there are a few unsuccessful attempts to do so) and the delights of traveling with female company.

In the personal battle between Stephens and Patterson, sexual display and competence are also at issue. At first Patterson openly protests at Stephens's actions, rejecting her authority: "I do not accept your command—now or ever." Later, coming to her cabin to effect a reconciliation, he exclaims, "Isn't it enough for you just to be a beautiful woman?" Furious that he has attempted to seduce her away from her command, the defiant Stephens challenges her lover to acknowledge the Wrens' worth and achievement: "Didn't we seize this ship from right under your highly superior, stuck-up male noses?" By the end of the film, when she must turn to him for help (a storm makes the Wrens seasick), Patterson finally acknowledges the legitimacy of her command, shifting from a celebratory sneer at the women's indisposition to concern for the ship, from a resumption of command to an acknowledgment of Stephens's authority. Thus he gives her an order, then corrects himself, standing to attention (slightly disheveled in his pajamas, the only image of male undress in the film) to formally offer the services of his men. On the bridge Patterson declares her to be the "best captain [he's] ever sailed with, and by far the prettiest" (figure 36, p. 170).

Petticoat Pirates is a contradictory film, characterized by simplistic sexism and an effective harnessing of a "battle of the sexes" format to comically challenge the limited definitions of women's work in circulation at the time. Comedy, sexual spectacle, and the mediating figure of Charlie Drake allow such issues to be addressed with relative safety. That *Petticoat Pirates* nonetheless poses some uncomfortable questions concerning military women is evident in the two British reviews of the film cited by John Hill. One, published in the *Sunday Telegraph*, a conservative broadsheet, includes this comment: "As any successful farce must be, this one is founded upon a genuinely ridiculous idea—that of women taking themselves in deadly seriousness as naval units." A second, from the rather more liberal *Observer*, comments, "For men who have a built-in aversion to women in uniform, it [the film's farce] was virtually insupportable."[31] An idea that was both ridiculous and insupportable for British men in the early 1960s, taking military women seriously, would persist and gain in political momentum in the decades that followed. Nonetheless it would be in comedy that the military woman would continue to appear most regularly in American and British film and television. Comedy, it would seem, provided a mode of narration and a generic setting that spoke to and made entertainment out of the military woman's persistently provocative presence.

MILITARY WOMEN AND SERVICE COMEDY 5

M*A*S*H and *Private Benjamin*

Throughout the 1970s and 1980s it was service comedies, both as films and on television, that most routinely showcased the military woman. The stereotypes developed in the 1950s and 1960s, from the military woman as a compelling sign of strength and independence to her iteration as a sexy nuisance, persist in this period. So too does the narrative concern with her impact on military men. Yet this was a period of immense change for military women in the U.S., changes that are registered in contradictory ways within the formulas of service comedy. In 1976 the service academies admitted female cadets for the first time, explicitly acknowledging that military women had a leadership role within the military. (The first women would graduate from the academies in 1980.) In 1978 the Women's Army Corps was disestablished, its members integrated into the Army to work alongside male soldiers, although a significant number of roles remained closed to them. At a policy level there were significant developments throughout the 1960s, yet as military reliance on female labor became increasingly evident these high-profile changes to the status and opportunities offered to military women were also framed by the more visible feminist activism of the 1970s. As a result of such social changes, the kinds of comedy elaborated around the figure of the military woman also begin to shift in this period. The comedies considered here are marked by an increasing degree of acceptance and respect for military women, in effect their normalization, and an intensifying misogyny, suggesting a move from themes of comic male confusion at women's presence to a rather more hostile rejection and exclusion.

This chapter centers on two commercially successful films, M*A*S*H (1970) and *Private Benjamin* (1980), as well as the television series that each generated. Though both films were significant box-office successes, the television series of M*A*S*H was far more successful than that based on *Private Benjamin*. M*A*S*H is the longest running television series to feature a military woman as a recurring character, Loretta Swit's Maj. Margaret Houlihan. The show demonstrates the continuing cultural anxieties associated with the figure of the military woman, often mobilizing an explicit disdain for female personnel. I look first at the film's presentation of military women within its overall anarchic, sexualized comedy. I then consider how the television series adapted the film's premise, particularly its staging of military women within a hybrid format combining situation comedy and drama. In both cases the female soldier is a figure of fun.

While M*A*S*H was pioneering in its combination of drama and comedy in the sitcom format, the *Private Benjamin* series is a more conventional coupling of sitcom and service comedy, avoiding the contentious topics dealt with in M*A*S*H. In a scathing summary of *Private Benjamin*'s political subtext Enloe observes, "Goldie Hawn was telling us cinematically that joining the military didn't mean killing Asians or even defending democracy from the communist menace: *Private Benjamin* instead showed a new American way for a girl to cope with youthful widowhood, escape clinging parents and stay physically fit: go to boot camp."[1] While Enloe's concerns are justified—both the film and the television series *Private Benjamin* echo contemporary recruitment materials more or less explicitly, portraying the Army as a healthy, character-building institution for women—my argument foregrounds the way military women are an accepted part of the Army in these comedies, exploring the extent to which they are represented in both new and familiar ways. The fact that both the film and the series *Private Benjamin* were produced during peacetime is of course significant. The early years of M*A*S*H were framed by the Vietnam War; *Private Benjamin*, by contrast, a show which situates military women as an established feature of Army life, is more decidedly the product of a postdraft era in which attempts to recruit larger numbers of women into the military were firmly in place.

M*A*S*H: AN ANTI–MILITARY SERVICE COMEDY

Released in early 1970, *M*A*S*H* the movie was a significant box-office and critical success for its director, Robert Altman. An adaptation of Richard Hooker's novel, published in 1968 and based on his experiences as an Army medic during the Korean War, this raucous comedy was widely read as a commentary on the contemporary Vietnam War. The film is set in a Mobile Army Surgical Hospital unit, the 4077th, which operates a few miles from the front line, primarily treating battle casualties. It centers on a group of disaffected Army surgeons who perform their medical duties effectively while disdaining military authority. At odds with this group is the film's only prominent female character, Maj. Margaret "Hot Lips" O'Houlihan (Sally Kellerman). The characterization of O'Houlihan as a *military* woman renders her a figure of fun on two counts: first in terms of the comic contradiction posed by any woman who attempts to assume authority, and second as a representative of the military authority against which the anarchic humor and carnivalesque qualities of the film's world is directed.

*M*A*S*H* begins with Capt. "Hawkeye" Pierce (Donald Sutherland) stealing a Jeep to take him to the 4077th; it closes with his departure in the same Jeep, marking Pierce as the film's key character and our point of entry into the world of the MASH unit. Pierce's anarchic attitude sits well with the ineffectual camp commander, Col. Henry Blake, and fellow doctors "Trapper" John McIntyre (Elliott Gould) and Duke Forrest (Tom Skerritt). Throughout the course of the film the group thumb their noses at a series of military authority figures, culminating in a somewhat disorganized football match between the 4077th and the 325th EVAC. Within the camp two characters serve as the principal foils: O'Houlihan and Maj. Frank Burns (Robert Duvall). Religion, sport, military regulation: these regimes of masculinity are thoroughly mocked in the antics of the male protagonists. While the protagonists' indifference to war suggests a distance from conventional ideals of masculine achievement (heroism, bravery), their constitution as a lecherous, misogynistic group underlines a continuing investment in male privilege. Moreover, although they are opposed to the business of war, in standing up to military martinets (male and female) the doctors show their courage and integrity. They embody the long-standing type of the "good doctor," always ready to apply their caring skills.[2] More generally their drinking and womanizing suggest a combination of fraternity humor and the authorized indiscretions that, as Carl Freedman notes, have long been sanctioned for active-duty servicemen.[3]

Noting the historical context in which it was produced (i.e., before the most significant impact of second-wave feminism on writers and performers, among others), Freedman claims that one of the key revisions the film *M*A*S*H* makes to Hooker's novel is the introduction of "a violent hatred of women."[4] He is not alone in drawing attention to the mixture of ferocity and contempt with which women are treated in the film. The humiliation and effective marginalization of O'Houlihan is the most striking instance of this process. As a woman with authority in a military system that the film, and its male protagonists, reject, O'Houlihan is a comic foil for both its strong misogynous and anti-authority impulses. Thus when she introduces herself to Pierce in *military* terms ("I like to think of the Army as my home"), he rejects her in *sexual* terms, dubbing her both "a very attractive woman" and "a regular Army clown." Pierce thus places her firmly on the other side of the film's "us versus them" structure in which the good doctors battle regulatory forces symbolized by the military.

As the 4077th's new chief nurse, O'Houlihan arrives a little way into the film's action. As she steps out of a helicopter and salutes, the audience is offered a view of suspenders and stocking tops. This image reprises the film's opening sequence at the motor pool, where (in the background) three Army nurses must negotiate a truck's tailgate and the muddy ground in their inappropriate (but regulation) skirts and court shoes; these women are both rule-bound and out of place. The first images of O'Houlihan economically sum up the role that she will play in the film's narrative. Her smart uniform and attention to military protocol (signaled here by her saluting) is in stark contrast to the male protagonists' refusal of both military attire and hierarchy (figure 37). Moreover the suggestion that underneath the surface O'Houlihan is a sexual woman (the fetishistic glimpse of stocking tops) prefigures the ways her character's uptight military attitude serves as a false appearance to be stripped away. An attractive and sexually active woman, she appears to wear her military demeanor as a disguise. The fact that she is keen to hide her sexuality facilitates the comedy subsequently constructed around her. In a film that stages, in William Paul's terms, "hip vs. square, the sexually liberated vs. the sexually uptight,"[5] O'Houlihan's condemnation of sexual activity

37. Major O'Houlihan's (Sally Kellerman) first appearance in *M*A*S*H* (1970).

as depraved seems to invite the sexualized humiliations that are visited on her.

While the opposition between Pierce and O'Houlihan implies a gendered "us versus them," many of the 4077th nurses are as anarchic as the male draftees, enjoying the revelry and participating openly in sexual relationships with the doctors. In rebelling against standards of appropriate sexual behavior, characters such as Lieutenant Leslie (who we see in bed with Colonel Blake) and Lieutenant Schneider (who Pierce persuades to have sex with the suicidal dentist "Painless" to give him back his sexual confidence) nonetheless occupy an appropriate female place as supporting (auxiliary) characters. Ultimately O'Houlihan too will be relegated to such a supporting role. Female characters who adopt a defiant attitude with respect to the male protagonists are dismissed with aggressive language, threatening behavior, and pranks. Such women are shown to be motivated by a petty commitment to regulations.

In a narrative economy that seeks to distance men from the category *soldier*, a comic commitment to regulations on the part of certain military women has a quite different effect from that in other comedies. The military woman is not mocked primarily for her misplaced ambitions, but rather for her *conformity*. For instance, the series of military women who challenge the authority of Pierce and McIntyre in the Japanese hospital scenes are finally deflated by McIntyre's crude demands for food and for "at least one nurse who knows how to work in close without getting her tits in [his] way." This aggressive naming of troublesome female body parts signals a departure from the comedy sustained around Crandall's "intrusive" breasts in the earlier *Operation Petticoat* or Stirling's comic consternation on the parade ground in *Francis Joins the WAC*. No longer even desirable, women's nonconforming (nonmale) bodies are simply a nuisance.[6] The pilot episode of the television series restates this physical animosity, with Pierce telling Houlihan in the OR, "If you don't move I'm going to have to cut around your B cups." Ultimately the fact that the Army gives authority to a woman (O'Houlihan outranks the core male group) serves to underline its absurdity.

The humiliation of O'Houlihan as a defiant military woman allows what Paul terms the "celebration of the animal in man" and thence a narrative of (male) "liberation from social constraints."[7] In the film's episodic structure there are two scenes in which O'Houlihan is publicly humiliated. Both involve jokes that make her body or sexuality public, and both involve nurses as silent participants, suggesting that these women's allegiance is to the male group rather than to each other. The first of these humiliations involves the broadcasting of O'Houlihan's lovemaking by the camp's loudspeakers, establishing the nickname "Hot Lips," which effectively undercuts her authority. The second has her exposed naked in the shower, the doctors seated before her as if for a performance, reinforcing their pleasure in mocking and taming her unwelcome presence through sexualized punishment. Although scenes in which men spy on naked (or seminaked) women are a staple of sex comedy (Charlie's voyeurism in *Petticoat Pirates*, say), *M*A*S*H*'s shower scene is, as Paul writes, significantly motivated by control and revenge rather than voyeurism.[8] Thus O'Houlihan is turned into a public spectacle as a way to undercut her claims to public status through her military identity.

Both scenes are framed by an effective collapse of military authority. The broadcasting of O'Houlihan's passionate encounter with Burns takes place in the absence of the camp commander, following a carnivalesque nighttime scene in which members of the MASH unit engage in drunken revelry. McIntyre is carnival king, carried aloft into the mess tent wearing an Uncle Sam hat as the gathered men and women sing "Hail to the Chief." O'Houlihan's rejection of this anarchy is effectively undercut by her subsequent sexual liaison with Burns; she appears to be a hypocrite. The shower scene extends this logic in telling fashion. Following her exposure, O'Houlihan storms into Blake's tent, where she finds him naked in bed, drinking wine with Lieutenant Leslie; overcome with emotion (itself played for comedy since it suggests an unmilitary lack of control) O'Houlihan screams what to her is the ultimate threat, that she will resign her commission unless action is taken against the doctors. While her status as a military woman is valuable to *her*, Blake's response is a scathing, dismissive acceptance that leaves her reeling: "Goddammit Hot Lips, resign your goddamned commission." Thus at the moment of her most extreme humiliation and distress, O'Houlihan is ultimately unable to make her rank *count* for anything. Protesting hysterically, her body wet, her hair soapy, and her robe disheveled, she is divested of both uniform and authority. In contrast to Lieutenant Leslie, whose sexual liaison with the camp's commanding officer places her in a position of both subordination and safety, O'Houlihan's status is ignored. For the remainder of the film she is a subordinate character, unable to command authority, space, or barely even a voice.

*M*A*S*H*, MILITARY WOMEN, AND SERIAL TELEVISION

Following the success of Altman's film, *M*A*S*H* was adapted into a long-running sitcom which would continue well past the Vietnam War. The show first aired in 1972 and ran for eleven seasons; the final feature-length episode was watched by an audience of 125 million in 1983. The series retains a popular following today and continues to play in syndication around the world. The film and television versions of *M*A*S*H* are, however, quite distinct. Altman's *M*A*S*H* was rated R, while the series reshaped the film's narrative trajectory (which followed Pierce's arrival and departure from Korea) and broad sexual comedy to both a continuing format and the constrictions of network television. As I have argued elsewhere in relation to *M*A*S*H*,[9] the sitcom is generically defined by a return to the same, a reiteration of the situation that brings together an often unlikely mix of characters and generates comedy; here that situation is a seemingly endless war and the absurd workings of military bureaucracy. In that context the unit's constant exposure to injured bodies and the absurdities of Army life generates and also explains a distinctive mix of humanistic outrage and adolescent male behavior, such as heavy drinking and practical jokes. The intense misogyny of the film, centered on O'Houlihan (now named Houlihan and played by Loretta Swit), continues into the early series of *M*A*S*H* but is increasingly qualified in terms that can be attributed in large part to the seriality of television and also to the attitudes of production personnel, the demands of particular performers to see their characters develop, and the more general impact of contemporary feminism. Nonetheless there remain firm continuities: the series pilot picks up from the film in establishing Houlihan's officious attitude with her comic expression of frustration at the male doctors' attitude: "Those two—they're ruining this war, for all of us!" In the early seasons, too, Houlihan's insistence on her rank produces only laughter, as when she complains, "They're making a mockery of my majority." For Swit, "one of the great challenges of playing the part of Margaret Houlihan" lay in keeping "her humorous, because Margaret is, more often than not, humor*less*. She is, in fact, the butt of the humor on the show."[10] Houlihan was to remain the butt of the joke for some time, although this shifted as she became more integrated into the group and notably more involved in the core group's competitive practical joking.[11]

Analyzing the film and series together highlights the complexities of viewing a long-running series as a single entity; during a long run an ensemble show develops in diverse ways, as production personnel, performers, and characters come and go. Perhaps what is most striking about the series is that over the course of its eleven years Houlihan's military woman was gradually incorporated or at least accepted into the boys' club that is the MASH unit. Although the emphasis remained very much on the male doctors, the commitment and talent of the female nursing staff, as well as their good-natured acceptance and rebuttal of repeated sexual advances, show the development of a sort of work-family unit.[12] The changing character and position of Houlihan is routinely acknowledged in popular and fan materials surrounding the series. David Reiss describes Swit's lobbying to end the comic relationship between her character and Frank Burns (Larry Linville) and the work of writers interested in developing the backstory of the Houlihan character. Reiss identifies two writers in particular, Linda Bloodworth and Mary Kay Place, who worked with Swit to develop her character's story "from childhood through boot camp."[13] Reiss attributes the season 2 episode "Hot Lips and Empty Arms" (15 December 1973), which reveals Houlihan's loneliness, to this kind of collaboration. The transformation at issue here works on at least two levels. First, a character who functions primarily as a figure of fun due to her status as a military woman is developed in more complex and emotional terms; second, there is a discernable shift away from comedy when it comes to *M**A*S*H's perspective on military women, Houlihan in particular. Tropes associated with the comic presentation of military women—such as masculinized female authority, frustrated sexual desire, and romantic isolation—remain but are treated differently.

The comedy centered on Major Houlihan has two gendered dimensions. On the one hand she is funny because her military identity suggests gender confusion: she is a woman associated with manliness and heavily invested in military authority, which she seeks (inappropriately) to impose on the male doctors. Her commitment to the minutiae of military life seems surreal and out of place given the work of the camp. On the other hand she is funny because her sexual desires and her sexiness are seen to be at odds with her military status and military life. The two are connected of course, since much of the humor sustained at her expense centers on her overinvestment in military procedures and protocol, an overinvestment supposedly belied by her nature as a sexual being and as a woman. There is something inherently humorous, it seems, about a conventionally attractive white woman so invested in an implicitly masculine military authority.

The comic contradiction that characterizes military women in numerous postwar comedies is played out in M*A*S*H through the tension between Houlihan's "masculine" and "womanly" qualities. When she aims to be womanly, alluring, or feminine, her more forceful, masculine, military persona frequently resurfaces to comic effect. Thus in "Soldier of the Month" (28 November 1975) she nurses the feverish Burns back to health, then slugs him. (Fearing death, he has made a will leaving his money to his wife and his clothes to Houlihan.) In her military persona, Houlihan's claims to authority often give way to her characterization as a shrew; one confrontation with Blake gives us the colonel's point of view through an extreme close-up of Houlihan's lips as she lectures him ("There Is Nothing Like a Nurse," 9 November 1974). The invocation of a nagging, loud, and dominating woman is familiar comic terrain, with Blake here inscribed as a cowering male. Houlihan's military demeanor regularly slips in episodes which show her not only nagging but hysterical, sexually demanding, furious, sad, sentimental, and drunk. A season 3 episode in which Burns, temporarily in charge, attempts to ban alcohol ("Alcoholics Unanimous," 12 November 1974) shows her torn between her allegiance to her lover and her secret store of liquor; her late-night search for drink brings her together with the male principals, who are defined by their social dependence on alcohol. Nonetheless as late as season 5 Houlihan is seen backing Burns in an overly rigid (in the show's terms) enforcement of regulations ("The Korean Surgeon," 23 November 1976).

Female masculinity serves as a put-down, frequently played for comedy in relation to Houlihan. There is the usual play with "Sir" and "Ma'am" designations. When Burns observes with glee, "This outfit is finally going to have a real man in charge," Pierce moves to shake Houlihan's hand in mockery of Burns's pretensions to manliness and Houlihan's inappropriate masculinity ("The Trial of Henry Blake," 3 November 1973). In the season opener that year, "Divided We Stand" (15 September 1973), when she rebukes McIntyre, saying "You are no gentleman," Pierce immediately chimes in with the observation "Good thing you are." In another season 2 episode Pierce and Houlihan are forced to work together (in the process laying the basis for the friendship that will develop between them) when their colleagues all succumb to flu ("Carry On Hawkeye," 24 November 1973). Houlihan, who outranks Pierce, attempts to assert her authority to no avail; furiously she protests, "You have emasculated me for the last time." Her anger is funny because it underlines both her aspirations to and inability to achieve masculine authority.

*M*A*S*H* also employs a quite distinct characterization of Houlihan as masculine in ways that are closely bound up with her military status and professionalism. In "Aid Station" (11 February 1975), for instance, she insists that she rather than Pierce should change the tire on an Army Jeep since, as he is a surgeon, his hands are an asset to be guarded. (The sequence positions Pierce as a delighted bystander rather than as unmanned by her capability.) Her professionalism echoes the more general representation of military nurses which, as we saw in chapter 2, is often framed in vocational terms, a dedication to the patient constructed as maternal and pure. It is through this aspect of Houlihan's character that *M*A*S*H* begins to move away from constructing her solely as a military martinet. This professionalism is explicitly coupled with her personal bravery, in turn reinforcing rather than undermining her status as military woman. There are certainly scenes in which comic effects are achieved by Houlihan's shrill panic at the prospect of capture, rape, and death. However, the series also conveys her professional calm under fire and her willingness to place herself in danger in the service of her patients. We've seen that the location of the military nurse at the front positions her distinctively in relation to the commonsense opposition between woman and soldier. *M*A*S*H* exploits this distinctiveness, situating Houlihan's career Army bravery against the more reluctant attitudes of the drafted male doctors. For instance, in "Aid Station" she volunteers for a dangerous assignment near the front; Pierce, who accompanies her, has by contrast drawn the short straw, in line with his characterization as reluctant draftee. A similar pattern occurs in the two-part "Comrades in Arms" (6 and 13 December 1977), which stages a brief affair between Houlihan and Pierce under fire. Initially antagonistic, the pair develop their intimacy in episodes that either take them out of the camp altogether or force them to work together by some other means.[14]

The growing friendship between Pierce's antimilitary doctor and Houlihan's career Army nurse is shaped by the shared terrain of professional commitment associated with representations of doctors and nurses and by the emphasis on comradeship so characteristic of military narratives. The television series based on *Private Benjamin* follows a similar pattern, drawing together its chief female antagonists into an unlikely friendship. Although Pierce does not volunteer to go to the front in "Aid Station," once there he is calm, efficient, and caring. They work well under intense pressure and enemy shelling, Pierce encouraging Houlihan to begin a surgical procedure without him, appealing to her knowledge and ability. Indeed before their arrival back at the camp Pierce stops the Jeep to confide his affection, praising Houlihan — "my favorite officer in the whole U.S. Army" — and kissing her on the cheek. The interactions between them serve to bring her character more centrally into the fiction. Although mapped in terms of developing respect, the relationship is also comically antagonistic; his suggestive comments are matched by her mugged expressions of outrage. When the nurses leave camp ("There Is Nothing like a Nurse," 19 November 1974) Houlihan formally salutes each of the officer doctors; Pierce's response is to sweep her off her feet in a kiss. Stealing kisses from Houlihan when she is at her most military is a regular motif, one that is reprised in the lengthy goodbye kiss between the two in the feature-length finale. The joke works comically by underlining the sexual possibilities of women and men working side by side, but it also foregrounds the particularity of the military woman in these fictions as, variously, comrade, antagonist, and sexual object.

Unsurprisingly it is through Houlihan's relationships with men that many of these themes are worked out. The open secret of her sexual relationship with the inept, selfish, and cowardly Frank Burns makes her a ridiculous figure in seasons 1 through 4. The pair are intensely committed to the signs and rituals of military life, repeatedly expressing outrage at the unmilitary appearance and behavior of the principals. Burns so clearly falls short of the mark that her attentions toward him make her seem both comic and foolish. A similar dynamic is at work in her various comic encounters with senior male officers: visiting dignitaries allude to past sexual encounters, and she fawns over military men, whether for their seniority or their muscular physique. Consider: Houlihan and Burns are overcome with passion as they sit together on the bed intended for use during General MacArthur's visit ("Big Mac," 25 February 1975); in "Quo Vadis, Captain Chandler" (7 November 1975) she swoons over the ludicrous Colonel Flagg; in "Iron Guts Kelly" (1 October 1974) the war hero dies in her tent; in "Margaret's Engagement" (28 September 1976) she announces her ill-fated engagement to Lt. Col. Donald Penobscott with the comic line "I couldn't love someone who didn't outrank me." Houlihan's fascination with weaponry is repeatedly played for comedy as she swoons over tanks and guns.

Houlihan's commitment to duty is elaborated in a comic monologue during which she packs her bag while Burns watches quietly, a range of expressions passing over his face. The monologue begins with her excusing him for not volunteering for dangerous duty, as she has done, acknowledging his marriage and (in passing) his mercenary reasons for remaining committed to it. She goes on to speak, in comic, self-aggrandizing fashion, of her own life and motivations:

> Well, I'm a married man too Frank: married to the Army. I don't want the future you offer—meeting behind garbage cans, and behind laundry trucks. When the war's over—and nothing good lasts for ever—you'll go home, home to your wife's bony arms. I'll still be in the service. I'm an Army brat, Frank: my father was a colonel and my mother was a nurse, and I was conceived on maneuvers. The Army's in my blood. I need its discipline, its traditions. I thrill to the sight of a precise parade. I could faint from looking down at my own brass. That's why I volunteered, Frank, to serve the Army I love. And don't you worry—I'm coming back, coming back to you for whatever time we have left together, because I'm not just Major Margaret Houlihan, Army nurse. I'm also Margaret Houlihan [her voice begins to quiver] frail, vulnerable, sensitive female—and if you touch one nurse while I'm gone, I'll cut your hands off! ("Aid Station")

This last passionate threat is sealed with a kiss, a moment held briefly in a freeze-frame that juxtaposes her physical and sexual aggression with his fear and passivity. The monologue reveals much about the way her character is a source of comedy in the early years of the series: her passionate nature coexisting with a commitment to discipline; her perverse pleasure in the opportunities of war; the sexual innuendo of military maneuvers; a self-proclaimed frailty backed up by the threat of violence; her self-designation as both a "married man" and a "sensitive woman." The sexualization and institutionalization of her relationship to the Army is also significant here, since in both comic and dramatic narratives involving Houlihan it is suggested that her material career has meant personal loneliness and loss.

Houlihan's coding as a sexually active and desiring woman is a recurrent source of comedy, as in the season 6 episode "Last Laugh" (4 October 1977), which sees her desperate to visit her husband in Tokyo. She projects her sexual need onto him, maintaining that he has "yearnings," when it is her own frustrations that are most evident. When the hapless Radar O'Reilly (Gary Burghoff) interrupts her attempts to convince Colonel Potter (Harry Morgan) to give her leave, she screams in his face, "Will you butt out, this is man talk!," before returning rapidly to her honeyed tones. Later she will again take out her frustration on Radar, pulling over shelves in his office and even kicking him; in self-defense Radar himself persuades Potter to grant her leave. The potent combination of military woman as sexually demanding and tough draws on an imagery of eroticized domination that is extensively prefigured in her relationship with the comically inept and cowardly Burns. The double episode that opens season 4, "Welcome to Korea" (12 September 1975), has Burns nominally in charge, though it is clear that Houlihan actually has the authority. Indeed he whines, "Oh gee, ever since I've been commanding officer, you don't let me do anything." Later that season, in "Dear Mildred" (24 October 1975), Houlihan sits on a table in her tent fixing her lips while Burns cleans her boots, an eroticized image of the woman on top. Most spectacularly, in "Lt. Radar O'Reilly" (12 October 1976), Radar delivers a gift from Houlihan's fiancé, a leather whip; she whoops with delight as she cracks it around her tent, causing Radar to flee in panic (figure 38).

This imagery of erotic authority draws on long-standing stereotypes of the sexy nurse. As Anne Karpf writes, "Apart from being good, bad, or background, screen nurses are also frequently sexy. In comedies especially, waddling precariously, their uniforms revealing curvaceous figures, nurses exude sexual availability, and use their access to the body of the male patient for erotic purposes."[15] Although Houlihan's professional capabilities are never questioned, her sexual and emotional im-

38. In the television series *M*A*S*H* Major Houlihan (Loretta Swit) gleefully wields a whip, a gift from her fiancé, in comic rendition of the woman on top.

pulses are repeatedly played for comedy, laying the ground for an undercurrent of suggestion that she has used her sexual attractiveness in order to secure advancement.[16] Here is a typical exchange from the season 3 episode "House Arrest" (4 February 1975). Houlihan has made a rare error in the OR (she is distracted due to the impending visit of a senior nurse) and Pierce has ordered her out. They discuss the incident as they wash up:

> Houlihan: I know my job. I didn't get to be major by just sitting on my duff.
> Hawkeye: Well, somebody did.
> Houlihan: Just what did you mean by that? [Laughter] I demand satisfaction!
> Hawkeye: [turning to Burns] Tired lately, Frank?

Houlihan's claim to experience and authority is undercut here by sexual innuendo, against which she can only express rage, reinforcing her ridiculousness and lack of authority. Her outrage is a great source of comedy in the series; her loud (even unruly) protests at individuals and objects that get in her way play out the comedy of a military woman who is simultaneously sexualized and womanly, tough and masculine. In this instance she appeals to Burns to defend her honor, which, predictably, he is unable to do.

Yet Houlihan's sexual demands are not exclusively played for comedy. Indeed as her character becomes more complex and more closely integrated into the group, her desires are granted a degree of legitimacy.

For example, in the season 7 episode "Major Ego" (6 November 1978), a feminist-informed narrative based on her emerging sense of self, she is seen delighting in a one-night stand with a visiting Army journalist but refusing to take the romance further. "Now that I've found a little freedom, I want to stay free," she declares. Her difficulties in finding a suitable partner ally her more closely to Pierce, but also confirm the incompatibility (for women) of military life and romance, a recurrent theme of military dramas. A subsequent episode, "Hot Lips Is Back in Town" (29 January 1979), explicitly turns on an association between sex and Houlihan's career. Having received her divorce decree, she determines to focus on her career. Though she is offered a promotion to colonel it is clear that this is contingent on sexual favors, a deal she is not prepared to make. No longer a grotesque figure, the show emphasizes the great personal cost of Houlihan's military career. And crucially, in becoming a more credible character, one who negotiates complex demands facing professional women, Houlihan is no longer primarily a comic figure.

COMEDY AND TRANSFORMATION: *PRIVATE BENJAMIN*

M*A*S*H's Margaret Houlihan is an "Army brat," combining an investment in military masculinity with elements of unpredictability and desirability marked as feminine. The film *Private Benjamin* articulates the comic contradiction of the military woman in a different manner; using a "fish out of water" formula, the film centers on the militarization of a hyperfeminine, spoiled (soft) young woman who seems entirely unsuited to military life. The image of Goldie Hawn as Benjamin, dwarfed by helmet, cape, and pack, drenched by the rain, wearing an expression somewhere between sullen and dazed, her makeup running, sums up the comedy of her inappropriately feminine character (figure 39). *Private Benjamin*'s tagline, "The army was no laughing matter until Judy Benjamin joined it," equates her enlistment with comedy. Like Jo in the comedy *Never Wave at a WAC*, Judy Benjamin's privileged background renders her a legitimate comic target. Her initial misguided attempts to secure an advantage over the other recruits—telling Capt. Doreen Lewis (Eileen Brennan) that she joined not *this* Army, but the one with the "condos and the private rooms"—set her up as a figure of fun who needs to be shaken up. The film recalls earlier movies of military women in other ways too, notably in its operation as a (comic) narrative of *transformation* in which military life and discipline result in the strength of character, toughening, and matur-

39. In *Private Benjamin* (1980) Benjamin (Goldie Hawn) is initially figured as physically unsuited to military life, her small frame dwarfed by her gear.

ing of a youthful, hyperfeminine female. Benjamin's hyperfemininity and naïveté is in turn pitted against the film's monstrous military woman, Captain Lewis. Marked as vengeful, militaristic in a small-minded sense, and inappropriately sexual—inappropriate due to her age and implicit mannishness—Lewis is a caricature of misplaced female authority.

While service comedy derives humor from individuals who play the system and from the absurdity of the larger institution, boot camp narratives are concerned with the formation of a military unit. Training camp films show men (and women) fighting each other and learning discipline, typically under the tutelage of a tough sergeant. Ultimately the recruits come together as a team, setting aside differences and civilian antagonisms. The genre, that is, stages transformation, a process for which women are regarded as having a particular affinity.[17] *Private Benjamin*'s comedic presentation of boot camp begins with the new recruits being introduced to tough drill sergeant Ross (Hal Williams). Ross drags a sleepy Benjamin off the bus and demands push-ups from her. When it is clear that she is in no condition to comply, he holds the waistband of her dress, pulling her up and down like a rag doll. Her petite frame, affluent background, and preoccupation with appearance all render her an outsider in the barracks; her presence is resented by the other recruits because her incompetence gets them all into trouble. Her initial disillusion culminates in a fight with the tough Pvt. Maria Gianelli and her decision to go home. When she is given the opportunity to leave with her parents (who are mystified by her enlistment), Benjamin is confronted with the promise of an infantilizing, carefully policed existence at home and resolves instead to stay, departing the scene with a brisk salute. The basic training section of the film charts her individual transformation, effectively into adulthood, and her incorporation into the group. The Fort Biloxi sequences include two contrasting montages of basic training: in the first Benjamin is out of place, ineffectual with her rifle, and tackling the assault course in an uncoordinated manner; in the second, following her decision to stay in the Army, we see a new sense of purpose: she polishes her boots under the blankets, runs in formation, handles her weapon proficiently, and engages in hand-to-hand combat.

Like the Esther Williams training camp musical *Skirts Ahoy!*, *Private Benjamin* begins with a wedding. Judy Benjamin is an affluent young Jewish woman who is about to marry a divorce attorney in fulfillment of her consumer-led dreams. But unlike the three female protagonists of *Skirts Ahoy!*, Benjamin goes through with her marriage (her second) at the film's outset. (She will reject a third marriage at the end of the film.) When her new husband dies on their wedding night, the distraught Benjamin is approached by an Army recruiter who has heard her bemoaning her fate on a radio talk show. Somewhat naïvely taken in by his promises of an adventurous life, she joins up. Her mistaken ideas about Army life provide the film's comic premise. Her vapid superficiality is emphasized in these opening scenes, setting up the comedy that will follow as she undergoes the rigors of basic training. Her perky femininity is a recurrent source of humor; when first handed her uniform, for instance, she inquires, "Is green the only color these come in?"

Militarization quite explicitly does not equate to masculinization for Benjamin. Indeed Linda Ruth Williams notes how effectively Benjamin "survives the rigors of her Mississippi training camp by marshalling the attributes of femininity in innovative ways."[18] In keeping with her comic successes, it is ultimately the Army that must adapt in the culture clash between Benjamin's consumer-led femininity and the austerity of military life. Thus during the war games ("the Super Bowl of basic training") Benjamin employs her initiative to fool the opposing team into surrender. The war games also provide the setting for scenes of female bonding; sent to guard a swamp, Benjamin and her unit sit around the campfire smoking a joint, giggling as they swap sexual histories.

The narrative focus of the basic training portion of the film is firmly on Benjamin's incorporation into the female group. Alongside this process the film enacts the expulsion or punishment of the two women (Captain Lewis and Private Winter) who most evidently embody the combination of military masculinity and hypocrisy held up for ridicule in a show like M*A*S*H. Private Winter is exposed half-naked after being caught with the opposing team's CO during the war games, a sexualized humiliation that recall's O'Houlihan's exposure in M*A*S*H. Benjamin's triumph in the war games is capped with a reprimand for Lewis and a thrilling flight with camp commander Colonel Thornbush. In the conclusion to the Fort Biloxi section of the film the group acts together to take their revenge on Lewis, the sort of anarchic reversal of hierarchy, with the triumph of enlisted personnel over officers, so characteristic of service comedy.

That women who aspire to military masculinity are misguided is further evidenced by Benjamin herself in her short-lived assignment to an all-male airborne unit. As the sole female member of Thornbush's elite parachute unit, she presents an impressive military demeanor, yet when required to jump from an airplane she panics, reverting to chaotic comic femininity. She finally overcomes her fear and jumps only when Thornbush reveals his passion for her, declaring, "There are other ways in which you can serve." Sexual harassment, even the threat of rape, is played for comedy here, underlining both the untrustworthiness of officers (a generic staple) and the danger of stepping too far outside gender norms. The confrontation triggers the end of Benjamin's engagement with military masculinity, her reassignment to SHAPE (Supreme Headquarters Allied Powers Europe), and a role in procurement, which she dubs "the one job I've trained for all my life." This knowing comic equation of supply work with the feminine pursuit of shopping as leisure signals the film's return to a reassuring version of the military woman who functions largely in an administrative capacity.

Following the teamwork exhibited in the war games, female comradeship is effectively absent from the remainder of the film. Benjamin is the only woman in the airborne unit and is subsequently stationed in Europe, where she is undercut by the vengeful Lewis and struggles to keep a sense of self in her developing relationship with Henri Tremont (Armand Assante), a French gynecologist. Forced to choose between her lover and her Army career, she chooses marriage; ultimately, however, she slugs her fiancé and walks away from the wedding (and her parents) in the film's final scene. Still wearing her bridal gown, Judy Benjamin moves into an unspecified but presumably nonmilitary future. The trajectory of the film thus suggests that military service has changed her to the extent that she resists being defined by marriage.

In mapping Benjamin's emergent sense of self with the acquisition of a military identity, *Private Benjamin* effectively contrasts her relationship with civilian men and with her family to her relationship with the Army. Her husband and later her fiancé are represented as ultimately repressive figures, as are her loving (but infantilizing) parents; in projecting their desires onto her, her parents and the men with whom she is romantically involved prevent her from developing a sense of self. In the Army, by contrast, her life is governed by the friendships she eventually develops with other recruits and a generically familiar antagonism with Captain Lewis. Thus the sentiment that underlies the comedy of *Private Benjamin* has to do with the transformative effect of military service, thematically coupled to a somewhat diluted popular feminism which suggests that women can be fully human without reference to their fathers or husbands and that the patriarchal institutions of the military allow a woman to evade the strictures of marriage. *Private Benjamin* effectively demonstrates the versatility and applicability of boot camp conventions for the "modern" figure of the military woman.

FEMINIZING SERVICE COMEDY:
TELEVISION'S *PRIVATE BENJAMIN*

The CBS television series *Private Benjamin* immediately followed the success of the film, airing from spring 1981 (with a short season of just four half-hour episodes) to 1983. The show would take a different direction, one more suited to serial situation comedy. Crucially Benjamin (Lorna Patterson) is not asked to choose between the military and romance, remaining in service throughout the series. Thus while the early episodes retread the basic training scenario, subsequently Benjamin is assigned to and performs effectively within a number of military roles, working alongside Captain Lewis and Sergeant Ross, played here, as in the film, by Eileen Brennan and Hal Williams. The situation which provides the recurring source of comedy in the show is not the place of women in the military, a situation which the show normalizes even as women's presence is defined in quite particular ways. The basic training episodes reprise the comic juxtaposition between Benjamin's hyperfemininity and privileged background and the physical demands of military life. "Benjamin to the Rescue" (2 April 1981) rehearses many of the comic turns from the movie, and Benjamin is once again portrayed as ill-suited to military life: she sleeps late, wears a cashmere sweater under her uniform for comfort, and inadvertently shoots Lewis's Jeep. However, we also see Benjamin vow not to quit and Lewis openly impressed that Benjamin (whom she terms a "tough disaster") has lasted so long. The second episode of the pilot season ("Jungle Swamp Survival," 9 April 1981) still emphasizes Benjamin's difficulties adapting to Army life. When even her friends counsel that "the Army's too much" for her, she expresses her determination to succeed, telling them, "I've gotta do this for me." As in the war games sequence of the film, here Benjamin and her friends triumph, capturing a soldier escaped from the stockade and rescuing the injured Captain Lewis on their way back to camp. Yet Benjamin is still defined as fundamentally unmilitary and feminine, reluctant to jump from a plane and then comically suspended as her parachute is caught in a tree.

The insistent repetition of Benjamin's incompetence during the six weeks of basic training doesn't sit well with the demands of situation comedy. Just as the film shifts from laughing at her incompetence to celebrating her capabilities and the value of female comradeship, the show shifts its focus to Benjamin's developing relationship with her peers and superiors, establishing comic situations linked to the peculiarities of peacetime Army life. There is certainly no suggestion that she or the other recruits will leave the Army, which is constructed as a sometimes chaotic but ultimately supportive, even familial space. It is not the contemporaneous *M*A*S*H* (which reached the end of its long run the same year as *Private Benjamin* was canceled), but *The Phil Silvers Show* that comes most readily to mind as a reference point for *Private Benjamin*. Both exploit the comic potential of a peacetime military setting, exploring the hierarchies and absurdities of a stateside posting. Her privileged background means that Benjamin, unlike Sergeant Bilko, is not interested in moneymaking schemes. Like Jo in *Never Wave at a WAC*, Benjamin's reasons for joining the Army are not economic; rather they are focused on feminist-informed themes of self-determination. As a result she is a sometimes anarchic but basically positive presence among the absurdities of military life, fixing the mistakes repeatedly made by the officers and managing relations with the press and general public. In "Astro Chimp" (14 September 1982), for instance, the self-serving Colonel Fielding organizes a parade for a retiring astronaut who turns out to be chimp; when Benjamin discovers that he is destined for a laboratory she intervenes.[19] In "Me, Me, Me" (1 April 1982) only Benjamin and Ross are immune to the hypnotic philosophy of self-interest offered by a visiting charismatic fraudster; together they save the day as self-interest threatens to erode military discipline. Other episodes show Benjamin mistakenly promoted to general ("Judy's Army," 21 September 1982) or working to safeguard Ross's future by sabotaging the robot that the brass hope to replace him with ("Ross versus the Robot," 18 October 1972).

Like Bilko, Benjamin is well able to work the system. But since she is neither self-serving nor avaricious in her scheming, the show insistently foregrounds themes of personal development through military service. Where the film contrasts Army life to marriage—the former liberating for women, the latter oppressive—the series rarely concerns itself with romance. Neither is the effect of military women on military men paid particular attention, unlike almost all other comedies featuring military women. Themes of female self-fulfillment through military service are presented in upfront fashion within each of the show's three credit sequences, chiming explicitly with contemporary recruitment campaigns directed at women. Credits for the four episodes in the pilot series featured a military locker stuffed with feminine possessions. Benjamin's voice introduces herself, explaining, "I was a debutante, I traveled all over the world, but I was bored, felt unwanted. The Army not only wanted me, they promised it would be wonderful!" As the image shows recruits falling in behind Benjamin, she explains that she is working on reshaping the Army in her own image: "Things aren't perfect in the Army yet, but I'm sure with a little time I can get them to do things my way." The second series credit sequence adapted this format, employing a theme song delivered as a cadence and featuring the line "Join the Army and you'll see / You will be all you can be," explicitly referencing the well-known Army recruiting slogan. Benjamin's intent to reshape the military is retained with the closing line of the song: "Look out, Army, here she comes!" The credit sequence for the final season again foregrounds Benjamin's military service as an alternative to a feminine career: Benjamin's voice-over returns, telling us that her parents had given her everything "except a purpose in life." In contrast to the tradition of anarchic, male-centered service comedy, a tradition in which the absurdity of military life is uppermost, service is here presented as character-forming and even incipiently feminist.

The sort of work-family model deployed in *Private Benjamin* is now a familiar feature of both sitcoms and television drama. Yet the show is unusual in focusing so centrally on women working together. As part of this process it works to distinguish between women, foregrounding the uneasy relationship between Benjamin and Lewis as well as deploying class and ethnic markers to suggest difference within the female group. Alongside the conventions of the sitcom, which depends on a play of seemingly diverse characters who comically interact, *Private Benjamin* makes use of the multiethnic group format familiar from numerous military movies, what Basinger dubs in relation to the World War Two combat film a "democratic ethnic mix."[20] Besides Benjamin, an affluent young Jewish woman, both film and series feature a white working-class southerner (Pvt. Barbara Ann Glass in the film, Pvt. Luanne Hubble in the series); an African American (Pvt. Moe in the film, Pvt. Jackie Sims in the series); and an ethnically identified white woman, the Italian American Pvt. Maria Gianelli in the first year, who is replaced by a Greek American, Pvt. Stacey Kouchalakas, in the second year. As with *M*A*S*H*, we occasionally learn a little more about these supporting characters, but the focus remains on the central group. Hubble reveals that she joined the Army because there were no good jobs in Tennessee, emphasizing an alternative view of military service than that sketched by Benjamin's search for a purpose in life. Sims borrows money from a loan shark to pay for an operation for her mother, suggesting the relative poverty of her family ("Undercover Judy," 3 December 1981). Although the series certainly makes comic use of fairly crude regional and racial stereotypes, these characters represent a minimal gesture to the economic circumstances underpinning women's increasing military service in the period, and indeed the types of women who were (and remain) most likely to serve.

In many ways *Private Benjamin* takes the presence of women in the Army as a given; it is rarely, if ever, a source of comedy. Following the early boot camp episodes, Benjamin emerges as a level-headed, pragmatic character who is able to master a confusing military world; her self-reliance, quick thinking, and abilities as a communicator enable her to get herself (and others) out of difficult situations. The film situates the newly militarized Benjamin in an elite, previously all-male unit before comically debunking this possibility and moving her to a post in procurement. The series too situates Benjamin as a military woman who struggles in basic training but serves effectively in a wide variety of desk jobs; her function as a military administrator thus complies with long-standing assumptions about appropriate roles for women in the military. It is worth considering in this context how the series situates Captain Lewis and Private Winter, the two women whom the film explicitly expels on the basis of their inappropriate investment in military masculinity.

Winter is, at times somewhat awkwardly, integrated into the female group, her enthusiasm for military procedures a standing joke (though an increasingly affectionate one as the series progresses). In "Are you Sure Mike Wallace Started Like This?" (28 January 1982) she relishes her new posting as an MP. Her aspirations to military masculinity provide the comic focus of one episode in particular, "Not for Men Only" (14 January 1982). Here the gung-ho Winter volunteers to try out for an elite unit, the Tigers, open only to men; the only male to volunteer does so for the additional money on offer. Angered at the discrimination experienced by Winter, Benjamin and Gianelli take the story to the base newspaper and a sympathetic female reporter, leading to a "Declaration of Grievances by Angry Non-Men." Despite a chewing-out from Lewis, Benjamin is unrepentant, reminding Lewis that she herself "broke new ground," before producing Winter, in a rather thin male disguise, as a candidate for the Tigers. Benjamin persuades Lewis to support this gender impersonation, speaking passionately of women's achievements in the military and asserting that Winter should either be part of the Tigers or have "the right to fail trying." In the extended comic sequence that follows Winter excels at all the events, taking first place over distance, assault course, push-ups, and terrain navigation; her performance is punctured, however, by her inability to swim. Consequently the feminine military woman Benjamin must rescue the floundering masculine military woman, underlining Winter's failure to embody the type to which she so desperately aspires. These events lead to the episode's punch line, in which the sympathetic Ross tells Winter, "You did win the right to fail." By orchestrating this narrative around the overtly militarized Winter, the series acknowledges contemporary debates with respect to gender exclusions, only to exploit them as a source of comedy. Moreover both Winter's and Lewis's repeated failure to effectively perform a more masculine military role—getting lost during exercises, for instance—is frequently contrasted to Benjamin's capability in the administrative and communications roles that she is assigned to.

It is the shifting relationship between Benjamin and Lewis and the humanizing of the latter that are the most marked innovations of the series, again largely a consequence of serial form. Lewis's role is more central, giving free rein to Eileen Brennan's exuberant performance.[21] Although she and Benjamin are sharply differentiated in age, class, and background, ultimately they end up working together, developing a genuine affection in the process. While Lewis may define herself in terms of military masculinity, she, like Benjamin, is effectively an administrator. Both must negotiate with the ambitions of Fort Bradley's commanders, notably Colonel Fielding, who lives in the hope that Benjamin's influential father will help him in his bid to become a general. Although *Private Benjamin* rarely addresses the specificities of American military women's experience, or the wider debates being staged in the media at the time as to women's proper role, the series does occasionally fashion feminist-informed comedy from the tensions of a recently integrated military. For example, the formidable Lewis bawls out one Sergeant Muldoon, who is dismissive of women in the military, with the injunction "Stay out of my sight until I can have you reassigned to a place where you belong—the sixteenth century!" ("So Long Sergeant Ross," 24 December 1981). Such instances deflect the joke away from Lewis to some extent and onto the sexism of certain military men. More generally, however, the series tends to imply that Lewis and Winter are held back as much by ineptitude as by such sexist attitudes.

The reconciliation between Lewis and Benjamin—their animosity drives the film, recall—begins in earnest in the fourth and final episode of the short pilot season, "Captain's Helper" (23 April 1981). Benjamin is assigned to be Lewis's temporary aide as part of a new program. Despite a series of slapstick incidents, Benjamin comes into her own when ministering to the sick captain. Not only does she feminize Lewis's apartment and arrange a romantic liaison with another officer for her, but she fixes a mean drink. Next morning a contented Lewis is roused by the brisk efficiency of her protégé Winter, replacing the flu-stricken Benjamin and in the process underlining the merits of Benjamin's less military but caring manner. Lewis subsequently visits Benjamin in the barracks; though she cautions against thinking they are now "buddy-buddy," a difference in their relationship is apparent. The first full season develops these themes: Lewis makes Benjamin squad leader (with disastrous results) and then her driver and aide (Benjamin drives the Jeep into the pool; "Judy's in the Driving Seat," 9 October 1981). This emergent relationship echoes the gradual humanization of Houlihan's character in the series *M*A*S*H*, by which she transforms from a representative of military absurdity to a sympathetically drawn core character. Nonetheless Lewis's character remains an essentially comic one. Significantly, the comedy is linked to the contrast between her ability to perform femininity and her (implicitly masculine) military identity; that is, Lewis articulates the comic gender confusion long associated with military women in film and television fictions.

Captain Lewis's characterization as a comic foil exploits not just gender confusion but her typically chaotic presence. More often than not the originator of problems, her attempts to fix things at the base usually lead to further complications. Lewis is both unruly and rule-bound (militarized), and her commitment to the military is a source of comedy and pathos. At times she represents a vindictive authority to be fooled and mocked. Indeed the series frequently derives laughs from her inflated sense of her own abilities, her commitment to discipline, and her repeated failure to get things right. In "You Oughta Be in Pictures" (27 September 1982), by contrast, which centers on the production of a film designed to recruit women into the Army, there is a certain power to her comic monologue, which includes the recollection "When I joined up women weren't even considered soldiers. We were WACs. . . . But I stayed in there, didn't I? Didn't I? I clawed my way right up to the middle, and now—dammit, it's my turn." But the film director wants to use Benjamin to sell the Army in terms of "youth, glamour, pizzazz," and Benjamin bridles at the way Lewis is rejected as a role model. Lewis's humanity and vulnerability are also revealed in episodes such as "The Talent Show" (5 November 1982), which depicts her awkwardness when visiting children (she has them stand to attention) juxtaposed with her compassionate treatment of one troubled youngster, and includes revelations about her own difficult childhood. In the final episode of the second series, Lewis confronts a future after retirement, and both she and Fielding confide to each other their fears about civilian life ("Real World," 12 April 1982). Again there is a gendered dimension to the comedy of a woman needing to be taught how to shop and manage a household. Women ought to be good at such things, it is implied, but Lewis simply isn't.

The series plays out the humor of Lewis's military woman at a number of levels, drawing on familiar stereotypes of partially repressed sexuality, ill-judged ambition, and manliness. Her characterization owes much to *M*A*S*H*'s Margaret Houlihan, in the evocation of a military woman defined in contradictory terms as excessively military and yet also womanly and passionate. This is literalized in the image of Lewis's two closets, one filled with olive drab, the other bursting with satins and feathers. At one point she confides in a portrait of Patton that hangs in her bedroom, "I am the perfect female soldier. I'm hard, I'm tough, I'm ruthless and I'm every inch a woman." Yet while Houlihan is consistently presented as a desirable woman, *Private Benjamin* generates cruel comedy through Lewis's inappropriate desire (inappropriate since she is not, in conventional terms, desirable herself). Thus in "Man on the Floor" (22 October 1981) canned laughter accompanies the suggestive line, delivered in medium close-up, "I'm not only a soldier, I'm a woman." The comedy here comes from the fact that she has misread the situation, but also from her conspiratorial alignment of herself with a sexual activity deemed fitting only for younger women.[22] Another episode features a running gag as Lewis repeatedly unbuttons her shirt (she is hiding some diamonds), generating comic expressions of surprise and horror from a series of men ("Beauty and the Brass," 12 February 1982).

Lewis's uncontrolled curly hair and dramatic red lipstick suggest a sexuality which is in turn played off against her military demeanor. She is described as a "floozy captain" in "Profile in Courage" (29 March 1982), an episode that purports to test the skills she and Fielding have learned at an antiterrorist seminar. Captured and bound, Lewis exclaims, "Do what you will with me physically, mentally, sexually [pause] six, seven, eight times." That the possibility of sexual violence is played for laughs here is quite in keeping with the casual misogyny of the period but also with the sexualized characterization of Lewis as an embodiment of the troubling and complex figure of the woman soldier. Although her sexuality is repeatedly emphasized, the series also plays with constructions of her military woman as manly. In "Judy Got Her Gun" Lewis and Captain Hickstratten get into a competition following his assertion, "It was a sorry day when they let women into this man's army." When Lewis protests that there is "a woman present," he looks around startled, and remarks, "I never think of you as a woman at all." An indignant Lewis proceeds to demand that everyone, including a group of male soldiers running past, drop and do push-ups. Her comic fury and her ability to exercise control over the troops is framed by the reassertion of the impossibility of the female soldier. Like M*A*S*H's Houlihan, Lewis is often portrayed as angry, an anger that comically underlines the supposed contradictions embodied by women in positions of (military) authority.

Many comedies featuring military women treat them as humorous by definition, using sexual imagery for laughs and to emphasize the implausible difference of the female soldier. The framing of women's achievements and authority in terms of a comic "battle of the sexes" format allows feminist themes to be raised, but not resolved. The comedies discussed in this chapter show military women performing effectively within specific roles: nursing, communications, and administration. Aspirations to move outside such familiar roles always fail and are presented as simply funny. Although it was an enormous success, *Private Benjamin* was the last high-profile Hollywood comedy to center on military women, though they figure as supporting characters in comedies such as *Stripes* (1981) and *Sgt. Bilko* (1996). Both *M*A*S*H* and *Private Benjamin* ended their initial run in 1983, the year in which around two hundred women deployed to Grenada. Some seven years later forty thousand women would be deployed in the first Gulf War, significantly shifting the visibility of military women on active duty. Indeed, as part 3 of this book explores, as military women become a more visible presence in popular culture and the news media, the generic location of their fictional counterparts shifts toward dramatic rather than comic genres. The Army becomes, it seems, no laughing matter for men or women in a period shaped by increasing levels of military deployment and an unprecedented media emphasis on scandal and trauma. The provocative presence of the military woman is reframed in genres such as the thriller, which stages narratives of threat, violence, and investigation.

PART THREE

This final section of the book traces the representation of military women since the 1980s, exploring the ways the intensely mediated and contested figure of the female soldier figures within contemporary film and television fictions. While the period since the Gulf War of 1990–91 has been characterized by a high level of media interest in military women, they appear relatively rarely as the central figures of film or television fictions, and almost never in high-profile feature films. (They may feature as ancillary or supporting characters.) At the time of this writing *G.I. Jane*, released in 1997, was the last Hollywood movie to feature a military woman as the central protagonist (although a remake of *Private Benjamin* is in development). Television movies, driven by issues and contemporary debates, have been more receptive. A number of television movies in the 1990s centered on military women, including *She Stood Alone* (1995), *Serving in Silence* (1995), and *One Kill* (2000). Across film and television there have been significant shifts in both the image of the military woman and the film or television genres in which we are most likely to encounter her. This generic shift is away from comedy and into genres such as the thriller, legal drama, rape-revenge, and war as well as scenarios of crime and investigation.

Although the cultural common sense which insists on the incompatibility of the terms *woman* and *soldier* remains very much in evidence, the military woman emerges in this period as more explicitly martial. This is unsurprising perhaps, considering the relatively high profile which debates concerning women's place in the military, and particularly their place in combat, have had in the American news media. The large-scale deployments of American women in the Iraq War and the established combat role of women aviators have further shifted that debate, with military and media seeking to retain ground combat as a distinctly male role. Many of the film and television texts explored in this section are acutely aware of this context and frequently stage debates more or less explicitly in the terms used by politicians, military personnel, and media pundits. My analysis is in turn framed by the widespread circulation of the military woman as an ever more intensely *mediated* figure within American popular and media culture. The strategies that explain and, I would argue, *contain* the presence of the military woman within film and television fictions are clearly related to the ways such women are figured in the news media. Chapter 6 offers an overview of this wider media coverage, identifying a series of recurrent tropes which typically associate military women with controversy and suggesting some of the ways film and television narratives have taken up these tropes. The controversies associated with military women—whether they are cast as ordinary or heroic or as victims—typically centers on gender, that is, on expectations of male and female behavior, aptitude, and aspirations.

Two issues in particular function as recurrent sources of controversy and scandal. The first of these is combat, which I address in chapter 7, teasing out the continuing significance of an opposition between combatant and noncombatant status for male and female personnel. The second issue which persists in both media coverage and film and television narratives has to do with sex and power: illicit sexuality, sexual harassment, and sexual violence or rape. The television texts discussed in chapter 6 suggest just how much debates about combat and sex as power are bound up with each other. Chapter 8 explores the figuration of military women as either avengers or investigators through a discussion of the rape-revenge narrative and the military woman as cop. In both instances military women are construed as outsiders and as potential victims of (military) male violence.

CONTROVERSY, CELEBRATION, AND SCANDAL
Military Women in the News Media

6

Since the 1980s there has been a relatively high degree of media interest in military women. A topic that has been deemed newsworthy in and of itself—the variation in gender roles in relation to women's work—has fed news stories ranging from policy and debate to scandal and humor. In turn the discourses developed in news media have impacted on and shaped film and television fictions featuring military women. This chapter begins with an exploration of how American news media have presented military women, focusing on the contradictory tendencies to celebrate and pathologize them. Two case studies follow; the first is concerned with the role of military women in fictional scenarios of military justice, the second examines fictions in which military women are effectively put on trial. Both sets of fictions clearly employ tropes established in news media, reiterating associations between military women and cultural controversy.

MILITARY WOMEN: CELEBRATION AND PATHOLOGIZATION IN AMERICAN NEWS MEDIA

There are at least five distinct types of stories or recurrent story elements identifiable within American network news coverage of military women:

- *Celebration*: Military women's achievements, presence, and deployment are regularly deemed newsworthy in and of themselves, a fact to be celebrated as a marker of progress.

Celebration of the military woman also serves as a sign of American modernity and democracy. Stories in this mode are not only contemporary; they also contribute to the memorializing work of groups of past military women long marginal within mainstream accounts, such as Vietnam War nurses, the WASP pilots, and POWS of the Second World War.

- *Debate*: Whether triggered by an incident during deployment (the death, injury, or capture of a military woman, for instance) or political or military intervention, news coverage repeatedly takes the form of debate on the viability of combat exclusions and the proper role of female personnel in the modern military. Such debates may be formal or informal, involving politicians, policymakers, servicemen and servicewomen, or concerned commentators.

- *Scandal*: In media coverage the scandal generated by military women's involvement in the humiliation and torture of prisoners in Abu Ghraib turned as much on the violation of gender norms as on the practices themselves. More generally, military women are repeatedly associated with sexual scandal. Stories of sexual misconduct and rape frequently cast military women as victims, whether of predatory men or of masculine military culture more broadly. Underpinning a fascination with sexual scandal is a preoccupation with the female body, construed as a problem, as out of place.

- *Testimony*: Here female military personnel "speak for themselves," typically arguing for a gender-blind assessment of their performance and the opportunity to simply do their work without special treatment. The testimony of male personnel, whether supportive of or antagonistic toward military women, is also regularly included in news features.

- *Professional and personal lives*: News media repeatedly highlight tensions between the professional and personal responsibilities of military women. The "problem" of pregnancy and the deployment of mothers are common themes. There is a degree of commonality here with the media presentation of working and professional women more generally, and in particular the trope of an elusive yet highly desirable "work-life balance."

These five story elements are by no means mutually exclusive; both celebration and scandal are typically coupled with debate, for instance.

Perhaps particularly relevant for thinking about the ways such news coverage impacts film and television fictions is the manner in which the body of the military woman becomes a site of contention and concern. Women's physical strength relative to men's is routinely scrutinized. This may take the form of "weak," "petite," or unreliable female bodies, or produce the specter of disturbingly strong (read "masculinized") women. The body of the military woman is pictured as disciplined and trained, but also as potentially unruly: menstruating, penetrable, pregnant or potentially pregnant. The body of the military woman has been claimed as a sign of American modernity; at other times it has been perceived as a problem requiring state intervention. Competing discourses then attempt to account for, naturalize, or problematize the female body, which remains a site of discomfort and even disgust.

A more detailed consideration of a particular example of the media coverage given to military women may help to illustrate how these five story types overlap and inform each other. To this end I examine an ABC News *Nightline* special devoted to a militarized all-male college, the Virginia Military Institute (VMI), which was broadcast on 20 February 1990. The Institute finally changed its male-only admissions policy some years later, in 1997, amid heightened media attention. The college's reluctance to do so provides an opportunity to rehearse wider debates. Ted Koppel, the program's anchor, introduces the special, speaking of the historic changes the U.S. has seen with respect to combat and locating VMI—and by extension the position of military women—in a dialogue between modernity and tradition. "It may seem curious, even quaint that we are still debating whether women should be allowed in combat," he begins. The implication seems clear: once appropriate, VMI is now outmoded, a point underlined by scenes of elaborate rituals involving traditional uniforms and weaponry which introduce the college. The college here stands for a nostalgic fantasy of military masculinity from which the nation, it is implied, has moved on. The discussion and commentary that follow include reference to the "bruising brotherhood" that characterizes VMI and fears that the integration of women will mean the loss of male comradeship (tellingly framing the "problem" of military women in terms of their impact on men). Maj. Gen. John Knapp, VMI's superintendent, insists categorically, "Nothing in the barracks, nothing in the process we use for cadet life has in any way ever been designed or allowed to continue with women in mind." Images of female cadets graduating from the service academies suggest that other institutions have adapted to military women, and headlines from Panama point to the deployment of those same women the previous year.[1] Authorities also comment: Brian Mitchell, the author of various books arguing strongly against women in the military,[2] suggests that upcoming defense cuts should focus on women since their presence in the U.S. military is a significant disincentive to male recruitment; Congresswoman Patricia Schroeder criticizes the premise of those official reviews geared at gauging the efficiency and capability of military women and attempts to debunk myths of male military chivalry.

Moving from the experts and policymakers to the individual soldier, the feature offers the confident testimony of Pvt. Cassandra Messick: "As far as physical, we have a lot of women here who can surpass some of the men. And as far as mental capabilities we definitely surpass them!" Surrounded by cheering women, Messick is clearly coded as a representative young, modern military woman. If the feature seems stacked toward modernization, a voice-over now seeks to qualify these views by evoking familiar anxieties: "But with women, many say, come problems. Romance, for example, and pregnancy, then child care. Not to mention the fundamental question of whether they're up to the job." In this way Messick's youthful assertions of military women's capabilities are almost immediately superseded by an assertion of the problems that women literally *embody*: emotional attachment, unruly bodies that become pregnant, and the responsibilities of parenting. (Men, it goes without saying, are deemed to have no place in any of this.) One "fundamental question," the ability of military women to perform a given function, is thus displaced by another: their reproductive potential. The fact of the female body thus functions as a sort of end point in this feature's articulation of the various story elements identified above. We see celebration, arguments are rehearsed, soldiers and students speak for themselves, but what to do about the scandalous female body persists as an unanswerable question.

Media insistence on women's vulnerability to rape and sexual harassment, whether as potential POWs or within the military's own academies and bases, represents an extension of these concerns with the "problematic" female body (concerns explored more fully in chapter 7). Military masculinity itself can be problematized only so far however, since it functions as a desirable goal to which military women are expected to aspire. As a consequence, it is repeatedly women themselves who are constituted as a problem, expressed in terms of their potentially disruptive effect on male military personnel. In this way conservative commentators cite instances of sexual harassment as evidence of the failure of gender-integrated training rather than speaking to a need for cultural change.[3] Popular culture too has demonstrated a remarkable capacity to acknowledge military women's exclusion and marginalization while retaining a more or less conservative view of these exclusionary institutions. An example from the late 1990s, when both The Citadel and VMI finally opened their doors to women, speaks to this playful doubleness.[4] An episode of the animated sitcom *The Simpsons* from 1997 has the smart misfit Lisa Simpson electing to join her unruly brother Bart at military school, in the process becoming the first female to join the academy ("The Secret War of Lisa Simpson," 18 May 1997). In a pastiche of boot camp and military school narratives, Lisa's fondness for discipline fails to endear her to the other cadets, who exclude her while welcoming the rebellious Bart. *The Simpsons* parodies the sort of narrative played out in films from *An Officer and a Gentleman* (1982) to *G.I. Jane*, released the same year, a film which manages to effectively castigate institutions perceived as anachronistic in gender terms while simultaneously reiterating the problematic status of the military and militarized woman.

Gender trouble remains central to news coverage throughout this period. Concerns over military women's gender status range from a discussion of inappropriate or insufficient physical strength to the significance of general appearance, clothing, and hairstyle. Writing of the media attention she received as a member of one of the first classes of women to attend West Point, Capt. Carol Barkalow recalls being asked, "Do you feel that you've lost your femininity?" She adds that some of her peers replied that "when they wanted to feel more feminine, they'd put on makeup or a skirt," but she felt differently: "Femininity was not a matter of how I looked or what I wore, but how I felt. . . . No one could take that from me."[5] Barkalow's attempt to redefine femininity in terms other than appearance flies in the face of institutional and media scrutiny of military women's gender in precisely these superficial terms. The need to accommodate the military to female bodies is repeatedly constituted as a problem, one implicitly or explicitly linked to combat exclusion policies understood as a way to regulate potentially unruly and troublesome military women.

When in 1976 West Point, the Naval Academy, and the Air Force Academy admitted their first female class members in response to a congressional order, media coverage speculated, "Why would a girl go to West Point?"[6] In covering this policy change, television news foregrounded and implicitly (at times explicitly) questioned women's physical and leadership abilities. Yet contemporary reports showed as much interest in sleeping and toilet arrangements, playfully highlighting the potential for sexual relations between male and female cadets while reassuring viewers that the leadership was as intent on "moral" as military regulation. A recurrent focus on toilet arrangements and separate living quarters in the decades that followed points to the persistent anxieties associated with the intimate proximity of male and female military bodies.

As combat exclusions came under increasing scrutiny the problem of where to place the military woman—professionally and personally—also intensified as a topic of media interest. An NBC news segment on 22 May 1985 reported on the "career crossroads" facing women who had graduated from the military academies. A variety of high-achieving women (all white) provided the report's examples: Capt. Ann Fields, one of the first women to graduate from West Point, who learned to fly helicopters but is "limited" by combat exclusion policies ("Let us do what we've been trained to do," she appeals); a pregnant officer; another seen juggling career and family commitments; and Lt. Crystal Lewis, who trains pilots to fight but is not permitted to fly in combat herself. The report ends with the image of Lewis looking on from the ground as planes fly past, the commentary underlining the gendered division of space and opportunity: "Talent is not yet enough to put her, or the others, in the pilot's seat." This imagery effectively evokes the figure of the grounded military women seen in films and recruitment materials from the Second World War, though now framed as a problem rather than an appropriate organization of space. The report thus suggests a failure to modernize, to make full and appropriate use of military women's skills and knowledge. Just as evident, however, is the report's juxtaposition of the "problem" of placing the military woman in an appropriate professional setting with the "problem" posed by pregnancy and motherhood. Ultimately such features tend to imply that it is the problematic female body rather than policy or military regulation that limits military women.

If the admission of women into the military academies underlined the problematic character of their exclusion from combat—surely an important aspect of the profession for which they were being trained as leaders—the various conflicts in which the U.S. has been involved over the decades that followed also tested and extended public understanding of the place and potential of military women in combat. Media coverage of the Gulf War reveled in images of military women, typically presenting them as extraordinary in spite of the women's insistence to the contrary. Thus Jeanne Holm reports the "incredulous" response of a CNN reporter to Maj. Marie Rossi's assertion, "We [military women] see ourselves as soldiers." Clearly, however, military women signified something exceptional rather than routine in contemporary news media. In what was a tightly controlled media context, the story of military women, mothers in particular, represented an attractive source of soft news stories.[7] Throughout the 1990s American military women were involved in peacekeeping missions in Haiti, Bosnia, and Somalia. During Operation Desert Fox in 1998, which sought to police the no-fly zone over Iraq, women aviators flew operational combat missions for the first time. Women also participated in combat operations the following year in Kosovo, with news coverage devoting as much time to this verifiable domestic milestone as to the purpose of the action itself. As the media image of the female soldier became more commonplace, her presence in or near combat was less likely to be the sole focus of news stories; nonetheless it remains remarkable, a facet of military culture to be commented on and concerned about.

In the 1990s public, media, and political debate concerning military women in the U.S. was framed by two distinct contexts: the largely positive media attention focused on military women as successful participants in the Persian Gulf War and an emphasis on military women as victims of sexual harassment within a male-dominated military. The events that took place at the annual convention of the Tailhook Association in 1991, and the scandal that unfolded in the years that followed, involved the U.S. Navy in a deeply embarrassing sexualized spectacle. The scandal centered not so much on the behavior of those young male naval aviators who had participated in the sexual harassment of women, both military and civilian, but on the seeming toleration of that behavior by senior naval officers. Ultimately the scandal would lead to the resignation of a number of high-profile officers; as late as 1994 the early retirement of Admiral Kelso was linked to the continuing reverberations of Tailhook. The revelation of what seemed to be routine sexual harassment, official complacency toward it, and the attempt to cover up the behavior of male officers contributed to a scandal which raised some fundamental questions concerning women's place in the military. Subsequent scandals involving the Army and Air Force suggested wider, perhaps even structural problems in managing a gender-integrated military. In 1996 accusations of rape and sexual harassment of female trainees at the Army facility in Aberdeen, Maryland, attracted media attention. The following year charges were filed against Sgt. Maj. Gene McKinney, the U.S. Army's top African American enlisted man; although he was subsequently acquitted, extensive media coverage concentrated attention on the potential for abuse within the ritualized context of basic training, as well as in the acutely hierarchical structures of military culture more generally. Also in 1997 the Air Force was at the center of negative publicity associated with the decision to press charges of adultery and disobeying orders against pilot Kelly Flinn. Politicians derided the charges against Flinn, arguing that they reflected a double standard in the treatment of the sexuality of military men and women.[8] In 2003 four former cadets went public with accusations that administrators at the Air Force Academy had punished female cadets reporting instances of rape and sexual harassment. Features and op-ed pieces in the *New York Times* and other newspapers continue to foreground the incidents of rape and sexual abuse experienced by military women during deployment on active duty in Iraq and Afghanistan.[9] The coexistence of celebration and victimization as components of popular discourse is evident in an article in December 2003 in *Vanity Fair* which featured an in-depth report on the allegations of systematic sexual abuse within the Air Force Academy, as well as a feature on the rescued POW Jessica Lynch as the lead in its "Hall of Fame 2003" celebrity profiles.[10]

The extent to which these two very different constructions (warriors and victims) effectively inform each other is one of the most striking aspects of mediations of the military woman in the past two decades. News media reports on sexual harassment seem invariably to lead to familiar discussions on women's role within the modern military. For some, sexual scandal provides evidence of the military's need to change; for others, continuing reports of rape and sexual harassment suggest that a gender-integrated military is simply unattainable. An association between women's independence and the possibility of sexual abuse is at the very least *implied* by media coverage which, in the wake of the Persian Gulf War, focused on the question of extending the opportunities available to military women, particularly with respect to combat. Sexual harassment emerges as both scandalous and routine, behavior to be reprimanded, and simply part of the job. Thus an ABC News report on 11 July 1992 on a presidential commission exploring the viability of combat duties for female pilots focuses not so much on women's capabilities, which are taken for granted, but on the impact any changes in policy might have on military men. Bob McLane (identified as "Top Gun Commanding Offier"), suggests that the key issue is "cultural change": "How do we introduce women into what has been an all-male environment?" The reporter's voice-over adds, "There's the additional problem of sexual harassment—whether men who are not inclined to do so will treat women as equals." In a post-Tailhook context of heightened media awareness, sexual harassment is understood as an issue of equality and acceptance, as a cultural question. Yet in foregrounding the aggression that defines and is required by military masculinity ("The women say they are just as aggressive as the men") the report implies that it is the task of military women to come to terms with and accommodate themselves to a culture that has defined itself as tough and aggressive in part through the exclusion of women.

Tailhook established an unsavory association between naval aviation and an unruly masculinity such that an NBC report later that month described the Navy as "in a class by itself in degrading its women" (21 July 1992). The achievements and potential of those military women (particularly aviators) pictured and interviewed in news reports are implicitly, and sometimes explicitly, set against a male military establishment that devalues them. The same NBC report that commented on the Navy's "degrading" treatment of "its women" rolled together a series of quite diverse incidents, introducing the item with the assertion, "Sexual harassment and abuse of women in the U.S. military is a rapidly growing problem." The linkage of women's advancement within the military and an increased level of sexual harassment, although it is not endorsed, is in many ways *assumed* in such journalistic discourses.

The high visibility of American military women in the Gulf War also functioned as a sign of modernity, implicitly or explicitly opposed to Muslim women, who signified a repressive patriarchy in media discourses. Observing a recurrent "contrast between the liberated American woman soldier and the veiled Arab woman," Cynthia Enloe points to the work of such constructions in maintaining a hierarchal relationship between nations and cultures, "implying that the United States is the advanced civilized country whose duty it is to take the lead in resolving the Persian Gulf crisis."[11] Such a pattern is exemplified by a prewar ABC report on

7 September 1990 which profiles Airman Kimberly Newberger, a young crew chief stationed in Saudi Arabia. Newberger describes how she must "be careful of what [she] wear[s]" in her current posting, while characterizing her military career more generally in terms of freedom and opportunity: "I took the twisted, bumpy path to adventure and travel—took me here." As Deborah Cohler, Susan Faludi, Deepa Kumar, and others have noted, a similar opposition between oppressed veiled women in Afghanistan and the freedoms of American women was extensively played out in the American media prior to the invasion of Afghanistan in 2002.[12] In contrast to such widespread assertions of gender equality, race is rarely mentioned in news reports on American military women. Although African American servicewomen may be pictured (and indeed are overrepresented as a group within the U.S. military) the specificity of their experience is not a subject for comment, and they provide testimony far less often than their white peers. Several scholars intrigued by media coverage of military women in the Iraq War have noted the discrepant levels of media attention accorded to the white POW Pvt. Jessica Lynch compared to other female members of the 507th taken prisoner or killed in the same events in Nasiriyah, the Native American Lori Piestawa and the African American Shoshona Johnstone.[13]

Lynch's high-profile rescue from an Iraqi hospital in April 2003 was an acknowledged feel-good story; supplied complete with video footage, in Carol Burke's words the Lynch rescue "revives the figure of war as theatre." Subsequent revelations that the commandos had met with no opposition, and indeed had expected none, punctured the power of the narrative somewhat, but not significantly. Indeed skepticism seemed to be most commonly expressed in the international but not the American press. To this extent the carefully stage-managed rescue functioned as a metaphor for the invasion as a whole, with the confident but ultimately unsustainable claims that Iraq posed a significant danger to the U.S. and the U.K. through its weapons of mass destruction. As Burke observes, "The Hollywood look, feel, and flow of the rescue did not go unnoticed by the American press, though they treated it as a reason for celebration rather than scepticism." In her analysis of media coverage of Lynch, Burke notes that "the familiarity of the story invited a hackneyed reiteration of gender stereotypes." Moreover, in keeping with Burke's analysis of military folklore, "the mainstream media relentlessly cast Lynch not as soldier but as civilian, not as an agent of liberation but as a surrogate for the women in the audience watching the evening news."[14] The words with which Lynch recalls responding to the commandos as they identified themselves, "I'm an American soldier, too," have a certain resonance here. Yet Lynch's own account, notably in her book, *I Am a Soldier, Too*, and a prime-time interview with Diane Sawyer, was only one among many competing stories.[15] As Naomi Klein wryly observed, "The real Jessica Lynch . . . has proven no match for her media-military created doppelganger, shown being slapped around by her cruel captors in NBC's movie *Saving Jessica Lynch*."[16] Lynch attempted to resist her characterization not only as a victim, but also as a warrior. A report published in the *Washington Post* on 3 April 2003 cited an official's comment that Lynch "was fighting to the death,"[17] a version of events she subsequently debunked. The spinning of her heroism and rescue produced familiar stories in many senses, not least the construction of a feminine, white woman as simultaneously victim and warrior.

What is most striking in the context of this study is the extent to which the media presence and contested image of the military woman would so explicitly form part of the Lynch story. The American media first promoted the idea of Lynch as warrior and subsequently as victim, a process that morphed into a self-regarding angst about its own myth-making and the amount of attention Lynch was receiving compared to (real) male soldiers. Susan Faludi effectively draws our attention to the repeated media scripting of Lynch as ultrafeminine (pretty, small, scared), a process that served to keep (military) women in their place, underlining once more an opposition between female noncombatants and male combat troops even in coverage which sought to celebrate her service.[18]

Once the scandal of the sexualized humiliation and torture of Iraqi prisoners at Abu Ghraib became widely disseminated and discussed in 2004, other military women, including Sabrina Harman but most particularly Lynndie England, quickly became synonymous with what an ABC News *Nightline* special on "women warriors" would term "a twisted tribute to gender integration in the U.S. military" (20 May 2004). A cartoon in the conservative British newspaper *The Mail on Sunday* bears the caption "Well at least we know the Americans have gender equality. We've been tortured by both men and women" (9 May 2004). In fact the media visibility of *both* Lynch and then England was accompanied by the voicing of deeply hostile sentiments toward military women and toward a feminism regarded as culpable for their inappropriate presence in war.

Lynch's petite body and England's pregnant body (as photographed during her court-martial) served as different markers of that inappropriate presence. England too was described as "petite," but also as unattractive (in contrast to Lynch) and masculine.[19] The British journalist Gary Younge suggests that Harman's and England's gender "made them easy to demonise," citing the conservative critic Ann Coulter's claim that the torture at Abu Ghraib offered "another lesson in why women shouldn't be in the military. . . . Women are more vicious than men."[20] That gender could effectively distract attention, at least in part, from the scandal itself (that is, the treatment of prisoners in an illegal and inhumane fashion) has much to do with the long-standing associations between military women and the scandal of gender nonconformity. The two case studies below explore some of the ways the disruptive potential of the military women has been incorporated, exploited, and contained in popular film and television fictions.

MILITARY WOMEN AND MILITARY JUSTICE:
A FEW GOOD MEN AND JAG

Though popular culture has frequently associated their visibility with a positive modernity, the coupling of military women with violence and combat has remained culturally troubling. Legal drama has provided a hybrid generic home for the military woman; as a lawyer she can stand not only for the modernity of the integrated U.S. military, but as a sign of the professional advancement of women in American society more generally.[21] This section takes as examples of this process a successful film, A Few Good Men (1992), and a long-running television series, JAG (1995–2005), both of which frame the work of the military woman within a courtroom setting. Both feature military women as lawyers, taking us into the offices of the Navy's Judge Advocate General Corps and into the workings of military justice. Demi Moore as the lawyer, Lt. Col. Joanne Galloway, is the only visible military woman in A Few Good Men; JAG foregrounds an exemplary military woman as a central character but also insists on women as an integral part of the Navy. Thus JAG seeks to manage a number of potentially contradictory factors, including respect for military tradition, a valorization of military masculinity, and an awareness of the legal, strategic, and moral issues at stake in a culture that systematically privileges men over women.

A Few Good Men uses the courtroom as a device to debate the kinds of behavior society requires, and even demands, of the men who serve in its military. The film begins with a precredit sequence depicting intense personal violence: at the U.S. naval base in Guantánamo Bay, Cuba, two Marines, Dawson and Downey, attack a fellow Marine, Santiago, who, we later learn, has been falling behind in his training. When Santiago subsequently dies, the other two are charged. The investigation and court case that follow focus on strategic uses of disciplinary violence within the chain of command. The defense suspects—but cannot easily prove—that the attack was the result of a direct order authorized from a senior officer. The debate that the film rehearses, then, has to do with the legitimacy of such illegal yet clearly sanctioned violence. Narrative resolution comes when Col. Nathan Jessop (Jack Nicholson) is goaded into a defiant public admission of his culpability, a dramatic scene counterposed by Dawson's more private realization that his actions were wrong, even though he was following orders.

Cynthia Lucia writes that *A Few Good Men* "fetishizes both the military and the masculine—ostensibly the subjects of its interrogation." Men and their relationship to military masculinity are at the center of the narrative. Yet it is the prominent presence of Lt. Col. Galloway which facilitates this thematic focus, foregrounding and reinforcing the combatant-noncombatant couplet in explicitly gendered terms. The first of the major characters to be introduced, Galloway is seen cutting across an elaborate display of drill, rehearsing to herself a request to be assigned as counsel for the two Marines (and hence to achieve greater professional visibility; figure 40). In the scene that follows, she will stumble over her carefully rehearsed words, signaling her failure to assert herself in public space. Her lack of certainty and her relative lack of authority will be a recurrent feature of the film. Lucia suggests that Galloway is consistently positioned as "a disruptive feminine presence," patronized and marginalized by her brilliant co-defense attorney, Lt. Daniel Kaffee (Tom Cruise). In line with her position as a military woman (and Moore's star status), Galloway's role is both central and peripheral to the film. Where Kaffee is glib and self-centered, she is an impassioned, deeply ethical character; she pushes her superiors, and later Kaffee, to look deeper into the case, although it is clear that the Navy would rather it be resolved quietly. Her reading of events proves to be the correct one, her suggestion of putting Jessop on the stand pivotal in winning the case, and yet, as Lucia notes, the film consistently adopts Kaffee's perspective: "Even though Jo is right, she con-

40. Galloway (Demi Moore) is introduced through a contrast with military men drilling in *A Few Good Men* (1992). She seeks greater professional visibility but is ultimately relegated to a supporting role.

tinues to appear wrong; even though Kaffee is wrong, he always appears right." Galloway's critique of masculine military culture—in the form of the violence that leads to Santiago's punishment and death—is acceptable only once mediated by a male military figure. Her attention to detail is valued by her male superiors, qualifying her as a researcher, but not as an attorney: "She's not cut out for litigation," one remarks. Galloway herself comes to realize that it is Kaffee's talents in the courtroom that their clients need, ultimately vindicating his judgment that her passion is "compelling" but "useless." Voluble outside the courtroom, on only one occasion does Galloway speak in court, an outburst that damages the case. Lucia analyzes this silencing in the context of other films featuring female lawyers in which "the female protagonist quietly is pushed to the narrative periphery by a (superior) male figure."[22]

The silencing and sidelining of Galloway in *A Few Good Men* are indicative of the cultural work surrounding military women in contemporary media culture. Since the mid-1990s media coverage has routinely construed military women as a problem for military men and for the martial culture that these men are able to so effectively embody. Fictions such as *A Few Good Men* and *JAG* exploit the presence of the military woman not so much to tackle issues of inequity as to elaborate stories in which military men are renewed and remasculinized. So, as Kaffee gradually finds his public voice, Galloway's idealism and professionalism trigger and sustain the narrative of remasculinization that the film stages around him. His alignment with a military woman (even one he openly disrespects) signals his location in a feminized arena and the need for the very renewal the film enacts. Throughout the course of the narrative he learns to step up and speak out; Galloway, by contrast, learns to keep quiet and to accept her ancillary status. This ancillary gender and military status is expressed in terms of a literal and metaphorical distance between those who inhabit a space dominated by the art of politics and talk, and those who serve in arenas of conflict and combat. *A Few Good Men* opposes the integrated naval and political elite of Washington to the all-male base at Guantánamo, inscribing in gendered terms a distinction between different forms of military service.

It is clear that Galloway's military woman is both a "disruptive feminine presence" (as Lucia puts it) and a woman deeply invested in military masculinity. As a military woman she is an outsider, and her attempts to assert herself generate male hostility. Yet she betrays the characteristic longing for acceptance expressed in numerous fictions showcasing military women. While fellow attorney Weinberg (Kevin Pollak) expresses his disgust at the Marines they are defending, characterizing them as bullies, Galloway's defense of the pair is unequivocal in its appeal to a masculine strength harnessed to national and personal security: "They stand on a wall and they say 'Nothing's going to hurt you tonight, not on my watch.'" Her endorsement of a protective military masculinity both aligns her with the code that Dawson and Downey attempt to live by and positions her as representative of the citizenry which benefits from that code. Ironically, while it is Galloway who is the lawyer most committed to military culture, as a woman she simply cannot, within the film's terms, embody its values. It is not that the film suggests that she has no place within the military. Rather, the military woman's value resides in her ability to take up a supportive role.

The military drama *JAG* repeatedly demonstrates the significance of this gender hierarchy and the extent to which it allows the imagination of an integrated military. The show's recurring female characters are lawyers: Lt. Kate Pike (Andrea Parker) and then Lt. Meg Austin (Tracey

Needham) in season 1, and Maj. and later Lt. Col. Sarah "Mac" MacKenzie (Catherine Bell) from season 2 onward.[23] While the show's male protagonist, Cmdr. Harmon Rabb Jr. (David James Elliot), a pilot turned lawyer, is explicitly enabled to perform in the air and in the courtroom, crossing and recrossing the supposedly secure categories of combatant and noncombatant, his female counterparts are more strictly coded as noncombatants. My discussion focuses on *JAG*'s characterization of the lawyer as exemplary military woman and, more broadly, the way the series engages with the military woman as a controversial and contested figure. The show was conceived in part as a response to the commercial success of *Top Gun* (1986) and *A Few Good Men*, hence the pilot-lawyer hero and the emphasis on military men and women working together in the context of military justice. From the beginning it was also shaped by the media attention generated by military women, alluding to or explicitly referencing a number of high-profile scandals.

Mac is deeply committed to military masculinity, a high-achieving woman shaped by a difficult childhood which was dominated by an alcoholic and violent military father (like her, a Marine). Yet she is also coded in familiar feminine terms; her emotional bonding with children and her desire to be a mother, and her enigmatic psychic powers, for instance.[24] Thus her military masculinity is at once "explained" in terms of her background (her father) and framed by more conventional female attributes. The show's legal fiction both conforms to and departs from the characterization of professionally successful women in American television drama more generally. The assumption that a successful woman cannot develop or maintain a romantic, heterosexual relationship is as commonplace in *JAG* as it is in other instances of postfeminist media culture. Because for women, it is implied, romance involves submission, the masculine military woman must by definition be single. Like Galloway in *A Few Good Men*, Mac is a powerful yet isolated figure; both are exemplary military women who thrive in the institutional context of Washington. These characters effectively figure the achievements of white American military women as well as indicating the arena in which such achievement is appropriate.

MacKenzie may show personal vulnerability, but she is constructed as a warrior more often than as a victim. Consider how she explains to her male colleagues her acute (and acutely gendered) awareness of personal space and personal danger: "A woman's intuition isn't a joke. It's a matter of survival" ("Defenseless," 9 December 1997). She does not draw on tales of combat here but describes the experience of being a woman in public spaces in terms of a constant expectation of violence; vulnerable to danger at every turn, women in general are advised to adopt her pragmatic, militarized strategies for self-defense. As if to follow up on her description of her everyday state of readiness, another season 3 episode presents her as the object of obsessive interest from a police detective who stalks and eventually abducts her ("The Stalker," 17 March 1998). Such frank acknowledgment of women's embattled position in a patriarchal culture suggests at least a feminist-informed understanding of hierarchies and institutions. Yet *JAG* is as intent on keeping military women in their allotted place as most of the other popular fictions discussed in this book.

On occasion *JAG*'s female lawyers finding themselves in dangerous situations, even what are effectively combat scenarios. The introduction of Lt. Meg Austin in the series 1 episode "Shadow" (30 September 1995) is indicative of how the show handles this. Rabb and Austin are paired to go aboard a submarine held hostage by an embittered computer nerd who is testing a new weapons system. Her unwelcome presence on the all-male submarine is justified by her expertise as a computer weapons specialist. Such a characterization echoes arguments in favor of expanding women's role in a modern, thoroughly technologized military.[25] Although Austin's expertise does indeed allow her and Rabb to win back the ship, she poses a significant problem to the mission by failing to disclose her claustrophobia. Sweating, hyperventilating, and panicky in the cramped submarine, she seems emblematic of the undisciplined and unreliable female body, a figure of abjection of the sort invoked by hostile commentators.

More often *JAG* situates its central female characters alongside other women on active duty in order to explore the effectiveness of women in combat and the position of military women more generally. The feature-length pilot episode ("A New Life") established both the formula of a male-female investigative military partnership and the dramatic potential of the military woman in a naval context, focusing directly on the questions posed by the military woman on active duty. Contrasting the masculinized and feminized bodies and modes of behavior of different military women, the pilot explores relationships between male and female personnel onboard ship, staging a debate about women's combat readiness and the effects of their presence on male personnel of different generations. Over the years many episodes would focus on issues relating to

41. The muscular pilot Cassie (Raye Hollitt) represents a masculinized image of the military woman in the *JAG* pilot episode.

military women which had received wider media coverage: their position while stationed in Saudi Arabia; their treatment in comparison to men; the difficulties facing a lesbian officer; the fallout from charges of adultery; and false claims of sexual harassment made by and against female officers. In this way the physical and mental capabilities of the female soldier are repeatedly interrogated in a manner that echoes ongoing news media coverage. Some acquit themselves, many fail, but all have something to prove.

The pilot episode begins with an aerial action sequence over the Adriatic and a confrontation between the older, experienced Admiral Boone, referred to as "Cag" (Terry O'Quinn) and his radio intercept operator Lt. Angela Arutti. A familiar generic opposition of youth and technology versus age and experience is explicitly gendered as Cag pushes Arutti and finds her wanting: "I wanted to see if you had the guts for a knife fight—and you don't." The show then proceeds to set up an opposition between Arutti, who is blonde and hesitant (feminine), and her muscular, mannish aviator roommate, Lt. Cassie Puller. Cassie is introduced taking part in a competitive weightlifting session in which she demonstrates greater strength than the misogynist Lt. "Ripper" Carter, who overtly regards her female masculinity as a threat to his male, military identity (figure 41). In this way the show early on sets up oppositions of different kinds between male and female naval personnel. The terms at stake include not only gender but age, experience, courage, bodily strength, and competitiveness, itself coded as a masculine quality possessed by some women but not all.

That is, the narrative effectively dramatizes and feeds back into the terms in which contemporary news media characterized military women as a problem for men and as somehow anomalous to cultural conceptions of gender.

JAG both acknowledges and incorporates into its ongoing narrative the media visibility and political significance of the military woman in American culture of the mid-1990s. The very media attention generated by military women serves as a recurrent plot device. Arutti's actions and emotions (her evident fear, participation in combat, decision to resign, secret marriage to a fellow RIO, and ultimately her murder) are all framed in terms of a media obsessed with military women and a Navy preoccupied with its public image. Lt. Kate Pike is assigned to the investigation on the basis of her gender and looks. Arutti is anxious about the prospect of becoming "a blurb on the evening news." With media attention focused on the "woman warrior," the Navy's investigation into Arutti's death is politically charged. Military men and women are portrayed as operating in a context policed, or at least closely monitored, by popular media and political intervention. Significantly this policing, and even the very presence of military women on active duty, is understood to be a product of the Tailhook scandal, the media repercussions of which I return to below.

The show presents the U.S. Navy as newly aware of the politics of language and behavior in a gender-integrated environment. Yet when individual women insist on the respect due to their position within the Navy, they are coded as lacking respect for naval tradition. Arutti scowls when congratulated on her first kill in sexual terms ("busting your cherry"); her stern response positions her as both outside the military fraternity and as an embodiment of deeply resented changes. Such changes are openly seen as a cause for regret by male personnel, including the male lead, Rabb. The pilot episode attributes the experimental presence of women on a battle carrier to the priorities of politicians rather than to military expediency. The attribution of inappropriate power and influence to female politicians (who are masculinized in a quite different fashion from military women) is a recurrent trope. In this intensely political and closely scrutinized context, individual military women are frequently cast as pawns in a game they do not control or even understand. In turn this complex situation has the potential to impact their judgment; thus, for instance, Rabb is characterized as effectively seeing beyond gender in a way that the military women with whom he works simply cannot.[26]

As mentioned earlier, like *A Few Good Men*, *JAG* exploits the presence of military women not only in terms of a current topic of interest but also to set in motion a more or less explicit narrative of remasculinization conducted around the male protagonist. Time and again the series provides opportunities for Rabb to demonstrate his distance from the military women with whom he works, showcasing his capability as a man of action, a pilot, and a combatant.[27] How might we make sense of such a shift in focus? Faced with the difficult prospect of sustaining recruitment to a volunteer military, Cynthia Enloe identifies a perception at work on the part of strategists that the "fundamentally masculinized culture of the military" be retained. Thus she notes that while the enlistment of women in certain areas provides a way of stemming the shortfall in recruitment, it is a strategy of which many are wary: "The military that enlists women must remain, it is thought, a military that is appealing to men. . . . Women recruits should not deprive men of the chance to serve in those posts held most precious to masculinity-seeking men."[28] From the pilot episode on, *JAG* exemplifies this agenda, demonstrating the limited integration of women into certain roles, pointing to the problems of their deployment, suggesting the limits of their leadership abilities, and noting the difficulties and problems of feminist rhetoric—never sustainable against the experience of military men—while castigating and expelling misogynous military men who are identified as too extreme to remain part of the new Navy. Thus in the pilot episode Cag, who openly expresses his lack of faith in women's combat capabilities, can be retained and valorized, while the more evidently irrational, murderous misogynist Ripper is excluded.

Precisely what is at stake with respect to the gendering of the combatant-noncombatant couplet in this structure is once more apparent in the season 2 episode "Crossing the Line" (31 January 1997). The episode opens with the raucous naval ceremony to which the title refers, which involves the humiliation of male and female "polliwogs" as the vessel crosses the equator; this crossing stands in for a rite of passage associated with an active service inscribed as both carnivalesque and masculine. Disgruntled Lt. Marilyn Isaacs doesn't take Navy ritual in the spirit intended, filing charges of sexual harassment against Cag, who has suspended her from flight duty; she claims that he has sought to discredit her as a way of discrediting all women in combat. The ritual associated with "crossing the line" is presented in the show as a part of naval tradition that has already been unduly compromised by an emphasis on zero tolerance. *JAG* lawyer

Mac tends to believe Isaacs; she lectures Rabb that in the wake of Tail-hook "the good old days are gone" and that "this is a new Navy with new rules." While the pilot episode expelled an extreme misogynous figure, "Crossing the Line" instead distinguishes between good and bad military women, between those who can accommodate themselves to naval history and traditions and those who cannot.

Along with Mac, the female RIO Lt. "Skates" Hawkes is as an example of the good military woman, adopting a pragmatic approach as she asserts both that "a woman who can't handle some jerk playing 'grabass' doesn't belong in the Navy" and that women who seek to be "one of the guys" are defined by loss and are required to "give up something . . . be less of a woman." Being "one of the guys" may involve accepting an uncomfortable level of physical contact. Equally it may involve a denial of the specificity of female experience or any forms of behavior that might be read as feminine. Isaacs seeks to sidestep the guys and the military culture they embody, exploiting her media visibility as a military woman and enlisting the help of Congresswoman Delong, a long-standing critic of the Navy and an advocate of extending more opportunities to women. In Washington Delong imperiously insists that Isaacs's flight status be restored. The interference of this assertive civilian woman (who patently does not respect male privilege or naval tradition) is, predictably, disastrous. Unwilling to take the advice of the experienced military men who counsel against it she proudly describes Isaacs as "a woman who's ready to go to war." In the botched landing that follows, the plane explodes and Isaacs is killed. The message is clear: it is experienced military men and accommodating military women who know best; the assertion of women's rights should not be allowed to override the judgment of ancient mariners such as Cag.[29]

The narrative trajectory of "Crossing the Line" suggests that a politically correct military has been achieved at the cost of naval traditions and that dealing with sexual harassment is simply part of the job of the military woman. Isaacs is doubly culpable in this context since she not only rejects the judgment of experienced military men, but exploits the Navy's (post-Tailhook) vulnerability with respect to issues of sexual harassment. The scenario enacted here points to deep-seated anxieties about female fitness for military service, concerns that center on the female body as undisciplined. Indeed in many ways *JAG*'s typical perspective on the questions raised by women in combat roles is difficult to disentangle from the show's articulation of military women as problematic bodies, disruptive or provocative figures who bring sex with them into a military setting, complicating (if not defiling) the supposedly simple rituals of communal male life. Since these issues—the legitimacy or otherwise of combat exclusions and the prevalence of sexual scandal—are so complexly entwined with wider media discourses, it is in no way surprising that they also inform each other in a show like *JAG*.

The heightened security in the wake of 9/11 and the military action in Afghanistan and Iraq which followed triggered a restaging of *JAG*'s ambivalent articulation of women's combat readiness and a forceful restatement of the necessity to retain military masculinity of the kind celebrated in the pilot episode. In an episode aired that fall season ("Dog Robber Part II," 27 November 2001) Mac confronts a case of harassment that leads her to argue for the reprimand of the male commanding officer, Colonel Presser, while simultaneously agreeing with her boss, Admiral Chegwidden that in the current context the military needs tough officers like Presser. The episode achieves its reframing of women in combat by employing a number of the show's staple elements. These include Mac's high level of commitment and ability to pass any test as an exemplary (but implicitly exceptional) military woman; an acknowledgment of discriminatory treatment meted out to military women by male peers and commanding officers; an unscrupulous military woman who manipulates media and public opinion; and anxiety that their expression of conservative views on gender might unduly compromise the careers of good male soldiers.

The plot develops as follows: relaxing at home, Mac watches a television show titled *Military Bloopers*, which features Capt. Sheila Grantham being bawled out on the course, conspicuously failing to achieve the physical standards required. This scenario raises the specter of an unfit female body and contrasts this with the capable military women represented by Mac watching at home. Following a complaint from Grantham, Mac investigates conditions at the training center. She scrutinizes Colonel Presser's insistence that male and female Marines be held to the same standards (to "separate the men from the boys") and concludes that the strategy has indeed contributed to a hostile environment for women. The colonel stands by his methods and angrily demands that Mac consider a future in which physically inferior women may have to fight for their lives.

42. MacKenzie (Catherine Bell) is *JAG*'s exemplary yet exceptional military woman.

Concerns for gender equality are effectively presented as a peacetime luxury which circumstances require the U.S. to set aside.

Against the specter of inadequately trained female Marines endangering themselves and national security, Mac agrees to take her annual physical fitness test while at the center. Of course her performance impresses both Gunnery Sergeant Smith ("Not bad for a lawyer") and Presser ("Not bad for a Marine"). Yet here, as elsewhere in the series, Mac is constituted as *exceptional* rather than representative (figure 42). As if to underline the point, it becomes clear that it was Grantham herself who leaked the video tape that triggered the investigation in the first place; by casting herself as a victim she had hoped to enhance her case. Mac's subsequent decision to charge Grantham with conduct unbecoming aligns her not with the humiliated military woman (who emerges as manipulative and media-aware) but with Presser and the high standards that he enforces. In the episode's closing conversation with Chegwidden, Mac asks whether he thinks there will ever be a female Navy SEAL. He replies authoritatively that this will not and *should* not happen, thus affirming a space appropriately reserved for the patriotic service of masculinity-seeking men. In this way the views of Presser are more or less explicitly, if regretfully, endorsed. When he tells Mac, "We can't carry Marines who can't cut it," the reference to female Marines is clear.[30] The response to 9/11 in a military drama like *JAG* highlights the distinction it has typically drawn, in common with wider media coverage, between the place of military women in principle and in practice. In acknowledging the skepticism of male military personnel and the importance of physical and emotional qualities (strength and courage) that military women are not typically deemed to possess—that they must repeatedly prove—*JAG* simultaneously interrogates and reiterates the perceived discrepancy between *woman* and *soldier*.

MILITARY WOMEN ON TRIAL:
SHE STOOD ALONE AND *ONE KILL*

How do the themes of harassment and unruly masculinity, which recur in popular journalism of the period, feature in film and television fictions of the 1990s and since? In what ways does the media presence of sexual scandal shape narratives of military women? The early years of *JAG* were very much informed by and even spoke directly to the somewhat tarnished image of the U.S. Navy with respect to gender equality that resulted from the Tailhook incident. The show tends to equate the enhanced position of women in the Navy with both modernity (it is a sign of the forward-looking character of American society more generally) and loss (elite spaces previously occupied only by masculine men seem compromised by the inclusion of women). By contrast, the television movie *She Stood Alone: The Tailhook Scandal* (first aired on CBS on 22 May 1995) approaches Tailhook from the perspective of Lt. Paula Coughlin, the naval helicopter pilot whose initial complaint and subsequent media interviews triggered the scandal.

In line with the conventions of the television movie, Coughlin (Gail O'Grady) is a heroic, if somewhat naïve, protagonist whose personal experience highlights a topical issue.[31] She is portrayed as a tough individual who stands up to her peers, her senior officers, and the naval traditions they embody. Ultimately she is praised by her ex-military father (and the film) for having changed the Navy. Yet the narrative also traces her exclusion from the Navy, a movement that seems inevitable once she has broken ranks to complain about her treatment. In line with wider media coverage, *She Stood Alone* contextualizes Coughlin's experience of sexual harassment within a military culture that is male-dominated and overtly hostile to women. The film characterizes her as an ambitious, capable, and successful woman; indeed her experience of sexual harassment is explicitly linked to her ambition. In this context two aspects of *She Stood Alone* are particularly significant: the construction of Coughlin as an *exceptional* woman as a way of intervening in and commenting on the commonsense opposition between *woman* and *soldier*, and the presentation of sexual harassment as part of a more general male hostility to any increase in the opportunities available to women within the military.

She Stood Alone begins with shots of Coughlin as a young girl out in the woods playing with a toy airplane that she holds aloft as she runs around. When real planes speed overhead, the excited girl asks her mother if one might be piloted by her father, and she expresses awe at the prospect. Her mother seems equally involved in the glamour of flight, telling the young girl, "That's why I married a pilot." A close-up of the girl's face has her saying quietly to herself, "Why marry one when you can be one?" We cut straight from this establishing scene to Coughlin as a young woman, now a naval officer and helicopter pilot, who tells a colleague, "I want it all," which here means command, combat experience, and a future in Washington "with a chest-full of ribbons." Thus the film positions Coughlin as an ambitious woman, a daughter in awe of her aviator father, and a woman deeply invested in military culture. Rejecting her mother's route of marriage to the military, she has sought to become a part of the institution. She deftly deals with an admiral's sexism while playfully distancing herself from "those feminists," suggesting her ease with male authority. When we next see her talking with her mother it is to confess feelings of anger and fear. The metaphor of military as family has become perverse as Coughlin speaks angrily of the officers who assaulted and betrayed her: "These guys are supposed to be my brothers." Ultimately she resents being treated as if she were a civilian, which is to say nothing more than a woman.

Coughlin is excited about attending Tailhook, seeing it as a chance to advance her career and meet the right people. (She does indeed get an introduction to the secretary of the Navy.) Yet at a panel designed to encourage an open exchange of views between naval leaders and junior officers, the hostility of military men toward military women is apparent. A uniformed woman asks the panel, "When are women going to start flying in combat?" The admiral's amused and evasive response is matched by derision from the floor as male aviators shout the woman down. The film links the public mockery of this young military woman, eager to question combat exclusions, to the sexual humiliation experienced by Coughlin later that night. Just as military women are let down by fellow officers and commanders in a public forum where they might have expected support, Coughlin's appeals for help during the incident itself, and subsequently in her attempts to seek redress, are ignored or laughed down.

Once she has made her complaint, Coughlin is effectively grounded and isolated from her peers, both male and female. Her boyfriend, Rocket, and her buddy Stick are both perplexed and angry about her decision. Having described Coughlin as "warrior class" early in the film, Stick subsequently delivers a contemptuous rejection of military women's claims to soldier status. His comments suggests not only that Coughlin has overreacted to male exuberance, but that such a reaction demonstrates how inappropriate it is for women to see themselves as combat-ready. Later he will attempt to reestablish a bond with her, offering an apology and a salute; that the gesture is rebuffed could be read as reinforcing the military woman's "failure" to understand or incompatibility with (male) military codes. The film's final scene has Coughlin's father reassure his newly civilian daughter that she is a "warrior" and that he is proud of her. Thus *She Stood Alone* attempts to reverse the conventional understanding articulated by Stick, suggesting that Coughlin's toughness—her warrior status—is bound up with her determination to pursue her complaint as much as her status as military woman. Yet as the film's title asserts, this involves her separation from the very military unit to which she aspires to belong and even ultimately to lead.

Military women more generally are presented as isolated and fearful in *She Stood Alone*. Fellow female officers tell her that the matter should have been settled in house, that sexual harassment "goes with the territory": "It does not pay to keep reminding these guys that we're different." During this last conversation Anita Hill's testimony plays on the television in the background, reinforcing a suggestion that publicly confronting male power and privilege is potentially costly. Nonetheless when Coughlin finally goes public it is with the support of the initially hostile Lt. Cdr. Evans, who has "kept quiet" about her own experiences of sexual harassment. Another hostile fellow officer confesses her experience of abuse following this public testimony. In this way, albeit tentatively, *She Stood Alone* suggests the possibilities of alliances between military women. Such bonds are potentially supported by the more overt feminism of a powerful female political figure in Assistant Secretary to the Navy Barbara Pope (Bess Armstrong), whose perspective is represented not as an uninformed antimilitary stance, but in terms of a fervent desire to modernize the military. While Pope insists that military women are a reality to be acknowledged and respected, she rails against the exclusive "cult of the warrior," which, she claims, "by definition excludes women." Despite its title, there is a relative optimism evident in *She Stood Alone*, not only in its concluding image of father and daughter, but in the offers of support Coughlin finally receives from other female naval officers. Such images of female comradeship are rare in recent military narratives. From the late 1980s onward film and television fictions have emphasized the isolation of the military woman in a gender-integrated but male-dominated environment.

She Stood Alone explicitly dramatizes the Tailhook scandal within a postfeminist media culture which routinely trades in the assumption that gender equality is already achieved and as a result is uncontroversial. The military is portrayed as out of step with civil society and in need of change. Both military women's professional isolation and their association with sexual scandal became conventional features of subsequent television fictions. The juxtaposition of sexual scandal and female ambition is clearly on display in *One Kill* (first aired on CBS on 6 August 2000), which stars Ann Heche as Marine Capt. Mary Jane O'Malley. O'Malley's affair with Maj. Nelson Gray (Sam Shepard) leads to his death and her trial for premeditated murder. Since Gray is married (although she does not realize this at first) the relationship compromises O'Malley's position; that he is unbalanced places her and her family in danger. A divorced mother of two, O'Malley is also characterized as a lonely, single, professional woman, an ambitious figure who employs the rhetoric of equality feminism and patriotism: "It's not my country if I don't fight for it."

The film opens by juxtaposing victim and warrior imagery. The first sequence stages the event that leads to Gray's death, his sinister, nighttime intrusion into O'Malley's home, accompanied by menacing music. Camouflaged as if for a military operation, Gray breaks into the house where he presents military tokens (an insignia and a salute) to O'Malley's young son. This collision of military and domestic tropes is strongly suggestive of imminent violence. Yet that violence is not seen; instead, as the bedroom door closes behind Gray, we cut to the credit sequence and an extended display of O'Malley's efficient progress through an assault course, effectively celebrating her athleticism. The film depicts her as an exemplary, high-achieving, aggressive, and physically able military woman who works in an almost exclusively male context.[32] That this celebration of female military muscle follows immediately after a sequence that suggests domestic threat is quite in keeping with the double focus of contemporary narratives featuring military women.

Though my comments foreground an association between military women and sexual scandal, questions of both women's combat readiness and the extent to which gender integration is achievable also clearly inform *One Kill*. Gray is initially brought in to monitor the training exercise in which O'Malley's convoy (she works in supply) will be involved. He is openly hostile, observing, "In a real war, women don't fight out front. I like to train people I can take with me." Her commander, who will later conspicuously refuse to back her, whispers to O'Malley, "I guess you'd better bring him into this century." It is O'Malley's subsequent success in the training exercise which garners the support of her macho military team, one of whom dubs her a "true Marine." While such comments imply that it is Gray whose attitudes are atypical among a more inclusive modern Marine Corps, the support of O'Malley's men is short-lived; the same lieutenant who praises O'Malley also propositions her. Later, at his instigation, all her men change their testimony in order to incriminate her. Like many other recent narratives centered on military women, *One Kill* constructs an exemplary military woman as an outsider. Indeed the film features a military establishment concerned to protect the reputation of a male war hero (Gray) and willing to sacrifice an exemplary female officer in the process. O'Malley's commanding officer explicitly warns her, "If you make me choose, it won't be you." The evocation of fear, secrecy, and conspiracy frames the position of the military woman (however exemplary) as extremely precarious. O'Malley's language suggests that she has become detached from the Corps, that, in standing up for herself, she risks losing a tenuous position within male military comradeship. In supporting O'Malley, the military lawyer Captain Randall feels that he too is breaking the rules; he confesses that he feels uncomfortable in going against what the Corps wants him to do. Just as one of the investigators in *She Stood Alone* comes to believe and support Coughlin, Randall will ultimately defend O'Malley successfully, ensuring that she has the right to keep her position. Yet O'Malley chooses not to exercise that right, and both films end with the exclusion of their female protagonists from a military career which had previously defined them.

As in the Second World War, the period following gender integration sees the military woman as a sign of modernity. Yet despite this commonality, the two periods are clearly different when it comes to the discourses surrounding military women. The shift is from a temporary necessity, an adjunct to conscripted male service, to high-achieving women seeking advancement in a professionalized volunteer military. Military women achieve significant levels of visibility in the news media, while in popular film and television they appear in markedly contradictory terms, simultaneously celebrated and tested (and thus implicitly needing to prove themselves), valorized and victimized. The genres in which military women appear register these contradictions, often figuring them as isolated rather than integrated. Whether that isolation has to do with the women's exemplary and exceptional status or a more threatening sense of being out on a limb, popular narratives work through anxieties about gender and about the consequences of feminism for women's working lives; thus in narratives that nostalgically celebrate military traditions and military masculinity the military woman is seen heroically confronting conservative institutions which require modernization.

CONFLICT OVER COMBAT

Training and Testing Military Women

7

Military culture secures gendered difference through an opposition between combatant and noncombatant personnel. Policies regarding military women are shaped in part by cultural
presumptions about gender, whether those presumptions have
to do with temperament, biology, or morality. While the military clearly requires women's labor, it limits the environments in
which they may work and the tasks they may undertake. Perceptions of military women as secondary (auxiliary) personnel, so
common in the rhetoric of the Second World War, thus persist in
an integrated twenty-first-century U.S. military. These presumptions have an impact on the working lives of women within the
military, the opportunities for reward and promotion that are
open to them, and the more general public recognition that is
tied to military service in American culture. They are also evident
in film and television fictions picturing military women.

Congresswoman Patricia Schroeder, a Democrat from Colo-
rado and an advocate for American military women, once characterized the testing and training of military women as a process
destined to be repeated until the "right" result (i.e., failure) was
achieved. In analogous fashion the fictional texts explored in this
chapter—all produced after 1980 and located within a military
that is to some degree integrated—enact a repetitive process by
which the military woman, constituted as a problematic presence, is *tested* throughout the course of the narrative. Whether

she emerges as an exceptional high-achiever, a liability, or a contradictory combination of the two, her presence is rarely taken for granted. In cinema and television fictions it seems that the military woman still requires *explanation*. In narrative terms she is also required to *prove herself* against an assumption of her inadequacy, whether professional or personal. The need to both test and explain fundamentally shapes the film and television narratives discussed in this chapter. These fictions also clearly draw on, reproduce, and revise genre conventions and the terms of the public and media debate outlined in chapter 6. All are concerned in one way or another with the possibility and potential consequences of combat roles for American military women.

The contested character of military women as noncombatants serving in a gender-integrated military makes their inclusion in war or combat movies tricky to manage. Some movies and television dramas do place women in combat scenarios. In *Wings of the Apache* (1990) a helicopter pilot, Billie Lee Guthrie (Sean Young), is part of a U.S. Army mission against drug cartels; her duties are in reconnaissance. (One year later Congress would repeal laws banning women from flying in combat.) In *Courage under Fire* (1995) a pilot, Karen Walden (Meg Ryan), *inadvertently* ends up in a combat situation. *Stealth* (2005), in which Lt. Kara Wade (Jessica Biel) flies an advanced Stealth fighter in a combat unit, takes place in "the near future," one which links futuristic technological innovations to female opportunity (figure 43). While in *Courage under Fire* the pilot is killed by her own (male) crew, in both *Wings of the Apache* and *Stealth* the female pilots are rescued by male pilots to whom they are romantically linked. That the three films all feature female pilots is itself noteworthy. This is the arena in which military women are perhaps most visibly engaged in combat activities. The role also has elite, high-achieving associations, in line with the typical characterization of film and television military women as exemplary and atypical. Additionally the distance of pilots from ground warfare allows a gendered redefinition of spaces that remain exclusively male or masculine.

On the ground, the pilot episode of *Over There* (Fox, 2005) features two female soldiers, Pvt. "Mrs. B." Mitchell and Pfc. "Doublewide" Del Rio; newly deployed to Iraq they are inadvertently caught up in combat. The belligerent Mrs. B. seeks privacy to defecate and ends up caught in a firefight. Most often film and program makers sidestep some of the complexities of military women's role in combat by making use of the training

43. Set in the near future, *Stealth* (2005) features a military woman as part of its high-tech flight program.

or boot camp narrative as a setting. I discuss these in the first section, before turning to a more detailed discussion of the staging of the accidental female combatant in *Courage under Fire*. Throughout I argue that a persistent concern with gender identity underwrites the scripting of military women in conflicts over combat.

BOOT CAMP: MASCULINIZING AND MILITARIZING WOMEN

Boot camp narratives stage the transformation of civilians into soldiers. Sometimes they show ordinary soldiers being inducted into specialized or elite units. The action involves conflict and typically concludes with scenes of actual combat or, more often, a training exercise that simulates combat (war games, a competition between platoons). Jeanine Basinger writes, "These conflicts represent the war these military men are being trained to fight."[1] Individuals demonstrate the skills and personal qualities they have learned (or enhanced) through the course of their training; the group's ability to work together is tested. Boot camp movies stage rites of passage as narratives of masculinization: boys become men, civilians become soldiers. Earlier chapters discussed dramatic (*The Gentle Sex*, *Keep Your Powder Dry, Parachute Nurse*), comic (*Never Wave at a WAC*, *Private Benjamin*), and musical (*Skirts Ahoy!*) variants of the boot camp narrative centered on women. In each instance the themes of transformation so characteristic of the genre are enacted by military women who discover a sense of identity and self-worth. In the process such films draw on the conventions of the woman's film, a genre that is strongly associated with themes of personal transformation. In the context of developing debates concerning the potential combat role of military women, this section considers the ways in which the conventions of the training camp narrative are inflected in more recent films, beginning with two quite distinct examples from 1981, both focused on young women in basic training: *Soldier Girls*, a documentary directed by Nick Broomfield and Joan Churchill, and an ABC television movie, *She's in the Army Now*. While *Soldier Girls* attracted positive critical attention, neither film had anything like the visibility achieved by *Private Benjamin* the previous year, yet both underline the renewed fascination with the military woman which followed integration. In different ways these two films are variations of the popular fictions considered so far; *Soldier Girls* is a documentary produced at a time when the genre did not have the high profile it does today, and *She's in the Army Now* is a low-budget genre production with limited distribution. Significantly both films depict the military service of working-class, Latina, and African American women, groups largely absent from the popular narratives of the period, which typically represent military women as white, high-achieving officers.

Comedy was the dominant mode in which postwar cinema figured the military woman. It is perhaps for this reason that *She's in the Army Now* was labeled a comedy for marketing purposes. In terms of the film's content, however, this is a perplexing designation. There may be a mildly comic chase sequence involving the central group of women driving off base in pursuit of Private Knoll's (Melanie Griffith) ex-husband, a cowboy caricature. But there is no laugh track or slapstick, no comic dialogue or innuendo, no music to counterpose the women drilling, or any other of the techniques so regularly deployed in popular culture to signal to the audience that the military woman is above all funny. Moreover dramatic events such as Private Marshall's breakdown and suicide attempt or Knoll's fears that she might lose custody of her daughter are not presented humorously. Even so, the video jacket proclaims that the film is "one of the funniest explorations of the armed services *ever*!" Perhaps military women, since they represent a sort of category confusion, are by definition humorous? The jacket blurb tells viewers that the film "takes a refreshing look at barracks life and the new breed of 'G.I. Joans' who have changed American Army life forever!," underlining the fact that the film sought to employ the comic novelty of military women as a marketing hook.[2]

The central figure in *She's in the Army Now* is Pvt. Cass Donner, a white woman whose voice-over guides us through basic training at Fort Jackson. Donner is an aspiring psychologist who sees the Army as a means to pay her way through graduate school; her last job offer, she tells us, was dancing in a strip club. Military service thus allows individual professional advancement and an alternative to sexual exploitation. Donner describes herself as "nonviolent by nature," remarking after her introduction to the M16, "I guess I never honestly believed that as women we would ever really have to be soldiers." Here Donner effectively articulates commonsense perceptions of the incongruity of the female soldier. Throughout the course of the film she must learn otherwise, acquiring discipline and leadership skills, and learning to value military life and service as more than the means to an end. Transformation is a central theme, then, but not in the fashion of *Private Benjamin* or those narratives from the 1940s and 1950s that pictured restless socialites finding self-worth in the ranks.

Alongside Donner, four other women make up the core group of *She's in the Army Now*: the ex-criminal Pvt. Rita Jennings; sensitive Pvt. Virginia Marshall; a southern single mother, Pvt. Sylvie Knoll; and a tough Latina, Pvt. Yvette Rios. The squad is instructed by the ambitious and demanding Sergeant Reed, assisted by Sergeant Barnes, to whom Donner is increasingly attracted. Donner's goal of acquiring an education is matched by Knoll's desire to provide for her young daughter. Jennings is attempting to dodge a Los Angeles Police warrant (the Army knows about this, but doesn't care) and to leave her criminal past behind. Marshall sees the Army as a sort of organized alternative to marriage, while Rios doesn't give a reason for enlisting; the film presumably relies on stereotypes of Latina toughness as sufficient explanation.[3] The group members thus have different levels and types of motivations for enlisting, but all seem first and foremost to want to improve their economic situation. Such an acknowledgment of the economics of women's military service is rare. The later *Lone Star* (1996), a film which foregrounds questions of race, ethnicity, and identity, is also rare in making this explicit in a scene in which Pvt. Athena Johnson (Chandra Wilson), an African American, expresses a resigned view of military service within the racial hierarchies of American society, describing it as "one of the best deals they offer."

The failing recruit is a stock character of boot camp narratives; this is usually a man who aspires to but cannot achieve the military masculinity embodied by the hero. Sometimes he will be guided by the tough but caring hands of others (as in *To the Shores of Tripoli* and *The Sands of*

Iwo Jima [1949]); sometimes he implodes (as in *Full Metal Jacket* [1987]) or is killed in combat. *She's in the Army Now* adapts these conventions, mapping the transformation of its female recruits to an appropriate military masculinity. In her role as demanding drill sergeant, Reed pushes the recruits hard, urging them to outperform their male peers; ultimately the resentful group will come to respect her and to regard the military as more than a route to economic opportunity. In this narrative of transformation those who are already tough learn discipline and teamwork, while those who are "soft" are challenged to masculinize. Thus Jennings's abilities as a driver and markswoman are channeled to military (rather than criminal) ends, and Donner learns to lead. On becoming squad leader she vows to employ the principles of group therapy in her command, a "soft" strategy that is destined to fail. Equally the fragile Marshall (deemed "soft material" by Reed) will break rather than toughen in the regime of boot camp. Significantly in terms of the contemporary iconography of the military woman, Marshall's inability to adapt to military life is signified by a marker of her femininity: her long hair. Perpetually falling down, Marshall's hair creates "an unmilitary appearance" which the closely cropped Reed instructs her to keep up or cut off. When the whole platoon is punished for Marshall's shortcomings, a group of recruits pin her down and cut off her hair in a brutal enforcement of group will. Unable to cope with the assault Marshall breaks down, attempting to take her own life in a sequence which sees her smear makeup over her face in a clownish parody of femininity. Her uncontained commitment to femininity effectively renders her incompatible with military life, an incompatibility dramatized in unforgiving fashion.[4]

The specificity of the women's experience in a predominantly male military is evident in interactions between male and female recruits. The sexual freedom and assertiveness of the female recruits signals their modernity (and heterosexuality); their reliance on each other is a sign of their emerging military identity. Knoll's position as a mother is also significant here, particularly if we recall that military women's motherhood (or potential motherhood) is so routinely cast as a "problem" in media coverage. Toward the end of basic training Knoll hears that her ex-husband has charged her with abandonment and is suing for custody of their daughter. Putting at risk their chances of graduating, the squad steal a vehicle and head to Knoll's hometown to settle the matter. Though they land in jail, a compromise is ultimately reached, with Knoll seeking to set at rest her ex-husband's fears about her newfound mobility, reassuring him of his rights as a father. This image of the mobilized mother prefigures what in the 1990s would be a staple of media coverage of military women whose deployment troubles normative conceptions of the family.

While military narratives, and perhaps particularly those concerned with basic training, do not present individuals in context (they are stripped of the signifiers of individuality associated with the outside world), differences of class, ethnicity, and race remain important. Donner may cite economic reasons for enlistment, but she is clearly differentiated from the rest of her squad in class terms and must learn to work with and lead others. In contrast to the comically sexualized white officers represented by Captain Lewis in *Private Benjamin* or *M*A*S*H*'s Major Houlihan, Sergeant Reed, an African American, is portrayed as a tough but ultimately fair leader; her relationship with the squad develops into one of mutual respect rather than hostility. Reed's expectations and ambitions are high (her actions push Marshall over the edge), but she also covers for the squad, demonstrating flexibility and solidarity. She serves as a variant of the tough black authority figure, a recognizable type from film and television since the 1970s. Indeed the following year Lou Gossett Jr. would win an Academy Award and a Golden Globe for his supporting role as Emil Foley in *An Officer and a Gentleman* (1982), taunting and challenging Zack Mayo (Richard Gere) into shape.[5] Robyn Wiegman reads the recurrent comparable trope of the black male cop as "establishing masculinity as the necessary force for the protection of U.S. culture and containing, in the process, the spectre of open black rebellion."[6] Since the 1980s the ethnic diversity of the U.S. military has been more obvious in military narratives. Yet black and Latina characters tend to be cast in stock or marginal roles which trade off stereotypical associations with toughness and violence. They have only limited access to the kinds of transformation narrative enacted by white military women and rarely appear in central roles.

The very prominence of African American servicewomen in the documentary *Soldier Girls* underlines their absence from (or marginality within) the majority of fictional narratives. In contrast to popular fictions, the film's vérité style doesn't foster a confessional mode or suggest the need to explain military women: we don't get commentaries on why the women of Charlie Company have enlisted. Although no mediating voice-over is offered, the film purposefully undercuts the glamour of re-

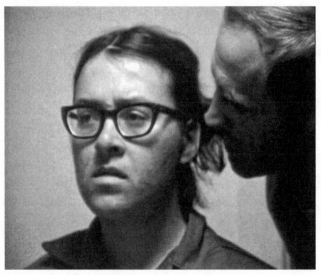

44. Private Alves is disciplined in the documentary *Soldier Girls* (1981).

cruitment images and boot camp scenarios. Instead of the usual emphasis on teamwork and personal transformation, the film foregrounds the
tedium of chores, sore feet, confused recruits, abusive sergeants, and the
necessary repression of emotion. In one notorious scene a survival instructor bites off a chicken's head and hurls the still mobile body toward
the recruits. More shocking in many ways is a scene in which recruits are
assured that, in the event of a nuclear accident or attack, they can simply
brush off radioactive dust or perhaps use water from their canteens. The
indifference toward the life and health of these recruits speaks volumes
of the value placed on their lives. One private sums up her disillusion and
exhaustion when she describes herself as "sick and tired." Two recruits,
Alves and Johnson, are shown being repeatedly disciplined. In one scene
Alves is surrounded by taunting figures who question her motivation, her
intelligence, and her sanity. (One suggests she should not have children;
figure 44.) Later Johnson will leave basic training; stepping outside her
place as subject of the film, she embraces the filmmaker, who has observed her throughout the grueling process.

Like the fictional films of the period, *Soldier Girls* inevitably opens up
the question of combat roles for female personnel; the year of the film's
release had seen heated congressional debate on whether women as well
as men should be registered should the draft be reintroduced. The film includes the women singing cadences of war: "I want to go to Iran. I want to

kill an Iranian." The recruits go through a simulated gas attack, suggesting that they are being prepared for combat. Yet toward the end of the film Abing, the drill instructor whose verbal violence is such a prominent feature of the film, expresses his fears that female soldiers might be placed in danger. He tells the filmmakers that he "never wants to see them in combat," adding, "There's no such thing as a safe line." As the film draws to a close Abing speaks with barely suppressed emotion of how much Army life takes away, how little remains to expend on family life (for which women conventionally are a sign). His words hint at the cost of militarized masculinity in a manner which the indifferent treatment of the recruits confirms rather than qualifies. The vérité style reveals aspects of the military as institution: its processes and procedures, its often brutal shaping of individuals. The kind of explanatory coherence offered in narratives such as *She's in the Army Now* and earlier versions of the female-oriented training camp film are absent from *Soldier Girls*. These young women may be seeking to improve themselves, but the film emphasizes their subordination and the restriction of their individual expression rather than the military as a site of aspiration, the "Be all that you can be" of the contemporary recruitment campaigns. Rather the film suggests the exploitation of those who have few options outside the military.

Popular fictions are intriguing markers of a cultural moment largely because of the work they do to craft stories out of the contradictions of lived experience. The fictional military woman is sketched in very different terms from the women seen in a documentary like *Soldier Girls*. Fictional military women have usually made an active choice to serve, and they are typically high-achieving individuals. Combat is presented not as labor undertaken by individuals without other employment options, but as an opportunity to which both women and men aspire. In the context of debates concerning military women it is the physical abilities of recruits as well as their suitability for military life that are explicitly being tested and developed in boot camp narratives. Over a decade after *Soldier Girls* and *She's in the Army Now*, the high-profile feature film *G.I. Jane* (1997) used the boot camp setting to frame a drama centered on an exceptional woman's performance of military masculinity, staging debates concerning women's suitability for a combat role. The action revolves around the central protagonist, Jordan O'Neil, as a test case for an integrated Navy. As Lauren Tucker and Alan Fried note, the film's American release coincided with the extensive coverage given to the admission policies and violent initiation rituals associated with VMI and the Citadel.[7] The film is clearly informed by the contemporary discourses and debates outlined in chapter 6: male soldiers express disgust at women's bodies; questions about the impact of woman's presence on military men are centralized; and anxieties about military women as victims in a combat context are voiced. A senator posits public anxiety about female bodies as a reason for restricting women's combat roles, proclaiming, "No politician can afford to let women come home in body bags." Male soldiers make comparable claims; speaking of O'Neil, Master Chief Urgayle (Viggo Mortensen) insists, "Her presence makes us *all* vulnerable."

Of all the boot camp narratives discussed in this book, only *G.I. Jane* features a military woman taking part in officially sanctioned combat. It is entirely consistent with the (improbable) logic of the film that the newly trained SEAL unit should happen to be on hand when their presence is needed to recover sensitive equipment from a plane that crashed in Libya, and that O'Neil should be included in the group. This scenario enacts a version of the accidental combatant plot which structures *Courage under Fire* and other films featuring military women who are drawn into combat. O'Neil's acceptance by her male peers is developed throughout the narrative, culminating in her bravery in saving Urgayle and his recognition of her as a comrade. The role of military women is explicitly discussed when McCool (Morris Chestnut), an African American, compares the bar on women in combat to the racial exclusions of the past. The film's dialogue quite openly argues for the place of exceptional (that is, in effect, masculine) women in combat, even as that case is repeatedly undercut by the intense hostility that O'Neil faces and by the film's invocation of the testing process.

O'Neil is isolated in a way quite different from the women of *She's in the Army Now* and the other boot camp narratives considered thus far, as she is the only woman to undergo the Combat Readiness Training Program and is thus quite literally exceptional. This very exceptionality renders her embodiment of gendered difference explicit and limits opportunities for female bonding and comradeship of the kind so characteristic of the female-oriented boot camp film of earlier decades. The brief scenes in which military women do connect with each other are typically viewed from a hostile, patriarchal perspective, most overtly when long-range photographs taken of a beach party cast suspicion on any kind of physical intimacy between servicewomen. *G.I. Jane* visualizes military women as professionally isolated. An early scene at the Naval Intelligence Center establishes both O'Neil's intuitive understanding of operational matters and her sense of professional frustration: she is the only woman on view in this sequence. There are a few precedents for this sort of isolation; for example, in the television movie *For Love and Honor* (NBC, 1983) Cpl. Grave Pavlik (Rachel Ticotin) is the sole woman assigned to the 88th Airborne Division.[8] Like O'Neil, Pavlik comes in for hostility from male peers and officers, although she finds support from a few of the more sympathetic male soldiers. A brief scene of the warmth and comradeship offered by her fellow female soldiers is in marked contrast to her isolation and vulnerability in the all-male barracks.

The key element shared by these two narratives is that a woman seeks entrance to an elite, previously all-male unit. Such intrusion into spaces commonly regarded as the sole preserve of what Enloe terms "masculinity-seeking men" represents a particularly acute challenge to gender hierarchy.[9] *For Love and Honor* moves toward narrative resolution with the formation of a core group that includes Pavlik; her drunken participation in a bar fight signals her inclusion in the masculine codes of the group. *G.I. Jane* also, albeit briefly, locates its military woman in the homosocial space of the bar, when her crew members finally invite her for a drink. O'Neil's exceptionality is additionally marked by her physicality, the spectacular transformation of Moore's body providing a way, as Linda Ruth Williams notes, for the film to work through its concerns regarding military women. Williams writes that O'Neil "wages and wins" a battle "first with her own body and second with fellow countrymen of a different gender over the issue of her body," a process in which "the spectre of feminine physical unreliability [is] pitched against the certainty of muscular prowess."[10] The transformation of O'Neil in *G.I. Jane* is both physical—she works out to overcome her body's female qualities—but also gendered, expressed most succinctly in the sequence in which she shaves her own head in an effort to assimilate (figure 45).[11]

Hair would become a significant point of differentiation between male and female soldiers in an integrated military. The length and style of a female recruit's hair must neither be intrusively feminine nor suggest mannishness. *She's in the Army Now* uses Marshall's long hair as a sign of inappropriate femininity, while *G.I. Jane's* O'Neil shaves her head in her attempt to resist being differentiated from the group on the basis of her gender. In her autobiography Nancy Mace describes her induction into

45. In *G.I. Jane* (1997) O'Neil (Demi Moore) shaves her head in an effort to figure military masculinity.

the masculinist and militaristic traditions of The Citadel in 1996 in the glare of media attention: "Nothing since my arrival had excited as much interest as the women's haircuts." During the summer Mace had served as the model, through computer imaging, for college authorities to arrive at a standard female haircut. The terms in which she describes her preparation for the experience are indicative of the overdetermined character of the moment:

> I tried to imagine how it would feel when my long hair fell to the ground, and reassured myself countless times that I was ready to be transformed into a "knob," the word used to describe the hairless state of Citadel freshmen. . . . I knew how traumatic the haircut was for male freshmen, and I wanted to experience the same sense of shock they did when watching their hair fall to the floor. It seemed only fair. One thing I was certain of: I was not going to cry. I felt strong, pumped up for the ordeal that awaited me.[12]

Mace's aspiration to be included in an institution she valorizes, and which in the book she repeatedly associates with her father (also a graduate of the college), strongly suggests the appeal of military masculinity. The perceived need to suppress emotion (and the reference to being physically "pumped up") in relation to a public ritual of transformation is part of Mace's thoroughgoing endorsement of military masculinity as positive and character-building. Yet the adoption of a female hairstyle, which fell short of the shaved heads of male cadets, signals the partial transformation of a female cadet's appearance. Her difference is evident in the need for computer modeling and trials and in the care and thought put into the process.

Enloe writes of the opening up of the military academies some twenty years before, "Figuring out exactly which hat, which jacket, and which bra a woman should be officially issued as she entered into a masculinized, militarized enclave of the state was thought necessary if that woman's entry was to sustain a militarized version of national security, not subvert it."[13] Drawing on Barkalow's *In the Men's House*, Marjorie Garber characterizes the response to the arrival of women at West Point as "institutional gender paranoia."[14] Both students and academy authorities are radically uncertain in the face of the potential erasure of gendered difference implied by women's entry to these elite spaces. The folklorist Carol Burke succinctly summarizes what is at stake here: "If head-shaving is essential in making the transition from civilian to soldier, then women should be subject to it."[15] In *G.I. Jane* O'Neil rejects dual standards, instead wearing standard-issue clothes and moving into the male barracks. She stakes her claim for inclusion in the elite force on the basis of exceptional achievement. Her provocative presence challenges male hierarchies by embracing militarized masculinity.

AN ACCIDENTAL COMBATANT: *COURAGE UNDER FIRE*

Courage under Fire investigates the events leading to the death of a medevac pilot, Capt. Karen Walden (Meg Ryan), during the Gulf War. Inadvertently drawn into combat, Walden ultimately emerges as a heroic military woman fully deserving the Medal of Honor which is posthumously awarded in the film's closing scenes. A high-profile film featuring A-list stars in Ryan and Denzel Washington, *Courage under Fire* suggests a rather different characterization of the military woman from that found in *G.I. Jane*. Nonetheless the extent to which a woman can effectively perform in combat—and enact the military masculinity combat requires in the movies—remains a significant theme. Indeed the narrative itself is shaped as an investigation into Walden's qualities as a soldier. The audience learns of her story through Col. Nat Serling's (Washington) investigation of her death to establish whether or not she merits such a distinguished medal. The investigation culminates in his discovery of mutiny by male soldiers who doubted the capability of their female officer. Having shot Walden, Monfriez (Lou Diamond Phillips) reports her dead rather than wounded, leaving her to be engulfed in the flames of an airstrike in

46. Though *Courage under Fire* (1995) offers conflicting versions of events, ultimately Walden (Meg Ryan) is presented as heroic in combat.

an attempt to cover his actions. Alongside this betrayal the film follows Serling's attempts to come to terms with his own failure in combat; in the opening scene his mistaken order results in the death of a close friend under his command.

Courage under Fire simultaneously celebrates the military woman in combat and questions the efficacy of this problematic presence, in the process drawing on and elaborating arguments familiar from popular news media: Walden's bravery is on display and is openly celebrated; the fact that her men fail to respect her command during crucial moments of danger under enemy fire rehearses familiar debates on the effect of military women on military men as well as evoking scandal as a context for telling military women's stories; the question of whether Walden was courageous or cowardly evokes wider debates on military women's suitability for combat; testimony is given, although as Susan Linville notes, Walden does not speak for herself;[16] finally, the evocation of Walden as (single) mother and soldier speaks to contemporary images of military women managing professional and familial responsibilities (figure 46). *Courage under Fire* acknowledges the intensely mediated character of U.S. military involvement in the Persian Gulf, insistently juxtaposing television images with the physical, material experience of war. Media coverage of military actions have a double significance in relation to military women, whose exploits, achievements, and failures are subject to extensive commentary by both journalists and politicians. An opposition between male soldiers and female soldiers is thus framed by the wider generic discourses of the war movie, discourses in which soldiers' stories are valorized even when particular conflicts are questioned. Military comradeship is contrasted to Washington's intrigues. My analysis expands on the diverse ways in which *Courage under Fire* works with these media tropes in order to center a military woman as an accidental combatant.

The film's defining formal feature is that Walden's story is told through a series of contrasting flashbacks so that the celebration of her bravery is juxtaposed with doubts as to its veracity. Because the film offers multiple versions of its heroine her image and legacy is a mediated and contested one. In one elegiac sequence, for instance, Serling contemplates a photograph of Walden. He imagines her singing softly, her crew silent in the tent around her; from this we segue to images of Walden with her daughter, which emphasize and even merge her identities as soldier and mother. Her image functions here as a moral anchor, signifying the good soldier whose toughness helps her overcome the odds in training, if not in combat. The film follows Serling's growing admiration and empathy for Walden, a recognition which represents (posthumous) inclusion and comradeship. A later sequence features idealized images of Walden graduating, a picture of ritual celebration introduced and overlaid by the taped words of one of the crew who, we later learn, betrayed her, speaking of her courage and decisiveness: "She never let her guard down, show any sign of weakness. But she was tough. She could handle it" (figure 47). Tough, a soldier, a good mother: Walden's records describe her as an "officer of exceptional moral courage." The exceptional woman's ability to achieve extraordinary things despite male hostility represents another sort of test, a process though which she must prove herself capable and worthy.

Both *Courage under Fire* and *G.I. Jane* end with an indicative contrast between a public ceremony in which gallantry is rewarded and a private one in which a courageous man passes his own medal to a woman who has proved herself in combat. Serling places a medal on Walden's grave; O'Neil finds in her locker a medal tucked into a volume of D. H. Lawrence's poems, a discovery followed by a silent exchange of looks between her and her erstwhile tormentor Urgayle. These ceremonies are moments of recognition and incorporation, testament that while official recognition has its place, it is just as if not more important to be recognized by one's peers. Thus although Urgayle is O'Neil's commanding officer, his

47. In *Courage under Fire* (1995) idealized images of Walden (Meg Ryan) graduating accompany a colleague's evocation of her as an exemplary military woman.

gesture of approval is distinguished from the machinations of politicians. And while the public recognition of her heroism is pictured as something of a superficial public relations opportunity, for Serling Walden is primarily a soldier to whom he wishes to do justice. Thus the film raises and attempts to set aside the cultural common sense of the female soldier as an anomaly or contradiction in terms. By constructing its narrative around an exploration of whether a tough military woman should be awarded the Medal of Honor, *Courage under Fire* repudiates the feminizing and superficial world of media and public relations and incorporates (albeit posthumously) a female soldier into the community of military honor.

Both *Courage under Fire* and *G.I. Jane* ostensibly argue for women to be included in the sentimental but also brutalizing brotherhood of the military while effectively reproducing the discursive terms in which that inclusion was so commonly questioned in the 1990s: their disruptive effect on military men and their unreliable, penetrable bodies. Thus both films feature key scenes in which male soldiers *disobey* their female officer's orders in a combat situation (whether actual or simulated). Monfriez's mutiny leads to Walden's death in *Courage under Fire*, while in *G.I. Jane* a soldier marked early on as putting himself above others gets the whole team captured during a training mission by ignoring O'Neil's orders. In *Courage under Fire* Monfriez screams at a recruit, "You never leave a man behind!" In leaving a *female* soldier behind, he simultaneously has and has not broken his own rule. In this way the films rehearse two of the standard arguments against involving women in combat situations: military women lack the right stuff, and military men will not take orders from women. These themes are relentlessly debated in media coverage, with longtime opponents of expanded roles for military women such as Elaine Donnelly suggesting that political correctness has compromised the nation's readiness. Indeed *Courage under Fire*'s artful structure allows it to condemn Monfriez's neurotic (and racially othered) masculinity while ultimately avoiding taking sides on a contentious issue. Instead argument is rehearsed and resolved through a discursive masculinity that renders Walden tough enough, just as O'Neil proves herself by triumphing over and then rescuing her commanding officer.

Consistent with a media emphasis on debate and questioning, *Courage under Fire* maps the acquisition of Walden's masculine and martial status by naming and questioning the plausibility of her heroism. Thus she is variously described as "a soldier," as "tough," as "afraid," a "wreck," a "fucking coward," and a "real good mom." This is also, inevitably, a sort of testing of Meg Ryan as a performer (Can she carry a dramatic role?) just as *G.I. Jane* was widely discussed in terms of Demi Moore's physical transformation and commitment to her performance as an aspiring Navy SEAL (her shorn head and developed muscles). It might seem that these questions pull each film in different directions. Yet the "ordinariness" so central to Ryan's persona actually secures the generic heroism she performs. The evolution of media interest in Jessica Lynch comes to mind here, the insistence on her ordinariness and her bravery when inadvertently caught up in combat, and her subsequent portrayal as a victim but still an emblematic ordinary "girl."

In both media coverage and film and television fictions the military woman is cast as simultaneously ordinary and extraordinary. Films and television shows tend to register that sense of the extraordinary by emphasizing high-achieving women. Their ordinariness is most often secured through motherhood. Of course many action movies cast strong female protagonists as iconic mothers. Indeed Williams writes that *Courage under Fire* "smoothes over the apparent contradiction of the maternal and the military with a montage of [Walden's] mothering skills, as she multitasks press-ups practice and child care simultaneously." And in her analysis of *G.I. Jane* as star vehicle, Williams speaks too of a "shadow of maternity cast by Moore's presence."[17]

Like Snapshot McCall's death in the war romance *Homecoming*, Walden's death leaves behind an orphaned child, reiterating the loss involved in combat casualties in terms of woman's role as mother. In the public ceremony at the White House the Medal of Honor is bestowed on Walden's young daughter; like Snapshot's son she will now be raised by her grandparents. This imagery chimes with the widespread media attention given to military parents in general, and military mothers in particular, during and since the Gulf War.[18] We've already seen how the specter of pregnant servicewomen has figured prominently in media coverage; a pregnant female body is read as unmilitary, unstable, and disturbing. Jeanne Holm notes that the coverage of military mothers serving in the Gulf became such a common feature of contemporary media that it was dubbed the "Mommy War."[19] "A Mother's Duty" was the cover story of *People* magazine on 9 October 1990; such images were not unprecedented, yet their visibility was distinctive. Military mothers make good copy, and they continue to form a media staple. A Christmas report for NBC (25 December 2002) focused on a veteran reservist serving in Afghanistan, cutting between footage of her (she carries a rifle at all times, we are told) and her husband, "now dad and mom" to their young son back home. She explains that in serving her country she is serving her son, thus mobilizing militarized motherhood in a patriotic, seasonal piece. The pilot episode of the television drama *Over There* also visualizes military motherhood in its opening sequence as Doublewide bids goodbye to her toddler son: "I'll be back—sometime next year." Later we see her husband and son watching a web video she sends home. As much as anything it is motherhood that underlines Walden's ordinariness in *Courage under Fire*. While centrally concerned with power and status, in the film becoming a soldier is insistently about remaining female.

Controversies over combat, and consequently the extent and character of women's military service, have played a significant part in shaping the media coverage of military women since the 1980s. In turn the tropes insistently reiterated in that coverage are evident in the film and television fictions that feature, or in some instances center on, military women. Boot camp narratives test them and situate military woman as part of a team. Films such as *G.I. Jane* and *Courage under Fire* celebrate the heroism of exemplary military women, foregrounding their gender ambiguity in the process, suggesting perhaps that an exemplary soldier cannot be an exemplary woman. Displacing feminist-informed concerns around equality in women's working lives, these fictions frequently foreground the scandalous difference of the female body, most frequently in tropes of pregnancy and motherhood. Sexual scandal frames the final chapter of this book, which looks at how film and television fictions of the past twenty years have cast military women as the subject of investigation and, conversely, as both avenging and investigative figures.

The narratives considered in this final chapter have been shaped by a variety of sexual scandals, from Tailhook to allegations of systematic sexual abuse at U.S. military academies and service-women's reports of sexual harassment and assault while on active duty. As with debates over women's combat capability, fictional accounts of military women are necessarily related to wider media coverage. As the American military, politicians, and news media attempted to come to terms with the implications of gender integration, how have popular fictions responded to the widespread imagery of and debate about military women? I explore two genres in which military women have figured in the past two decades. The first of these is the rape-revenge narrative, a feminist-informed derivative of the thriller and horror genres, which stages a woman's sexual victimization and subsequent revenge. The second consists of genres of crime and investigation; a number of films and television dramas portray military women as investigators, often, although not always, as military police-women, a strategy which capitalizes on the established figure—in television at least—of the tough female investigator. Since the rape or murder of military women features prominently in the crimes investigated in these fictions there is an element of overlap between the two. Both sets of fictions also share the figuration of military women as exceptional but isolated. Such isolation is fundamental to rape-revenge narratives. An outsider status is also exploited when the military woman is cast as an investigator; the cop or private eye has license, albeit limited, to question the powerful. Although part of the military, investigators can address themselves to all ranks; their position entitles them to ask inappropriate questions, to quiz their superiors, to suspect dishonesty rather than honor, and to use devious means to achieve their (legitimate) ends.

The association of military women with hostile environments and sexual assault echoes the wider media presentation of the American, and to a lesser extent the British, military. Media discussions of the limits placed on military women's combat role—and the challenges mounted to those limits—often lead to or become entwined with sexual scandal. The American films and television shows considered here are contextualized by a heightened media interest in the sexuality of servicewomen, made manifest in debates concerning lesbians and gays in the U.S. military, the scrutiny of a masculinist military culture of sexual harassment, and a variety of high-profile cases involving charges of adultery or misconduct against military women. Sexual aggression has been framed within these political, legal, and cultural discourses as an inherent part of military culture. Such a perspective is clearly articulated in a show like *JAG*, which I've argued seeks to distinguish masculine military playfulness from extremes of misogyny. It underpins a case in 1982 to which Susan Jeffords refers, that of a female Army reservist raped while confined to barracks, and the subsequent rejection of her claim for damages since the rape was "incident to service."[1] More recently news stories concerning high levels of rape and sexual harassment of military women on active duty have repeatedly foregrounded these women's isolation. In an op-ed piece for the *New York Times* in 2008 Helen Benedict wrote, "The Department of Veterans Affairs faces a pressing crisis: women traumatized not only by combat but also by sexual assault and harassment from their fellow services members."[2]

Although military women are frequently presented as women in peril and as needing protection from their male peers, military masculinity is nonetheless typically valorized in the narratives considered here. As Carol Burke notes, the publicity in 2003 relating to reports of sexual assaults at the Air Force Academy were "met with calls for gender segregation from conservatives, many of whom hold that women shouldn't be at the academy in the first place."[3] Indeed the fictions explored here both condemn the misogyny of military masculinities and reinforce widely circulating discourses of the military woman's problematic or even inappropriate presence. Her difference troubles the uniformity of homosocial space, and she is in turn blamed and punished for that effect. It is not coincidental, then, that two recurrent themes developed in this chapter have to do with the gender identity of the military woman. On the one hand she is associated with sex; she embodies a sexuality with the potential to disrupt established masculine hierarchies. On the other she is associated with androgyny and gender confusion; as tough and ambitious, "one of the boys," the fictional military woman can function as a soldier to the extent that she is not a woman.

RAPE AND SEXUAL VIOLENCE: THE MILITARY WOMAN AS VICTIM AND AVENGER

Images of rape or sexual threat in recent military dramas draw on well-established narrative patterns (across a number of genres) which cast a raped woman in the role of avenger. The contradictory victim-warrior status of the avenging woman in popular movies such as *Kill Bill* (2003) resonates with the typical characterization of the military woman as skilled and violent yet perpetually under threat from those around her.[4] In such narratives rape validates and explains female violence. The military woman who is raped by her fellow soldiers is portrayed as betrayed by a masculine culture in which she had sought inclusion. Rape reveals a deep-seated hostility toward women on the part of military men in these fictions, while attempts to cover it up—or even legitimize it—speak to the wider misogyny of these institutions.

In repeatedly linking military women's experiences of abuse to a desire for advancement, military rape narratives draw on a postfeminist rhetoric that assumes equality is achieved but presents professional achievement as unfulfilling and inappropriate for women. Sarah Projansky argues that rape emerges in films depicting "independent women . . . interested in masculine careers" as "a mark of women's essentialized bodily gender difference that must be overcome before they can succeed in this masculine world."[5] Thus in military rape narratives women are raped (or threatened with rape) when they are too successful; this is the case, albeit in different ways, in *The General's Daughter* (1999), *G.I. Jane* (1997), *Opposing Force* (1986), and *Rough Treatment* (2000).[6] All four involve military women making claims to roles and opportunities associated with military men and masculinity. All take place against the backdrop of training narratives, with women seeking entry into previously all-male or predominantly male terrain. In *The General's Daughter* Elizabeth Campbell is raped while a cadet at West Point. The simulated rape of O'Neil in *G.I. Jane* is contextualized by her outsider position as the first woman to enter Navy SEAL training. Lieutenant Casey in *Opposing Force* is also the first woman to take "the toughest escape and evasion course in the military." In the British television drama *Rough Treatment* Eve Turner (Daniela Nardini) is one of only two women in the 23rd All Arms Command course. In these contexts, rape or the threat of rape serves to discipline and punish military women. As Projansky succinctly puts it, "The feminist argument that male exclusivity encourages rape becomes a *new postfeminist logic* that women's pursuit of independence and equality leads to rape."[7] Female excellence, we come to understand, is in itself provocative.

Carol Clover, Sarah Projansky, and Jacinda Read all understand cinematic rape-revenge scenarios as informed by, and to some extent engaging with, feminist analyses of rape. Thus Clover notes that the revenge tradition which emerges in the 1970s articulates rape as a question of power rather than sex.[8] Projansky argues that at least some films in this cycle have the potential "to be understood as feminist narratives in which women face rape, recognize that the law will neither protect nor avenge them, and then take the law into their own hands."[9] The construction of rape as agency identified by Projansky is in sharp contrast to earlier representations. Consider, for example, the treatment of the rape of a young military nurse in the film *In Harm's Way* (1965), whose setting is the Second World War. Against the advice of an older, wiser nurse, Maggie (Patricia Neal), the newly engaged Annalee keeps a date with Commander Eddington (Kirk Douglas), who rapes her; traumatized and fearing she might be pregnant, Annalee subsequently commits suicide. The film constructs Annalee in contradictory terms as foolish, vulnerable, and yet provocative. Eddington comes to regret his action only when he discovers that Annalee had been engaged to the son of his friend and colleague Rock (John Wayne). Clearly Annalee has no value to Eddington (or indeed the film) other than her association with an honored mariner. In line with this logic the matter is also settled between men; Eddington undertakes a heroic suicidal mission, but Rock insists that there be no posthumous decoration, ensuring an unofficial retribution for Annalee. The raped (military) woman is thus discreetly mourned and avenged, but she herself has no agency within the narrative.

The experience of domestic or sexual violence works to legitimate and contextualize female violence and agency in numerous popular narratives. Indeed Clover argues that "female self-sufficiency, both physical and mental," characterizes the rape-revenge genre.[10] While Clover reads the avenging woman in terms of "masculinization," Read suggests that "the avenging woman is frequently eroticized rather than masculinized."[11] The potential fluidity of the raped and avenging woman's gender identity is resonant for a consideration of the military woman, a figure understood as troubling gender hierarchies. Her avenging violence is framed by her status as a soldier, the very status that generates male resentment and hostility. Significantly, then, both *Opposing Force* and *G.I. Jane* feature military women responding to rape or the threat of rape in a manner that tests and valorizes their combat-ready status. O'Neil's defiance and ability to fight back in *G.I. Jane* demonstrate her courage and endurance, effectively ensuring her integration into the male group. By contrast, both *Rough Treatment* and *The General's Daughter* depict raped and vengeful military women as either excluded from or actively seeking to undermine the military. Despite the specificity of the military woman as a figure associated with legitimate violence, Projansky's description of a cross-generic trend appearing after 1980 and depicting "rape transforming a woman into an active, independent agent—allowing a woman to take control and not play the victim" retains relevance for the fictions considered here.[12] Military rape narratives construct military women as already "active, independent agents," yet their capacity for action is repeatedly limited.

It is not the case that the movement of military women from supporting roles to protagonists does away with the figure of retributive men who avenge rape (the role undertaken by Rock, John Wayne's character in *In Harm's Way*). Men continue to play an important role in the films considered here: some testify to the validity of women's complaints, witnessing the violence and indignity of rape; some honor their female colleagues, including them in an elite group; some investigate the (mis)treatment of military women, standing up for them against the misogynous military men from whom they are, in the process, distinguished. For Jeffords the narrative structure, point of view, and editing of *Opposing Force*— editing that aligns the spectator with the suffering male witness to rape rather than the military woman who is raped—work to other and reject the bad masculinity of the military man as rapist, retaining and valuing the military masculinity of the good men who object, investigate, and defend. Writing in the context of the Persian Gulf War and the high-profile images of American military women associated with that conflict, Jeffords discusses *Opposing Force* as a military rape narrative that stages *male* outrage in a way that allows "the film to avoid any recognition of the systematic mistreatment of women in the military." In this way, rape "becomes an occasion for the reform and reproduction of masculinity."[13] Comparable structures are at work in several of the examples considered here, suggesting that representations of military women and concerns about the masculinity of military men are intimately linked.

Opposing Force centers on a simulated POW camp which forms part of an Air Force training program; Lieutenant Casey (Lisa Eichhorn) is the sole woman on this tough escape-and-evasion course. The film's roots lie as much in exploitation as in military drama, and its promotion foregrounds themes of violation and abuse alongside the promise of action.[14] In line with the combat controversy narratives explored in chapter 7, and indeed wider media attention to the role and function of military women, Casey's motivation for undertaking the training becomes subject to scrutiny. Even if she succeeds on the course, we are informed, she will not secure a posting since the unit has a combat function. Casey responds to this paradox in the aspirational terms of the exceptional woman: fully expecting the situation to change, she wants to be trained and prepared for a new role. From the beginning she faces male scrutiny and hostility. Abandoned by her partner as soon as they land, she teams up with the older, injured Logan (Tom Skerritt), a decorated Vietnam veteran seeking to requalify for flight duty. Both are outsiders, a connection expressed by Casey in crude physical terms: "You've got a limp and I've got tits—these aren't great things to have in the military." Logan's damaged body and Casey's female body are thus equated by Casey herself, unproblematically replicating contemporary assumptions that women's bodies render them unsuited to certain aspects of military service.

Once captured, the "prisoners" are subjected to a program of physical and psychological torture by the increasingly erratic Becker. Becker isolates Casey from her male peers, exploiting and heightening their hostility toward her. He then rapes her, reasoning, as Jeffords puts it, that "this is the parallel to men's fears of humiliation, homosexuality, pain, and so on" and that "he must help her overcome any anxiety she might have about rape by desensitizing her to it."[15] Such perverse logic is not unrelated to wider discourses surrounding the dangers that women in frontline situations might face. As Jeffords notes, a preoccupation with the rape of military women by enemy forces is by no means new. In having Becker rape Casey as part of her training, *Opposing Force* simultaneously echoes these arguments and prefigures the increasingly public accusations of rape and sexual harassment of military women that preoccupied media coverage in the early 1990s and has remained in the news. Not one of the films considered here shows military women raped by a national enemy; instead they are raped, or rape is threatened, by their own forces. The metaphorical language of the "sex war" in this way displaces the rape by an ethnic or national other so routinely invoked as a reason to keep women out of combat.

G.I. Jane replicates the scenario played out in *Opposing Force*, although in different terms. During a comparable exercise designed to simulate capture and torture, Urgayle threatens to rape O'Neil, forcing her over a table and cutting her belt with his knife. In contrast to Becker, who wishes to educate Casey privately in the experience of rape as torture, Urgayle chooses to stage his assault publicly for the benefit of the captured men; O'Neil's fight back (culminating in her scornful, bloodied challenge "Suck my dick!") seems equally staged for her male peers. Both Casey and O'Neil seek to bargain their status as exceptional women into opportunity and acceptance. A decade apart, both films seek to manage cultural assumptions that ambitious women erase sexual difference. In *Opposing Force* Becker insists on the difference of the military woman, using rape as a marker of her specificity. Thus although Casey is told to expect no "special treatment," Becker explicitly tells her that her gender makes this an impossibility: "You're not like anyone else here—you're different."

If in *G.I. Jane* the threat or simulation of rape completes the formation of a group identity, Casey's rape in *Opposing Force* triggers the rejection of the terms of the exercise by Logan's good soldier. As Jeffords argues, Logan's response to the rape of a military woman tells us that Becker is not typical of military men. Just as significant, his anger facilitates Casey's adoption of an aggressive military masculinity, inscribing the exceptional woman as soldier: "By taking Casey's voice here, Logan permits Casey to become more soldierly, more 'masculine.'"[16] During their escape Casey engages in combat, finishing off the villainous Becker. The film ends in slow motion and then a freeze-frame, fixing the image of Casey as avenger, her face fixed and determined as she points her weapon toward the camera. The moment exploits and juxtaposes two popular cultural images of violent women: as soldier and as one who seeks revenge for a sexual assault. While the scenes of Casey in combat suggest her readiness for full inclusion in the military, her final remarks continue to emphasize that she is an outsider with an uncertain future.

Many of the themes evident in these two American films are also present in the British television drama *Rough Treatment*. Although the national contexts are distinct, in *Rough Treatment* the military woman also functions as a sign of self-determining female identity and as a challenge to male privilege. Salacious scandals of adultery had also made headlines in the popular press in the U.K., and investigative journalism had criticized a military culture characterized by bullying and sexual harassment. (A lead story in the *Independent on Sunday* in 2005 suggested that half of RAF women had experienced sexual harassment, for instance.)[17] *Rough Treatment* features a prickly, competitive, and often unappealing female protagonist in Eve Turner (Daniela Nardini).[18] As the frequent shots of her running suggest, she is a self-made woman, who has learned to discipline her body in order to achieve her goals. Turner works in Army Intelligence and is one of only two women to take part in the 23rd All Arms Command course. Her success on the course attracts the particular ire of Andy Parkhurst (Gregor Trutter), who openly objects to Turner's presence as a woman. His outspoken protest ("Bloody ridiculous—women officers. Playing at it") invokes a familiar question: Why prepare military women for leadership functions relating to ground combat when they will not be deployed in these roles?[19] Various answers have been offered to that question (defensive training, the difficulty of distinguishing combat and noncombat arenas and roles, the significance of women's role in peacekeeping duties, the importance of women in a volunteer military), and yet such fundamentally gendered assumptions relating to women's secondary status remain firmly in place; here they also crucially inform Turner's construction as rapable. Parkhurst's response to the shooting exercise, in which Turner outperforms him, is to sneer, "You'll only ever be a pretend soldier"; however accomplished, as a woman she cannot ever "really" be a soldier. For Summerfield (Edward Atterton) the rape that he and Parkhurst subject Turner to is also play; she receives flowers from him the following day, the card inscribed with a careless message, "Thanks for being such a good sport." Clover's comments on the cinematic construction of (gang) rape as "a sporting competition, the point of which is to test and confirm an existing hierarchy" between men, are surely pertinent here.[20]

48. Eve Turner (Daniela Nardini) refuses to give ground in *Rough Treatment* (2000).

Projansky suggests that the analogy between rape and sport has become so familiar since the 1990s as to constitute a new stereotype.[21]

In the role of exceptional woman, Turner is a provocative presence par excellence: she is a crack shot, one of only three soldiers to evade capture during the exercises, and openly displays her pleasure in besting military men. Her provocative presence is contrasted to another female recruit's more pragmatic approach to a male-dominated environment: she has consensual sex with one of the men who will later rape Turner and shows no desire to compete with the men. She cautions Turner about her antagonistic behavior and expresses surprise at the latter's evident pleasure in "that cowboy stuff, leaping around with guns." Turner, however, is determined to assert herself; she resolutely and unapologetically inhabits public space, refusing to give ground during the exercise or in the scenes that lead up to her rape (figure 48). And since she is in no way willing to play a vulnerable role, she lacks credibility in the subsequent court case.

It is in this scenario of female success and male resentment that Turner is raped. Clearly *Rough Treatment* seeks to confront and reject the cultural commonplace of a provocative woman who "asks for it"; Turner's drunken celebration of her achievements, her loud rejection of Summerfield while they dance together, and her initiation of sex with another solider all work to set up her character as sexual, independent, and stubborn. Thus when Summerfield and Parkhurst drunkenly interrupt Turner and another officer, Fellowes, having sex in the sauna, she insists on the right to occupy any space she chooses. Fellowes, by contrast, gives ground, leaving Turner to the two men, who rape her in turn. Parkhurst's sexual violence is explicitly retributive; after sodomizing her he gloats, "She doesn't look so bloody pleased with herself now." Summerfield enacts a more casual misogyny, yet both characters clearly make assumptions concerning Turner's status as a sexually available and rapable (military) woman.

The multiple traumas Turner experiences from the rape, the lost court case, the subsequent death of her father, and a devastating accident initiate her transformation from exemplary military woman to violent civilian driven by revenge. The positive transformation narratives associated with boot camp are here effectively reversed such that mental and physical trauma wrest her from the military while unleashing her capacity for violence. She is constructed in the familiar generic terms of avenger, of her own rape and her father's death (it is implied that the ordeal of the court case is a factor in his sudden death). Her status as a (former) military woman now simply serves to equip her with skills in marksmanship and operations that she puts to effective use in her campaign. Ultimately, however, *Rough Treatment* pulls back from the violent conventions of the subgenre, suggesting in the process that militarized masculinity offers no straightforward resolution for women. In her pursuit of vengeance Turner risks being consumed by it. *Rough Treatment* not only shifts genres, from military rape narrative to revenge drama, but also calls into question the violence that underpins both. It seeks to problematize the fetishistic violence of rape-revenge narratives in favor of a more complex coming to terms with hurt and loss. Yet in the process the military woman is once more constructed as an unviable category, and Turner ultimately is reinscribed in the terms of domestic femininity.

A different kind of double narrative is at work in *The General's Daughter*, which revolves around the investigation of the title character's rape and murder. The spread-eagled, naked body of Capt. Elizabeth Campbell is discovered by a remote vehicle in an urban warfare training site; she has been strangled. Despite the appearance of the crime scene, it is subsequently discovered that Campbell was not raped at Fort Hadley but seven years before, while a cadet at West Point, a crime her father asked her to keep quiet. Though the film reveals that she has been fueled by a desire for revenge, Campbell is inscribed primarily as a victim (figure 49). Indeed *The General's Daughter* seems to suggest that military women are

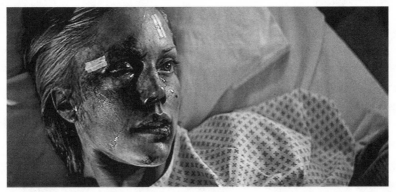

49. *The General's Daughter* (1999) centers on Elizabeth Campbell (Lesley Stefanson) as a vengeful victim of rape and of her military father's refusal to act on her behalf. The film pictures her in flashback, beaten, raped, and traumatized.

a marginal presence in need of the sort of paternalistic protection the general has failed to provide for his own daughter. Through a process of investigation and a series of flashbacks, Campbell emerges as a tormented and vengeful figure. The investigation of her past and private life produces a proliferating list of suspects and uncovers deep male hostility toward military women. One captain, who describes himself as an unwilling participant in the West Point rape ("I tried to save her, I did everything I could"), tells the investigators that his male peers "hated" Campbell: "They hated that she was smarter than them. They hated being out there with someone who had to squat to piss." Such visceral resentment at the intrusion of high-achieving women, expressed in terms of disgust with (and assault on) their bodies, is also indicative of the film's double strategy with respect to the portrayal of gender and military culture, its simultaneous endorsement and critique of military masculinity.

Adapted from a best-selling novel by Nelson DeMille first published in 1992, *The General's Daughter* exploits the currency of the topic of military women, yet suffuses that topic with an aura of sexual scandal, dwelling on the details of Campbell's sex life and graphically portraying her experience of rape. The film thus both expresses and disavows an aggressive hatred of women and their provocative and disruptive bodies. Two issues addressed by DeMille in his foreword to the novel contextualize the production of such a darkly ambivalent story from a historical moment characterized by the media celebration of the achievements of American military women.[22] First there is Tailhook, described by DeMille as "rocking the nation" at the time *The General's Daughter* was first published in the U.S. This confluence understandably led interviewers to link the two events, reading the novel of rape and revenge through the lens of Tailhook and a perception that military culture was systemically sexist. The writer's discomfort with this contextualization, and with the media's role in pressing the Navy for change in the fallout from Tailhook (which he describes as "an hysterical witch-hunt"), is evident. His concern about the media's elevation of military women (and denigration of military men) is given another, more personal dimension. The positive visibility of military women in the early 1990s is contrasted to media coverage of an earlier war: "Like most Vietnam veterans," he writes, "I was a little surprised and a lot annoyed at how the news media reported this war, as opposed to *my* war." DeMille's feelings of unjust treatment at the hands of the media are reflected by and projected onto contemporary military men: "Of course, many male soldiers, sailors and airmen felt a little left out, and certainly veterans of my generation felt totally disenfranchised and retroactively snubbed and unfairly portrayed." Holm too points to the resentment of military men at the laudatory focus of Gulf War media coverage on military women's achievements, suggesting the sort of coupling of female achievement and male resentment so typical of film and television fictions.[23]

The film reiterates this double discourse, and in the exploration of the life and death of a military woman we see a male military unable to cope with her presence. *The General's Daughter* casts Campbell as a victim, a woman betrayed by her fellow soldiers, her father, and the military. She is also associated with illicit sexuality, pictured as a dominatrix, as promiscuous, in short a figure of scandalous, undisciplined sexuality. Promiscuity provides her with a weapon against her father; having had sex with almost all his male staff she threatens to bring down his reputation and to destroy the public image he has so carefully crafted. An association between military women, sexual scandal, and unwelcome media attention was already firmly established by the early 1990s. Thus it is appropriate that Campbell's manipulation of appearances, of official fears to do with bad publicity, should structure the plot of *The General's Daughter*. Her story metaphorically speaks to wider issues of women's military service, yet it remains a family matter, a paternal betrayal that "explains" this particular military woman's pathology.

In line with Projansky's identification of a shift of emphasis in representations of rape such that men's "ability and desire to *see* the rape" are constructed as feminist acts, the film foregrounds not Campbell herself but the process by which Warrant Officer Paul Brenner (John Travolta) comes to see the rape and to understand its explanatory role.[24] In his first encounter with the general, Brenner is told that he must decide where his loyalties lie: "Are you a soldier or a policeman?" On this occasion Brenner replies that he is a soldier; ultimately the instincts of the detective will win out, however. *The General's Daughter* hints at perversity and criminality beneath the veneer of an ordered military society. The capable military woman that the film investigates is rendered abject. Campbell's final pleas to her father are defiant ("I want to hear you say it happened"), condemnatory ("You never helped me"), and desperate ("Daddy, please help me"), standing for the film's construction of military women as demanding victims. Military masculinity seems hopelessly bankrupt, with Elizabeth's brutal rape part of a continuum that includes General Campbell's personal betrayal, the attempts of his staff to cover up his daughter's (and their own) sexual behavior, and a more generalized hostility toward military women. Yet if military men clearly resent and desire Campbell, the film also tries to vindicate military masculinity and military men. Thus in the closing montage Brenner honors Campbell's coffin as it is loaded onto a plane, a brave male soldier saluting a dead female soldier who has been vindicated, even avenged. In the process male military masculinity is also valorized and honored (figure 50).

In his investigations Brenner is reluctantly partnered with a military policewoman, his former lover, Warrant Officer Sarah Sunhill (Madeleine Stowe), who is described variously as a rape counselor and rape investigator and who never (unlike Brenner) appears in uniform. Sunhill describes Brenner as someone who knows nothing about women; it is she who discerns an inconsistency in Campbell's West Point file, identifying her as a high achiever whose performance fell off significantly following the unrecorded rape. Yet Sunhill occupies a supporting role in the film, in accordance with its focus on male military masculinity; she plays no part in the accounting that comes toward the end of the narrative, being conspicuously absent from the scenes in which Brenner confronts the general about his behavior. Instead her role is a far more conventional one; her military cop is constructed as a victim on two occasions, both of which involve her returning to the murder site at night. On the first of these she is assaulted and threatened with rape; later she is held hostage in a minefield

50. Brenner (John Travolta) honors Campbell's coffin in *The General's Daughter* (1999).

and must be saved by Brenner. Thus if Brenner is aligned with Campbell because both have been let down by a father and leader they esteemed, Sunhill is aligned with her as the object of military men's violence. Both women are strong, smart, and capable, yet one dies and the other is attacked twice. In the logic of the film it is these women's very intelligence that seems to endanger them.

These four fictions all involve narratives in which rape or the threat of rape is used to put military women in their place, to remind them of the gendered character of the hierarchies within which they seek to assert themselves. Exemplary military women stand out, their presence construed as inherently provocative. In exacting revenge, these raped or assaulted military women employ a variety of skills that showcase their violence, engaging a strong tradition in popular culture which figures the raped or wronged woman as a figure of agency. At the same time these narratives emphasize the precarious position of military women within patriarchal systems such as the law and the military. They also forcefully suggest that the main danger facing military women comes in the shape of their male comrades. Narratives which frame military women as investigators exploit precisely this outsider status.

THE MILITARY WOMAN AS "FEMALE DICK"

In her study of the female investigator in fiction, film, and television, Linda Mizejewski points to the impact of state intervention in opening up careers in law enforcement to women in the U.S.; as with the integration of military women, change "came from outside and . . . pushed outsiders in."[25] More recently the female investigator has become a commercial asset in television crime series, an integral part of any number of ensemble shows and even the chief protagonist in series such as *Cold Case* (CBS, 2003–10), *The Closer* (TNT, 2005–), and *Close to Home* (CBS, 2005–7). Mizejewski writes, "Television is exactly the place where we see how forcefully the female investigator has become part of our cultural 'central casting.'"[26] This shift suggests that what Mizejewski playfully terms the "female dick" no longer evokes the sorts of cultural contradictions persistently associated with the military woman. Or rather that such contradictions have been effectively contained and even commodified.

In recent years popular fictions have regularly cast the military woman as an investigator or as a member of the military police. *The General's Daughter* and *Basic* (2003) are thrillers which situate their most compelling and successful female soldiers as military cops. The British drama series *Red Cap* (BBC, 2001–4) also makes its protagonist a military police-woman (the Royal Military Police being known as Red Caps). The television movie *Inflammable* (CBS, 28 November 1995) features Marg Helgenberger as Lt. (j.g.) Kay Dolan, investigating an attempted rape and then a murder at sea. (The film clearly trades on the success of the high-profile Navy lawyer narratives *A Few Good Men* and *JAG*.) In this context I want to consider how the generic conventions and stock characters of crime, murder-mystery, and thriller allow for an articulation of female agency within the military. The existence of a military police force (and, in the U.S., the Code of Military Justice) underlines the extent to which the military functions outside of civilian society, operating by different rules and depending on a conviction that the military has the right and the ability to police itself. Even so, many military narratives portray an institution reluctant either to change or to admit flaws, such that uncovering the truth has the potential to compromise the investigator's career. MPs are thus frequently presented as outsider figures; like women in the military more generally, there is a suggestion that MPs are not "really" soldiers at all.[27] *Red Cap* foregrounds this tension extensively; indeed it is one of the show's central themes. In the pilot episode Capt. Gavin Howard rebukes Sgt. Jo McDonagh (Tamzin Outhwaite) for her rashness in interrogating an officer on her own initiative. Howard explains that the squad walks a "fine line" between "serving the Army and investigating the Army." Such a scenario is particularly resonant for military women, who are often portrayed as being committed to an institution which remains uncertain about their presence and role.

As both policewoman and soldier, McDonagh's ability to think through cases is bound up in her hands-on approach; she impulsively leaves the office to follow up leads alone more than once. Her soldiering skills, an ability with vehicles and weaponry in particular, are repeatedly underlined in this context. (Her previous assignments were as a bodyguard.) Her tendency to go out on her own and to pursue her instincts troubles her superior, Sgt. Maj. Burns; yet her behavior is quite in line with the dedication of cop protagonists in television drama. Like nursing, police work is frequently represented in terms of vocation; it is work associated with tenacity, selfless labor, and personal loyalty. It is also, like nursing, a profession with a distinct, distanced relationship to the military business of killing since, in its idealized fictional form, police work involves speaking for victims, seeking justice on their behalf.

As both insider and outsider, the tough female investigator suggests a different association between female agency and masculinity than that embodied by the military woman. Popular culture understands both in terms of a kind of male impersonation, so that the description "female dick" is in many ways unsurprising. Both tough female investigators and tough military women are characterized in popular narratives as women with balls, women with dicks, or "ball-breakers." In *Inflammable* Dolan's position as an investigator gives her the license to tackle the atavistic CPO Duke Miller on his sexism; in response he rails against "feminist ball-breakers." Staff Sgt. Harriet Frost in *Red Cap* is also referred to as a "ball-breaker."

Lines of authority and contestation are plainly at work in *The General's Daughter*, a film that, as I've argued, tends to marginalize military women and associate them with victim status. As a rape counselor and rape investigator, Warrant Officer Sarah Sunhill is defined in terms of a specialization associated more commonly with the civilian police; thus the film reiterates the position of women in the military as victims of sexual assault.[28] The one scene in which Sunhill successfully asserts her authority makes effective use of the iconography of television's tough female cops, when she locates and confronts one of the men responsible for the gang rape of Elizabeth Campbell at West Point. The scene takes place in a locker room, a masculine setting that recalls the recurrent analogy drawn in popular fictions between rape and sport (figure 51). Sunhill may not be in uniform here, but neither is the man she interrogates; the crow-

51. Military woman as "female dick" in *The General's Daughter* (1999): Sunhill (Madeleine Stowe) asserts her authority as an investigator, confronting a soldier suspected of rape.

ing male group, wearing only towels, are reduced to vulnerable figures who rapidly disperse when she produces her badge. During the interrogation that follows Sunhill mobilizes (false) forensic evidence to gain information before triumphantly revealing her deception. Tough, provocative, powerful: Sunhill exploits her power to intimidate the male soldier, forcing him to sit when he tries to leave and asking him in hard-boiled fashion, "How scared are you right now?" Her coding as a (military) cop in this sequence, and more than that, as a female cop avenging another woman's rape, allows her to assert her authority in a manner quite in contrast to those numerous fictions showing military women's inability to make their rank count with male peers and subordinates. Because neither acceptance nor leadership is at issue in this scenario, male resentment has no immediate consequences for the chain of command. The female investigator, such fictions imply, may use male resentment and hostility to her advantage.

Red Cap's Jo McDonagh is initially an unwelcome presence in the unit, so that she too faces resentment. Although she must battle for recognition and inclusion, she is not the only woman in the unit, nor the series' only military woman. Along with the enthusiastic but relatively junior figure of Corporal Ogden, the show takes care to feature a more established female character from whom McDonagh is clearly differentiated; Staff Sgt. Neve Kirland and Sgt. Harriet Frost perform this role in the first and second season respectively. The prickly, competitive Kirland and Frost at times tend to confirm Staff Sgt. Roper's contemptuous assertion "Women don't like women they work with; it's genetic, something to do with the need to compete." Yet the strategies adopted by both women, and indeed by McDonagh herself, are contextualized by their habitual isolation within the unwelcoming institution in which they work.

Inflammable stages contemporary public interest in military women, making use of thriller conventions and an investigative format. Dolan's arrival onboard ship via helicopter is indicative of the film's sexualized working-out of military hierarchies. Capt. Jack Guthrie (Kris Kristofferson) greets Dolan's arrival to investigate an attempted rape on the ship with the derisive comment, "Behold the legacy of Tailhook." Guthrie tells Dolan directly that she is a "showpiece," her presence nothing more than "a public relations stunt to make the Navy look politically correct," a judgment the ambitious Dolan herself seems to accept. Here, as in *She Stood Alone*, narratives of sexual assault and female ambition are linked. As the film opens a young sailor, Tanya Santos, is assaulted while working in the cargo hold. (She will later be murdered.) Yet as Projansky writes, Santos herself and the attempted rape ultimately become marginal to the central narrative of Dolan's attempts to establish herself within the military.[29] Characterized in familiar terms as an isolated, tough professional woman, Dolan works both to avenge a murdered military woman and to advance her own career.

From the beginning *Inflammable* is constructed as a narrative foregrounding the change and loss associated with military women. The film opens with a ritualistic "crossing the line" performance in which CPO Duke Miller, preparing to retire from a Navy he no longer recognizes, appears as Neptune. Miller's hostility to women at sea marks him as a figure associated with the traditions of the past; he is repelled by what he regards as "women trying to prove they're men," and claims that Santos brought her fate upon herself. Ultimately his anachronistic military masculinity is partially redeemed as he assists Dolan to defeat the real villain, the ship's seemingly exemplary white military woman, Warrant Officer "Charlie" Porter (Park Overall). That it is a military *woman* who is revealed as Santos's killer displaces the significance of Miller's involvement in the attempted rape. It was, he claims, a "prank," a disciplinary message intended for Santos's lover, not even the woman herself. Miller's misogyny is thus reframed as misguided rather than murderous.

Male hostility toward military women fosters an atmosphere of threat and danger appropriate to the thriller; *Inflammable*'s title refers to this charged atmosphere with the potential for violence on one hand and sexual possibilities on the other. An evident sexual attraction between Dolan and Capt. Guthrie (it is later revealed that they had once been lovers) further emphasizes the erotic possibilities of a gender-integrated crew. Military women are presented as bringing sex onboard ship with them. Santos's sexual relationship with another sailor is associated with her attempted rape. The staging of Dolan's arrival emphasizes her legs as she steps out of a helicopter. The intimate moments shared between Dolan and Guthrie compromise her status as independent (military) woman, emphasizing instead her sexual availability. Despite her self-characterization as an ambitious woman who needs to build a sense of self, personally and professionally, she succumbs to her (sexual) impulses in a fashion more reminiscent of an erotic thriller than investigative fictions. Dolan is thus both the narrative's key protagonist and a provocative (eroticized) presence who troubles the world of the ship.

If authoritative military women are cast as ball-breakers by resentful men, they are also frequently described as women with balls, associated with male anatomy through their toughness. As with O'Neil's affirmation ("Suck my dick!") of her masculine military identity in *G.I. Jane*, these military women overlap with Mizejewski's evocation of the "female dick."[30] In both investigative and military narratives, agency is associated with men and masculinity through a language that equates physical violence and positions of authority with the body. Capt. Julia Osbourne, the military policewoman played by Connie Nielson in *Basic*, exemplifies this pattern. Described by Cynthia Fuchs as "the exemplary outsider,"[31] Osbourne's military demeanor and commitment to duty are undoubted; she pushes and questions when easy answers are offered to the mystery, suggesting that she is both a good soldier and a good cop. Osbourne's toughness is signaled by conventional signs of military masculinity, such as her heavy boots, cropped hair, and capacity for violence. When she intervenes to protect the DEA investigator Tom Hardy (John Travolta) from a suspect the two are interrogating he rebukes her, "Next time I want to borrow your balls, I'll ask you." A subsequent scene shows the two literally slugging out their battle for authority. The erotic coding of this physical conflict suggests that neither the performance of masculinity nor androgynous styling is enough to displace the military woman's association with sex. *Basic*'s costume designer joked, "She [the actor who portrayed Dolan] practically wanted me to put a sock in the trousers." Roselyn Sanchez, who plays the tough Latina ranger Nunez in the movie, also comments in amused terms on the shock of seeing herself in military masculine guise: "I'm a man, I'm a little boy, I'm a boy in this movie."[32] The blurring of gendered categories is evident in Sanchez's description; subsequently the film reveals that her character is impersonating a boy as part of an elaborate undercover operation. Sanchez's performance of a military woman as tough is framed by both ethnic and gendered representational codes.

The most benign version of this sort of gender confusion is to cast the military policewoman as "one of the boys." The erasure of femininity isn't specific to military policewomen or investigative narratives; as discussed in earlier chapters it is evident in nursing narratives and combat scenarios. It is used extensively in *Red Cap*, which portrays McDonagh as a physically capable woman who is ill at ease when called on to perform femininity. The jealous wife of a colleague with whom McDonagh pursues a fitful romance sneers at her as "a bloke with tits." McDonagh, called the unit's "little pit bull" by Kenny Burns, has her military identity effectively mapped onto her gender identity. The pilot episode shows her on the shooting ranges engaging a paratrooper in a fist fight. (He escapes and her split lip is prominent for much of the episode.) In the later episode "Fighting Fit," she holds her own in a fight, taking on and defeating a corporal whose bullying and extortion have led to the death of another soldier. In "Payback" she wears a cocktail dress undercover, yet needs Staff Sgt. Neve Kirland's help to dress for the occasion.

Although *Red Cap* refuses the more fantastic scenarios of female agency played out in action cinema, McDonagh humorously describes her reasons for joining the Army to the affable Sgt. Hornsby in Hollywood terms: "When I was a teenager I saw *Terminator 2* and I wanted to be Linda Hamilton. . . . I wanted to have a gun, run around in cool clothes, taking out bad guys." She then appends a more conventional explanation: "I don't know, three brothers—I suppose I always wanted to be a boy." Between these identifications with a strong fictional woman and her male siblings, McDonagh is produced as a masculine, military woman. That her inscription as masculine woman has implications for both her personal and professional life becomes clear as the series progresses. Her characterization as "one of the boys" is both productive and problematic, as it is for McMurphy in *China Beach* and for other fictional military women. Individual episodes often close with an image of McDonagh alone. Sometimes she smiles; at other times she seems mournful or apprehensive. On a few occasions she is incorporated into the group, but the emphasis on her outsider status is more insistent. Both her uncertain position in the professional group and her romantic isolation are conveyed in the final sequence of "Fighting Fit," in which she is walking to a ceremonial function in full dress uniform. From a distance she sees Roper and Burns arrive with their wives, conducting the rituals of polite kissing. This is one of only two scenes in the entire series to show McDonagh wearing a skirt or dress (in the other she is undercover); here the long skirt of her dress uniform distinguishes her from the military men in her unit, though all wear the distinctive red jacket. Her difference and sense of exclusion are made apparent, registered both in the uniform that is meant to signal equality between military personnel but which here marks difference, and in the difficulty of imagining an equivalent to the military wives who accompany Roper and Burns.

McDonagh's masculine military demeanor and her status as one of the boys result in her ultimate exclusion from the possibilities of romance. We learn in series 1 that her assignment to the Special Investigation Branch followed an assignment as a bodyguard in Algiers, during which a colleague with whom she was romantically involved was killed when her gun jammed. A growing attraction to Roper leads nowhere after he reconciles with his ex-wife. In "Betrayed" she impulsively sleeps with a civilian contractor, subsequently revealed to have been involved in the deaths of a group of soldiers in the Special Air Service. Although for a brief moment she is seen delighting in an afterglow of sexual satisfaction, giving in to romantic or sexual impulses ultimately compromises her professionally. With the exception of Corporal Ogden, whose marriage to Hornsby ends the series, military women are portrayed as either single or involved in failing relationships. A female captain, a rape victim in "Cold War," is a loner whose vulnerability leads her to agree to a weekend liaison with the man who subsequently imprisoned and assaulted her; another female captain has an affair with an enlisted man that leads to her death (she is murdered by her jealous husband); in "Friendly Fire" pictures of a married female colonel kissing a male sergeant appear on the front page of a tabloid newspaper.

Marked by her experiences, McDonagh works hard to earn the respect of male and female colleagues, but this is no easy process, despite the actress's assertion that her character is "a woman in a man's world but the man/woman thing isn't an issue."[33] Throughout the series McDonagh feels the pressure of her position as single woman, as someone who stands out. Early on in the pilot, after she has taken the unit's dog into her barracks bedroom, she discovers a collection of male soldiers gathered outside her door on all fours, comically panting; her response is a smile and good-natured dismissal. Later, after she has been busted to corporal, she receives unwelcome sexual attentions from Sgt. Sam Perkins, who arrives with an offer of help but proceeds to make a clumsy pass. This scene also takes place in the quasi-domestic (supposedly safe) space of the barracks; she is able to handle herself once more, punching Perkins in the throat. Yet the scene emphasizes her sense of isolation; a brief follow-up shot shows her sitting in her room, alone and crying. As the series develops, McDonagh attracts a more complex sexual obsession from her coworkers. First there is the problematic mutual attraction, built on initial antipathy, between her and her married but separated colleague Roper. As the second series draws to a close, this dynamic is rendered more complex by a scenario in which her boss, Burns, becomes fixated on her. Burns characterizes her as a femme fatale, a trap for vulnerable men such as he. It is telling perhaps that *Red Cap*'s tough military woman ends up involved in sexual intrigue, the object of an obsessive interest that requires both quick thinking and decisive action on her part. In this the show clearly draws from and reproduces a long-established set of stereotypes, constructing the military policewoman as a provocative presence and a challenge to military men and to persistent cultural concepts of masculinity.

The generic relocation of the military woman to the thriller and to investigative scenarios in recent decades effectively exploits her outsider status. Popular film and television fictions figure the agency of the military woman as avenger and investigator while continuing to suggest the failures of integration. While transformation is certainly a theme of the rape-revenge films, the fictions explored in this chapter emphasize isolation rather than community. They are extremely ambivalent when it comes to culturally insistent questions of the military woman's gender identity. She is often scripted as boyish, independent, and masculine (not really a woman). Yet the emphasis on sexual scandal and the potential for sexual violence tells a different story, one which insists on the primacy of sexual difference, the continuing presence of gendered hierarchies in key institutions such as the military, and the provocative character of female demands for inclusion in those institutions.

Soldiers' Stories has described a trajectory from the rhetoric of the Second World War, which inscribed military women as auxiliary, a temporary necessity of "total war," to a contemporary context in which scandal and intensive media interest frame the military woman. In describing the shifting representation of the military woman in popular film and television, the book has moved across very different generic locations, from dramatic war stories and romantic narratives of heroism to the comic and musical performances which achieved box-office success during the Second World War and which continued to showcase military women in the postwar period. More recently, in the context of a gender-integrated military and a wider media emphasis on controversy and scandal, other genres have featured military women as central and supporting characters: dramas using boot camp scenarios or inadvertent adventures in combat to test military women; action narratives in which women are an integrated part of special units; rape-revenge narratives inscribing women as victims and avengers; thrillers and legal and investigative fictions which trade on the very isolation of military women established in other genres. The broad generic shift detailed in this book—from drama through comedy to crime-centered fictions— is absolutely in line with wider media coverage which celebrates military women and yet insistently frames them as provocative, whether to military men and masculinity specifically or to deep-seated ideas about gender identity, social status, and work. Representations of military nursing also span the period; nurses are integral to the waging of war but often are pictured as somehow disconnected from its prosecution. The heroism celebrated in many nursing narratives draws from other popular fictions in which nurses are selfless, nurturing figures; military nurses are similarly devoted to their patients.

Though *Soldiers' Stories* has dealt with diverse genres, a number of common stereotypes and character traits have emerged. In line with contemporary recruitment campaigns the military woman is often presented as seeking adventure and opportunity, and transformation is a recurrent theme. Military service may allow romance, but family and domesticity are largely reserved for civilian life. In the wake of the gender integration of the U.S. military, those narratives that did center on military women have tended to figure them as single, childless, and exceptional high achievers rather than ordinary women or mothers. That said, relatively few fictions of the past few decades have focused on military women. Instead, maintaining the auxiliary associations evident in earlier periods, they appear as supporting or peripheral characters in action-led scenarios, battle for justice in television movies, and appear as troubled characters in television series such as *The L-Word* (Showtime, 2004–2009) and *Army Wives* (Lifetime, 2007–). At the same time that media interest suggests the military woman provides a compelling image, hers is a *story* that seems difficult to tell. Indeed the filmmakers Meg McLagan and Daria Sommers comment on their attempt in a documentary on female veterans, *Lioness* (2008), to escape some of these media clichés: "While the reality of the changing role of female soldiers was playing itself out on the ground in Iraq, here at home the image of the female soldier stagnated in the public imagination, polarized between Jessica Lynch at one extreme and Lynndie England at the other."[1] Among many instances of this opposition between Lynch and England would be *Newsweek*'s description of England as the "anti–Jessica Lynch."[2]

The use of Lynndie England's image to stand for the scandal of Abu Ghraib is the most recent instance of a repeated use of the military woman as an overdetermined sign of impropriety.[3] Whether she is figured as a feminine victim, an amusing conundrum, or a perverse, masculinized bully these images build on a deeply ingrained cultural assumption about military women's inappropriate presence. They speak to the persistence of that cultural common sense in which the female soldier is a contradiction in terms, in which she is either not really a soldier or not really a woman.

Interviewed in Errol Morris's documentary *Standard Operating Procedure* (2008), England reflects on events without escaping the logic of these gendered types; she casts her younger self as a victim, a vulnerable young woman who had merely done what men had asked of her. Sabrina Harman, who claims that she used photographs merely to record events in Abu Ghraib, also remarks that she doesn't know what she would have done differently—except perhaps not join the military in the first place. Were military women a distraction from the scandal or, as Henry Giroux suggests, a convenient scapegoat?[4] In *Over There* the character Double-wide references Abu Ghraib explicitly, asking her fellow soldiers, as they listen to an interrogation nearby, whether they could get into trouble for just being there. Her question poses a pessimistic yet self-interested choice between quiescent conformity and a risky questioning of one's superiors. The journalist Frank Rich characterized the more general phenomenon at work in media as the "downsizing" of the torture scandal, that is, its widespread coverage in the press but absence from the image-driven television news.[5] Rich believes this has much to do with the limits of representation in a conservative cultural climate squeamish about reproducing some of the details of the abuse. Court-martial proceedings following the events in Iraq centered on the image, specifically the photographs which had been leaked and circulated in the international press in May 2004. Subsequent revelations have made clear the extent to which such treatment of detainees was normalized, shifting the question from how military women perform—so much a feature of the media coverage which took shape in 2004 as commentators responded to the photographs—to how the U.S. military and other organizations routinely conducted interrogations. In media commentary on their stories and personas both Lynch and England served something of a diversionary function. Above all, military women are a newsworthy subject, perhaps more so than the abuse and torture of detainees by American (and British) troops in Iraq or in military bases such as Guantánamo Bay.

Carol Burke writes, "Military culture is made, not born; it has a history." She contends that the future of military culture in the U.S. "should be directed toward serving democratically approved ends," a process that for her necessitates the full inclusion of women and recognition of the extent to which the rituals and traditions of military life work against this goal.[6] For many military women and their advocates, and for much of the news media too, the full(er) integration of women into the institutions of the U.S. military has to do with gender equality. Equality of opportunity underwrites a rhetoric of democracy and citizenship that is central to Western political culture (feminism as a historical project, now supposedly complete; civil rights as once contested but now seemingly secured). Yet it is also clear from a variety of media texts that integration has the fearful potential to symbolically *erase* gender differences. Representations of military women exemplify the policing of a hierarchical concept of gender, in which both femininity and female bodies are associated with disgust. Thus Billie Mitchell writes, "Military women voluntarily put up with a subculture that abhors their presence in it."[7] The insistent message of recent popular narratives is that military women must adapt themselves to masculine military culture, rather than the other way around. Today media constructions of military women continue to negotiate the meanings of the terms *woman* and *soldier*. For all the reports that tell us she is one of the team, just "one of the guys," her difference marks the military woman as noteworthy and as inherently provocative. And for popular narratives the female solider undoubtedly remains a contradiction in terms.

A PROVOCATIVE PRESENCE

1. *Picture Show*, 24 October 1953, 15. WRAF stands for Women's Royal Air Force.
2. Doherty, *Projections of War*, 159.
3. Meyer, *Creating GI Jane*, 3.
4. Ibid., 86–87.
5. See H. Patricia Hynes, "On the Battlefield of Women's Bodies: An Overview of the Harm of War to Women," *Women's Studies International Forum* 27 (2004), 431–45.
6. Meyer, *Creating GI Jane*, 20. Meyer makes reference in this context to John Costello's study, *Love, Sex and War*. Significantly, in terms of a contemporary repertoire of images of military women, Costello also refers to an interest in Russian women as soldiers (61). In Britain, too, Soviet women were an object of some fascination, as seen in the film *Tawny Pipit* (1944), which features a visiting sniper.
7. "British Women at War," *Life*, 4 August 1941, 70.
8. Lant, *Blackout*, 86.
9. Solms, "Duty, Honor, Country," 27.
10. Suid, *Guts and Glory*, 218.
11. Suid cites John Wayne's apparent discontent with the female character introduced, at the studio's insistence, into *The Fighting Seabees*: "For Wayne, the addition to the script 'took all the reality out of the picture. They really had a fine picture, kind of a lost patrol story to begin with. But it just ended up the usual type of film'" (ibid., 219).
12. The most sustained discussion of the genre is offered by Jeanine Basinger in *The World War II Combat Film*. Basinger explores in some detail the various hybrid forms of the combat film, including the musical and the women's picture.
13. Enloe, *Does Khaki Become You?*, xvii.

14. The WAAC was established in 1942. The following year it was assimilated into the army as the WAC, its members achieving full military status and benefits.

15. Crockatt, "Citizenship and Identity," 23.

16. Feminist scholarship on the First World War belies the exceptional role women carved out for the Second World War. See, for example, Kimberly Jenson's study, *Mobilizing Minerva*.

17. Gledhill and Swanson, *Nationalizing Femininity*, 3.

18. Summerfield, "Women and War," 307–32.

19. Phillips, *Engendering Democracy*, 6.

20. Lant, *Blackout*, 59.

21. Billie Mitchell, "The Creation of Army Officers," 37.

22. Enloe, *Maneuvers*, 247.

1. AUXILIARY MILITARY WOMEN

1. Most, though not all, of the women's services in this period were auxiliary in character; some changed during the course of the war in response to the difficulties of integrating auxiliary forces within the regulations and disciplinary mechanisms that governed military life.

2. Another in the same series shows an ATS driver with the text "Ceaselessly new vehicles roll off the production lines. Army units await them, the ATS deliver them." The ATS was formed on 27 September 1938 and subsequently given equal military status with men in April 1941. See Collett Wadge, *Women in Uniform*.

3. Meyer, *Creating GI Jane*, 19–20.

4. These contradictions are by no means absent from contemporary cultural and political life. Indeed they are in many ways formative of the pervasive postfeminism associated with discourses of gender in the U.S. since the 1980s, a set of connections I examine in the third part of this book. See Yvonne Tasker and Diane Negra, eds., *Interrogating Postfeminism: Gender and the Politics of Popular Culture* (Durham: Duke University Press, 2007).

5. The Women's Auxiliary Air Force was formed on 28 June 1939 and came under military regulation in April 1941. Women were fully integrated with the RAF in 1994.

6. As a member of the Mechanized Transport Corps, Johnny is a civilian rather than a member of the armed services, although women were drafted into the MTC following the introduction of conscription. MTC drivers served in Europe and Africa. See Collett Wadge, *Women in Uniform*, 376–78.

7. Kennedy, *The Life and Death of Colonel Blimp*, 66.

8. It is the realist Theo (Anton Walbrook) who voices the latter sentiment, observing, "Do you remember, Clive, we used to say 'Our armies are fighting for our women, our children and our homes.' Now the women are fighting beside the

men. The children are being trained to shoot. What's left is the home. But what is the home without women and children?" As Meyer demonstrates, precisely such questions were being posed in the debates that accompanied the establishment of the WAAC (*Creating GI Jane*, 19–21).

9. "How to Enlist More Women in the U.S. Navy," a handbook for procurement personnel, held at the National Archives in Washington. From the beginning the Navy made intensive use of advertising and publicity techniques, as Meyer records in *Creating GI Jane*, 64.

10. Meyer, *Creating GI Jane*, 59.

11. Ibid., 60.

12. Ibid., 20.

13. The ATA was a mixed auxiliary service, set up in September 1939 and first admitting women the following year. See Collett Wadge, *Women in Uniform*, 381–82; Walker, *Spreading My Wings*.

14. It is intriguing that the work isn't characterized as either demanding, tough, or skilled in this context; these terms were often used to signal specialized (male) occupations against which there was the most resistance to female involvement.

15. Worrals appeared in eleven books, the first (*Worrals of the WAAF*) published in 1941 and the last (*Worrals Investigates*) in 1950. See Ellis, *By Jove, Biggles!*

16. *Worrals of the WAAF* was serialized in the *Girl's Own Paper* from October 1940. In their study of girls' fiction, Mary Cadogan and Patricia Craig write, "Girls who read the *Girl's Own Paper* must have realized that if they joined the WAAF they were unlikely to have adventures as exciting as Worrals's. For those who wanted factual information there were endless articles describing life in the various women's services and voluntary organizations" (*You're a Brick, Angela!*, 279).

17. When shortages of male personnel in the ATA led the RAF to allow some thirty WAAFs to join, Escott reports, this number were selected from some fourteen hundred volunteers (*The WAAF*, 18). Escott was a squadron leader in the WAAF.

18. The Coast Guard is a civilian authority but comes under the Navy in time of war; the acronym SPARS comes from the Guard's motto, "Semper Paratus—Always Ready" (Holm, *Women in the Military*, 27).

19. Lant, *Blackout*, 99.

20. Ibid., 84.

21. From *News Chronicle*, 8 November 1941, reproduced in Games, Moriarty, and Rose, *Abram Games*, 24.

22. Games et al., *Abram Games*, 60.

23. Of course, wartime recruitment aimed at men also offered the enticement of professional opportunities, particularly as services sought to compete with each other. A Navy poster from January 1944 proclaims a free $27,000 education, flight training, and "a chance at a Commission for men from 17 to 18 years

of age." While the WAVES received equal pay, in the U.K. both WAAFS and ATS members received two-thirds of the male wage.

24. Indeed reputedly the ATS avoided using the acronym WAAC following the contempt heaped upon the women of that organization during the First World War.

25. Waller and Vaughan-Rees, *Women in Uniform*, 6.

26. Meyer writes, "It is no coincidence that the whispering campaign against the women's corps gained momentum at the precise moment that the WAAC was trading its marginal status for full membership in the Army" (*Creating GI Jane*, 38). In *Stateside Soldier: Life in the Women's Army Corps 1944–1945* (Columbia: University of South Carolina Press, 2001), 4, Aileen Kilgore Henderson cites male disapproval of her enlistment, worrying in her journal, "Am I getting into something that will transform me into a disgraced monster?"

27. Costello, *Love, Sex and War*, 65.

28. Recruitment for the WAVES also employed imagery which suggested familial approval of the daughter's decision to join up. In one poster a little girl in pigtails looks wistfully at the framed photograph of a young woman in uniform; "Wish I could join too," reads the text. In the same series a father sits at a desk having just unwrapped a signed framed photo of his daughter in uniform; the caption reads, "Proud—I'll say."

29. Feminist scholars have shown that these assumptions had (and have) a material impact on the working lives of military women. Meyer writes that assumptions relating to the need to maintain the femininity of WACs resulted in their assignment to inappropriate jobs and to a lack of flexibility in their use during the Second World War, citing as "the most extreme example" of this process the case in 1944 of "100 white Wacs trained as mechanics. . . . They had been requisitioned from the United States specifically for work in technical jobs and were assigned to the maintenance division to work in the tool crib and the parachute rigging department. When a high-ranking male officer discovered that they wore trousers and shirts on the jobs, however, he reassigned them to jobs where they could be 'dressed as women.' Consequently, these Wacs were transferred to the Supply Division where they were given desk jobs for which they had no training" (*Creating GI Jane*, 84).

30. Recruiters were directed to probe the reasons behind an application: "One question recruiters were encouraged to ask was if part of the applicant's motivation was to 'be with other girls?' This question was aimed at 'catching' women of 'questionable' character, in particular lesbians" (ibid., 157).

31. Waller and Vaughn-Rees write, "The WRNS, from quite early on, was the hardest to get into; at their wartime peak they numbered no more than 74,000, compared with 170,000 Waaf and 198,000 ATS. Because of this they were able to impose a strict two-week probationary period for new Wrens and eventually limit recruitment to women having family connections with the Navy. This

very exclusivity made the WRNS the first choice of many volunteers, and some accounts show that there was a decided pecking order in the minds of many outsiders" (*Women in Uniform*, 6).

32. Quoted in ibid.

33. Harris, *Women at War*, 46.

34. Moore, "From Underrepresentation to Overrepresentation," 117, notes that fewer than one hundred African American women served in the Navy, although unlike in the WAC, these women served in integrated units from the start.

35. Meyer, *Creating GI Jane*, 66–68. While there are photographs and other records, there are no recruitment materials of the period specifically addressed to or even acknowledging black women in the U.S. National Archives.

36. Jarrett-Macauley, "Putting the Black Woman in the Frame," 119–26.

37. Ben Bousquet and Colin Douglas, *West Indian Women at War: British Racism in World War II* (London: Lawrence and Wishart, 1991), 82–106.

38. Jarrett-Macauley, "Putting the Black Woman in the Frame," 120–21.

39. Bousquet and Douglas cite the December 1943 issue of *Picture Post*, which emphasized the respectable and highly educated nature of the thirty women (*West Indian Women at War*, 107).

40. On the deployment of respectability as a defense of women's military service, see Meyer, *Creating GI Jane*, 62–70. Bousquet and Douglas report the frantic efforts to reject Bahamian applicants to the WAAF before the reassuring news that the sixteen women were, in the words of an Air Ministry telegram, "white women of excellent type" (*West Indian Women at War*, 92).

41. See, for example, the letters gathered in Litoff and Smith, *We're in This War Too*.

42. *Keep Your Powder Dry* credits a WAC technical advisor. *The Gentle Sex* was supported by both the War Office and the ATS.

43. On British screens the film's exhibition was also linked to local recruitment drives, literalizing the connection between narrative fiction and recruitment films. At a showing in Derby the ATS arranged a march past of some thousand ATS together with a band during the intermission and set up a recruiting office in the foyer later that week ("A Thousand Smiles," *Kinematograph Weekly*, 9 September 1943, 41). A gala performance of the film in Salisbury was attended by Joyce Howard, an ATS band who opened the show, and "civic, ecclesiastical and military personages of high rank," including U.S. military officers ("Acclaiming the Ladies," *Kinematograph Weekly*, 9 September 1943, 31). For a discussion of the film's spotty production history, see James Chapman, *The British at War: Cinema, State and Propaganda, 1939–1945* (London: I. B. Tauris, 1998), 208–11.

44. Review of *The Gentle Sex*, *Manchester Guardian*, 27 July 1943. On the film's success, see Lant, *Blackout*, 231; Chapman, *British at War*, 211.

45. Review of *The Gentle Sex*, *The Star*, 10 April 1943.

46. "Odeon Premiere of 'Gentle Sex,'" *Kinematograph Weekly*, 8 April 1943, 34.

47. Lant, *Blackout*, 90.

48. Robinson, *Sisters in Arms*, 28. For a more recent iteration of these views, see Cornum, "Soldiering." Cornum writes of her time at Officer Cadet School in 1978, "I liked running in formation. I liked doing things as a group. The Army sort of took on the feeling of family" (4).

49. Burke, *Camp All-American*, 25.

50. Basinger, *The World War II Combat Film*, 92, traces this convention back to films of the First World War, terming it the Quirt/Flagg relationship, after the opposed characters in *What Price Glory?* (1926).

51. Lant, *Blackout*, 102.

52. In the case of the ATS, we might note, there was widespread dissatisfaction with the predominance of titled women (county ladies) in senior positions. While the secretary of state for war may have denied recourse to class-based hierarchies in appointment and promotions, such a perception was nonetheless widely held.

53. The male voice-over that closes the film does not fail to mention pay and conditions, appealing to material interests along the lines discussed above in relation to British and U.S. recruitment materials.

54. Lant, *Blackout*, 60.

55. Many of these connotations continue into the postwar period, doing much to inform the career-glamour of roles such as flight attendant, as evident in British comic strips directed at girls such as *Angela Air Hostess* or the series of American books following the adventures of an air stewardess, Vicki Barr (published between 1947 and 1964).

   Incidentally, Carol Harris writes, "So smart was the uniform that after the war, the British airline BOAC bought up surplus WRNS clothing, including the tricorn hats, for the uniforms of their stewardesses" (*Women at War*, 91).

56. Lant, *Blackout*, 106.

57. Most notably instances of women who cross-dressed in order to serve. See Wheelwright, *Amazons and Military Maids*; Young, "Confederate Counterfeit."

58. Kirkham, "Fashioning the Feminine," 158.

59. Enloe, *Maneuvers*, 263.

60. Lant, *Blackout*, 104.

61. This would have been used during the initial training period, when recruits and the Navy judged each other's suitability.

62. As this suggests, popular culture did register the sense of dislocation experienced by former servicewomen who found themselves abruptly returning to the limitations of peacetime femininity following the war. These uncertainties find expression in as conservative a space as Agatha Christie's crime fiction.

Christie centrally features a returned Wren, Lynn Marchmont, in her novel *Taken at the Flood* (1948). Lynn finds it difficult to adjust to civilian life, missing the excitement of service. Contrasting herself to her stay-at-home farmer fiancé, she muses, "All through the years of war Rowley had never been more than a mile or two from home. And she, Lynn, had been to Egypt, North Africa, to Sicily. She had been under fire more than once" (34).

63. Holden and Olsen had appeared together the previous year in the critical and commercial hit *Sunset Boulevard*. Holden's character dies in that film, so audiences might well have brought to the pairing expectations of doomed romance.

64. Indeed Ian Christie characterizes *A Matter of Life and Death* as concerned with "rebuilding the idea of 'Britishness' after a war won only with American aid, which would spell the end of Empire" (introduction to Powell and Pressburger, *The Life and Death of Colonel Blimp*, xiii).

65. Lant, *Blackout*, 52, 53.

66. Basinger, *World War II Combat Film*, 290.

67. For discussion of the WAC's attitude toward pregnancy, whether of unmarried or married women, see Meyer, *Creating GI Jane*, especially 115–17.

68. Ibid., 58. Meyer also describes the difficulties experienced by potential WACs in getting release from employment, suggesting reluctance to support female military service.

69. Ibid., 69.

70. Glancy, *When Hollywood Loved Britain*. Glancy gives the American publication date of the novel as April 1941, reporting conferences on the script as early as July the same year.

71. Koppes and Black, *Hollywood Goes to War*, 225, 233.

72. Glancy, *When Hollywood Loved Britain*, 137.

73. Glancy suggests that the casting of the American star Tyrone Power as Clive Briggs, together with the fact that he makes no attempt at a British accent, effectively displaces or dilutes the vivid class anger expressed by his character: "His grievances sound as though they are those of an American Anglophobe or isolationist rather than a working-class British soldier" (ibid., 140). Power's Irish background perhaps also colors his character's antipathy toward the English aristocracy in the film.

74. Lant, *Blackout*, 114, 145.

75. In the novel, Glancy notes, the two sleep together and Prudence becomes pregnant.

76. An illicit seaside sojourn similarly brings mixed emotions in *D-Day, the Sixth of June* (1956) when Val Russell (Dana Wynter) learns of her fiancé's injuries via a newspaper headline.

77. Glancy, *When Hollywood Loved Britain*, 138.

1. Reeves, "The Military Woman's Vanguard," 73, 112.
2. See ibid. for a discussion of women's involvement as nurses in the Crimea, the American Civil War, and other conflicts. Cynthia Enloe writes that, whatever the official policy, female nurses "have served in combat regardless of official prohibitions banning their presence there. They have served in combat not because of unusual individual bravery—the stuff of nursing romances—but because they have been part of a military structure that has needed their skills near combat" (*Maneuvers*, 223).
3. Enloe, *Maneuvers*, 216–17.
4. Ibid., 218.
5. Lachie tells Patricia Neal's nurse in *The Hasty Heart* (1949) that she is "a lovely, lovely angel." Neal plays the nurse as a nurturing, but also a socializing figure; by kissing Lachie she accepts him into the social world from which he has been excluded (by illegitimacy) for most of his life.
6. Hallam, *Nursing the Image*, 20.
7. Ibid., 10.
8. Ibid., 136.
9. Reeves writes, for instance, that "nurses in Vietnam . . . saw more death and destruction than the average soldier." Improved rates of extraction of wounded personnel meant "increased casualty loads of patients who often would not survive." She adds, "Nurses hated 'playing God' during triage—setting aside the men expected to die, the 'expectants,' and treating the more survivable cases" ("The Military Woman's Vanguard," 109).
10. The notion of choice (like that of vocation) of course negates the fact that most nurses serving in Korea had joined the reserves at the end of the Second World War with little inkling, as Reeves puts it, "that they would be called up again so soon" (ibid., 106). While all the female American nurses who served in Vietnam were volunteers, some were also reserves. Reeves reports that Army Reserve nurses were called to active duty in 1968 (108).
11. Summers, *Angels and Citizens*, xiv. In the context of the expansion of military nurses in the First World War Enloe points to the confluence of large numbers of wounded with "many middle-class women's picture of nursing, especially nursing abroad, as a multisided opportunity" (*Maneuvers*, 214).
12. Such imagery clearly informs popular nursing fictions aimed at girls. Julia Hallam characterizes the appeal of the *Cherry Ames* books in precisely these terms of agency, as well as familiar themes of selfless sacrifice: "The opportunities afforded by nurse training are those of travel and adventure rather than a life of dedication to professional ideas and values" (*Nursing the Image*, 55). There were eighteen books in the series, several with a military setting.
13. In terms of the stereotypes Hallam identifies, Carter is also something of a

battleaxe, subjecting Winters to a painful and unnecessary mustard plaster treatment. Evelyn Johnson's (Kate Beckinsale) willingness with the needle in *Pearl Harbor* (2001) is a more recent enactment of this scenario.

14. Forbush must overcome her prejudice concerning de Becque's mixed-race children; she chooses marriage and a maternal role, seeking to inculcate table manners in an indication of her continuing conformity. In the television version (2001), in which Glenn Close stars as Nellie Forbush, her military status and her professional role as a nurse are much more evidently foregrounded. We do not see Forbush in military uniform in the 1958 version; in 2001 she is rarely out of it.

15. Enloe, *Maneuvers*, 220.

16. Doherty, *Projections of War*, 161. *Cry Havoc* was adapted from Allan R. Kenward's stage play *Proof through the Night* (1942). See Dick, *The Star-Spangled Screen*, 134. Basinger, *The World War II Combat Film*, 226–40.

17. See Reeves, "The Military Woman's Vanguard."

18. Norman, *We Band of Angels*, 124.

19. For many nurses, the process of incorporation into the military was associated with public recognition and material benefits. See Enloe, *Maneuvers*, 218; Summers, *Angels and Citizens*.

20. On the woman's film, see Basinger, *A Woman's View*. On themes of costume and transformation in the genre, see LaPlace, "Producing and Consuming the Woman's Film."

21. The concerned therapist who invites confession or admission is another staple of the woman's film, as in the Bette Davis vehicle, *Now Voyager* (1942).

22. She is subsequently paired off with Kansas, the Marine played by newcomer Sonny Tufts whose naked torso featured extensively in promotion for the film with the associated line, "Hold on to your hearts, girls!"

23. While this seems foolish in the context of the film, it is worth noting the relative luxury of the life lived by prewar military nurses stationed in the Pacific.

24. Norman writes, "The nurses of the Philippines became the first American military women to wear fatigues, as field uniforms were called, on duty" (*We Band of Angles*, 22).

25. These conventions of transformation and trial operate effectively in relation to male characters too. In the prewar sequences of *They Were Expendable* we see a leisured world in which naval officers drink and dine in their pristine white uniforms. By the end of the film, their equipment and their clothing are in tatters.

26. The couple aren't actually married at that point; indeed Davy returns to the hospital not only to the confusion of evacuation, but to McGregor's warning of a dishonorable discharge.

27. Exhibitors were urged to take advantage of the recruitment drives and the desperate need for nurses and to get the message included in sermons and news-

paper editorials. Others got in on the act, according to the exhibitors manual, which provides details of an extensive magazine campaign for the cigarette company Chesterfield, with images featuring the three stars, text urging women to enlist as nurses, and the tagline "At home and over there it's Chesterfield."

28. Both John Wayne's Rusty Ryan in *They Were Expendable* and Robert Ryan's character in *Marine Raiders* are reprimanded for allowing such feelings to guide their judgment. Wayne's character wants to stay behind to settle his unfinished business, but he is reminded that the needs of Navy and country come first. Ryan's character is intent on exacting personal revenge against the Japanese troops, making him unreliable in the eyes of his commanding officer.

29. Basinger, *World War II Combat Film*, 239.

30. Koppes and Black, *Hollywood Goes to War*, 100.

31. Norman, *We Band of Angels*, 129.

32. Hallam, *Nursing the Image*, 36.

33. See ibid., 71. The benevolence of the good doctor legitimates his social superiority—he uses his power for good—and in the case of *Homecoming* this implicitly sanctions both the erasure of the (white) woman as a figure of agency and the reiteration of master-servant relations between black and white Americans as represented in the Johnson household by the loyal and unchanging figures of the maid Sarah (Jessie Grayson) and the butler Sol (J. Louis Johnson).

34. The armistice was signed 27 July 1953; *Flight Nurse* was filmed from 14 May to mid-June 1953 and premiered the same year.

35. Holm, *Women in the Military*, 150–55. Holm makes clear the flawed character of the military's guiding assumption that large numbers of women could be recruited on a voluntary basis for the Korean War effort (whereas men were drafted). On the domestic ideology of the 1950s, see Elaine May, *Homeward Bound: American Families in the Cold War Era* (New York: Basic Books, 1988).

36. Wells, *Cherry Ames*, 10. At the end of the story Cherry receives a citation. Between 1947 and 1964 Wells also coauthored a series of girls novels featuring Vicki Barr, a flight stewardess, further exploiting the glamour of aviation, albeit in a civilian context.

37. Enloe, *Maneuvers*, 222.

38. Basinger, *World War II Combat Film*, 242.

39. A similar incident occurs in Wells, *Cherry Ames, Flight Nurse*: "The men were scared. Cherry was scared, too, but she dared not let them see it. Eighteen helpless men looked to her for courage. She was actress now—actress, leader, mother—as well as nurse" (111).

40. Enloe, *Maneuvers*, 199.

41. Levine, *Wallowing in Sex*, 173–74.

42. Kayla Williams opens her provocative account of her year in Iraq with the assertion that Army women cannot escape definition as either sluts or bitches. See *Love My Rifle More Than You*, 13.

43. Susan Jeffords writes, "The popularity of Vietnam representation in contemporary American culture—films, novels, personal accounts, collections of observations and experiences, political and social analyses, and so on—cannot be questioned" (*The Remasculinization of America*, 1).

44. Enloe, *Maneuvers*, 229. The memorial takes the form of a sculpture of three nurses, one of whom holds a wounded man in her arms.

45. Seanz, "*China Beach.*"

46. Vartanian, "Women Next Door to War," 201.

47. Howell, "Reproducing the Past," 171.

48. Vartanian, "Women Next Door to War," 194.

49. *M*A*S*H* too has Hawkeye Pierce construct a memorial, making use of a shipment of 500,000 tongue depressors (the unit had asked for 5,000). He has inscribed each with the name of a patient and assembled them into a tower, which he then blows up ("Depressing News," 9 February 1981).

50. Series 1 of *M*A*S*H* featured an African American doctor, Capt. "Spearchucker" Jones, played by the former football player Timothy Jones.

51. Blood supplies had been racially segregated as recently as the Second World War.

3. MUSICAL MILITARY WOMEN

1. The film was based on the troupe with whom Sid Caesar toured during the war, working to evoke wartime entertainment for a postwar audience.

2. Fischer, *Shot/Countershot*, 138.

3. Burke, *Camp All-American*, 27.

4. See Wills, "Women in Uniform."

5. Ibid.

6. Allen Woll writes, "Unlike the majority of wartime films, the soldier of the musical comedy was rarely seen overseas in a combat role" (*The Hollywood Musical Goes to War*, 84). On the utopian qualities of the Hollywood musical, see Richard Dyer, "Entertainment and Utopia," in Altman, *Genre*, 175–89.

7. There is a thin line between film and film star performances in alternate venues tied to war, such as the USO; this overlap is evident in a film like *Four Jills in a Jeep* (Fox, 1944), which reconstructs the USO tour of its four female stars: Kay Francis, Carol Landis, Martha Raye, and Mitzi Mayfair.

8. Dale, *Comedy Is a Man in Trouble*, 175. Dale specifically discusses Hutton's performance in *The Miracle of Morgan's Creek*, a film in which the transgression of convention with respect to female sexuality is very much at issue.

9. "How to Enlist More Women in the U.S. Navy," a handbook for procurement personnel, held at the National Archives, Washington.

10. Woll, *The Hollywood Musical Goes to War*, 94.

11. The U.S. military was finally desegregated by presidential order in 1948.

12. Knight, *Disintegrating the Musical*, 16.

13. According to Donald Bogle in *Toms, Coons, Mulattoes*, 118–21, such numbers were designed to exploit the attraction of black entertainers while avoiding the need to integrate the performers within the narrative; such scenes could also be easily excised for those white audiences who might object to seeing black performers on-screen.

14. See Koppes and Black, *Hollywood Goes to War*, 84–90.

15. Although neither mentions *Here Come the WAVES*, useful discussions of Crosby's blackface numbers in *Dixie* and *Holiday Inn* can be found in Rogin, *Blackface, White Noise* and Knight, *Disintegrating the Musical*.

16. Rogin, *Blackface, White Noise*, 195.

17. Ibid., 86.

18. In their USO comedy dance number for *Skirts Ahoy!* Debbie Reynolds and Bobbie Van briefly adopt Polynesian-style masks, referencing racial masquerade in rather different terms.

19. Basinger, *World War II Combat Film*, 244.

20. Williamson, "Swimming Pools, Movie Stars," 7.

4. WOMEN ON TOP

1. Rowe, *The Unruly Woman*, 19.

2. Dale, *Comedy Is a Man in Trouble*, 125, 100–101.

3. Landay, *Madcaps, Screwballs*, 98, 105.

4. It is a commonplace of Hawksian scholarship that the director's comedies depict a world torn apart by gender. As V. F. Perkins writes, "Most of all Hawks likes to upset the relationship between the sexes" ("Comedies," 21). Also relevant here is Naomi Wise's observation that while Hawks's heroes need to learn, women, in the comedies at least, are presented as "already mature at each film's beginning" ("The Hawksian Woman," 114).

5. Bell-Metereau, *Hollywood Androgyny*, 60.

6. Perhaps just as acutely, Rochard must accept his treatment as someone who is not an American citizen: his status as "alien," and the later sight of the Statue of Liberty, directly reference immigrant experience. Early on he shakes his head after a conversation with Gates, muttering to himself, "American women," suggesting that it is her Americanness that is at issue as much as her status as a military woman. Grant's status as an Americanized European is perhaps acknowledged here, although in the movie he makes no attempt at a French accent.

7. For a discussion of military husbands, see Enloe, *Maneuvers*, 153–97.

8. Bell-Metereau, *Hollywood Androgyny*, 23, 43, 45. Bell-Metereau judges the film repressive in its use of cross-dressing, contrasting it negatively to the screwball *Bringing Up Baby* of the 1930s and the later Billy Wilder movie *Some Like It Hot*.

9. Ibid., 62.

10. The film's British title, *The Private Wore Skirts*, once more centers on the supposed mismatch of female clothing and military status.

11. Basinger, *A Woman's View*, 178.

12. Dale, *Comedy Is a Man in Trouble*, 52.

13. General Omar N. Bradley appears, briefly, as himself.

14. This commercially successful and somewhat formulaic series began with *Francis the Talking Mule* (1950), which introduced the core characters in an Army setting. This was followed by *Francis Goes to the Races* (1951); *Francis Goes to West Point* (1952); *Francis Covers the Big Town* (1953); *Francis Joins the WAC* (1954); *Francis in the Navy* (1955); and (with Mickey Rooney replacing O'Connor) *Francis in the Haunted House* (1956).

15. While the episode title suggests Hogan's centrality, it is worth noting that it is also sometimes referred to as "Personal Transportation Provided," a title that foregrounds the Jeep over which Bilko and Hogan compete. Such an association between woman and object or commodity means that Bilko must effectively choose between two different commodities or pleasures.

16. In Steven Cohan's words, Tony Curtis as Holden is a "boy who was not a man" (*Masked Men*, 309).

    Although realism is not at stake with respect to *Operation Petticoat*, a small group of eleven Army nurses and one Navy nurse did indeed escape Corregidor via submarine, the USS *Spearfish*; Elizabeth Norman discusses their experiences, including the difficulties—comic fodder for *Operation Petticoat*—in living together in the cramped conditions of a combat vessel (*We Band of Angels*, 118–21).

17. Rowe comments on the equation of unruly women with the grotesque and unclean connotations of pigs (*The Unruly Woman*, 39–43).

18. This rhetoric of Congress legislating against nature was also deployed in *Force of Arms* (1951), discussed in chapter 1; recall William Holden's snide remark, "WACs ain't women. They're officers and gentleman—Congress says so."

19. The pilot was first broadcast on NBC on 4 September 1977. In the U.K. this television movie was given the title *Petticoat Affair*, while in the U.S. it was later reissued as *Life in the Pink*. The series itself was canceled in its second season, after airing on NBC from September 1977 to October 1978.

20. Hill, *Sex, Class and Realism*, 171, 170.

21. National service, required for men over eighteen, was in operation in Britain from 1 January 1949 to 31 December 1960.

22. "Dr. Godwin Prescribes a Change of Mood," *Kinematograph Weekly*, 15 January 1959, 22.

23. The phrase appears in an AB-Pathé promotional spread in *Kinematograph Weekly*, 14 May 1959. The piece also reminds us that the film features "some of Britain's most beautiful girls."

24. An illustrated report on the film's premiere includes images of Wrens at the

Warner Theatre in London; Mary Talbot, chief officer of the WRNS, was also in attendance, along with other "top naval brass." "Warner-Pathe launches 'Petticoat Pirates,'" *Kinematograph Weekly*, 7 December 1961, 12–13. *Operation Petticoat* also declares its gratitude to the Department of Defense and the U.S. Navy.

25. British naval women would finally serve at sea for the first time in 1990.

26. Review of *Petticoat Pirates*, *Kinematograph Weekly*, 23 November 1961, 25.

27. This was the second of a series of films for which he was contracted to Associated British.

28. Hill, *Sex, Class and Realism*, 171. In the introduction to his book Hill contrasts the critical neglect of a film like *Petticoat Pirates*, with its unusual "treatment of sex roles," with the valorized and "aggressively misogynistic" attitudes deployed in the canonical *Look Back in Anger* from the same period (3).

29. King, *Film Comedy*, 111.

30. Review of *Petticoat Pirates*, *Kinematograph Weekly*, 23 November 1961, 26. The same page features a half-page advertisement for a nudist film, *Naked as Nature Intended*, indicating that contemporary film productions sought to exploit the female body in a variety of contexts.

31. Alan Dent, *Sunday Telegraph*, 3 December 1961, and James Breen, *Observer*, 3 December 1961, both cited in Hill, *Sex, Class and Realism*, 208.

5. MILITARY WOMEN AND SERVICE COMEDY

1. Enloe, *Does Khaki Become You?*, xvi. In her study of women directors, Barbara Koenig Quart expresses her frustration at what she perceives to be Goldie Hawn's dilution of feminism: "*Private Benjamin* has the appearance of a feminist fable for the masses, as well as a light and pleasing entertainment," yet Quart is unsettled by the inscription of militarism as a marker of women's independence. She is also troubled by the figure of Lewis and the decision to construct the film's "only other important woman" as "the heroine's arch enemy" (*Women Directors*, 86–87).

2. For a discussion of the "good doctor" type in a British context, see Karpf, *Doctoring the Media*.

3. Freedman, "History, Fiction, Film," 90.

4. Ibid., 92.

5. Paul, *Laughing Screaming*, 98.

6. Paul reads the scene as an indication of male rejection of the dependence associated with women and nursing more generally (ibid., 104).

7. Ibid., 102.

8. Ibid., 104.

9. Tasker, "Comic Situations/Endless War."

10. Cited in Reiss, *MASH*, 96.

11. For example, her character is involved in several versions of the shower gag at others' expense; in "An Eye for a Tooth" (11 December 1978) she steals Pierce's

and Hunnicut's towels while they are in the shower, gathering the nurses with popcorn to await their naked return to the swamp.

12. As the series went on, episodes became more explicit about the work–family ethos. Two season 6 episodes, "Mail Call Three" and "Potter's Retirement," show characters (Klinger and Potter) speaking of the 4077th in familial terms. For a useful discussion of work–family patterns in recent medical drama, see Heller, "States of Emergency."

13. Reiss, *MASH*, 98.

14. Freedman notes that "during the last seasons she almost displaces B. J. as the most important character after Hawkeye" ("History, Fiction, Film," 103).

15. Karpf, *Doctoring the Media*, 210.

16. The pilot episode, for instance, has Houlihan phone one General Hammond to report the activities of Pierce and McIntyre. The camera zooms in on his face, cuts to a shot of him eyeing her up during their time at Fort Benning, and then to a brief shot of them kissing passionately.

17. Linda Ruth Williams discusses this point in relation to both *Private Benjamin* and the later *GI Jane* in "Ready for Action."

18. Ibid., 173.

19. In an episode of *The Phil Silvers Show* ("The Court-Martial," 6 March 1956) we see a chimp inducted into, and court-martialed from, the U.S. Army.

20. Basinger, *World War II Combat Film*, 61.

21. It is worth adding that Brennan achieved some critical success with her supporting comic performance; she was nominated for an Oscar for the film and was nominated for an Emmy in each of the series' three seasons, taking the award in 1981. She took a Golden Globe for her role as Lewis in 1982 and was nominated once more in 1983.

22. On the comedy of age-appropriate sexuality, see Sadie Wearing, "Subjects of Rejuvenation."

6. CONTROVERSY, CELEBRATION, AND SCANDAL

1. During the U.S. invasion of Panama in 1989 intense media scrutiny was trained on an incident involving Military Policewoman Capt. Linda Bray. Bray led an assault that turned into a more substantial fight than anticipated; her role served to highlight the peculiarities and inconsistencies of official definitions of combat. Holm reports that Bray was so distressed by her fellow officers' response to media coverage of the incident that she left the Army (*Women in the Military*, 399, 434–36).

2. See, for example, Brian Mitchell, *Women in the Military*.

3. Burke, *Camp All-American*, 51.

4. The Citadel voluntarily (albeit under pressure) admitted its first class of women in 1996. The courts forced VMI to open its doors to women the following year after a lengthy legal battle.

5. Barkalow and Rabb, *In the Men's House*, 47.

6. A female reporter asks this rhetorical question in an NBC report that aired 27 February 1976.

7. Holm, *Women in the Military*, 442.

8. In *Creating GI Jane*, especially chapter 5, Meyer explores in some detail the double standards applied to male and female soldiers with respect to sexuality in the Second World War. More specifically, Enloe discusses the implications of Tailhook, Aberdeen, and Flinn in *Maneuvers* (276).

9. See, for example, Helen Benedict, "For Women Warriors, Deep Wounds, Little Care," *New York Times*, 26 May 2008; Sara Corbett, "The Women's War," *New York Times*, 18 March 2007.

10. Clara Bingham, "Code of Dishonor," *Vanity Fair*, December 2003; Krista Smith, "Jessica Lynch," *Vanity Fair*, December 2003.

11. Enloe, "The Gendered Gulf," 217.

12. Cohler, "Keeping the Home Front Burning"; Kumar, "War Propaganda"; Faludi, *The Terror Dream*.

13. See, for example, Kumar, "War Propaganda." Some journalists too commented on the wider media omission. For instance, in "A Wrong Turn in the Desert" Osha Gray Davidson asked, "Why has the Hopi soldier been all but forgotten?" observing of Piestewa, "If she had been born a century earlier, the United States government would have considered her an enemy" (66).

14. Burke, *Camp All-American*, 222, 225.

15. The Diane Sawyer interview with Lynch aired on Veteran's Day, November 2003.

16. Klein, "The Year of the Fake," 10.

17. The *Washington Post* report is reproduced and discussed in Bragg, *I Am a Soldier, Too*, 157–61.

18. Faludi, *The Terror Dream*, 165–95.

19. For a detailed discussion of American media coverage of military women and men involved in the scandal, see Gronnvoll, "Gender (in)visibility at Abu Ghraib." Errol Morris's documentary *Standard Operating Procedure* (2008) alludes to the specific ways female soldiers were employed in interrogation. Both male and female participants interviewed for the film present themselves more or less passively, as doing what they were told to do.

20. Gary Younge, "Blame the White Trash," *The Guardian*, 17 May 2004.

21. This is a central argument of Cynthia Lucia's study *Framing Female Lawyers*.

22. Ibid., 161, 162.

23. The first series was aired on NBC in 1995, but the network did not pick it up. It began its long run on CBS the following year, when the character of Mac was introduced.

24. In "Capital Crime" (8 January 2002), for instance, Mac "sees" the murder of another military woman, using her vision to guide her to the body and to assist

in the investigation. This device chimes with a number of contemporary crime and investigative shows which credit female protagonists with psychic powers.

25. In *G.I. Jane*, Jordan O'Neil's background in intelligence performs a similar function, despite the thoroughgoing physicality of the militarized masculinity played out in that film.

26. Rabb frequently exhibits the objectivity required to see past gender issues in a fashion that military women cannot. In the pilot episode he bluntly tells Lt. Kate Pike, "Your gender is blinding your objectivity." In "Head to Toe" (5 February 2002), an episode revolving around dress restrictions for female military personnel based in Saudi Arabia, he suggests that Mac has a "tendency to over-compensate when faced with a female client." A season 5 episode, "Mishap" (30 November 1999), bears this out when Mac takes a tough line on the culpability of a female RIO, Skates. In "Promises" (28 March 2000) Rabb defends a female seaman by suggesting that her female commanding officer was unreasonably tough on women when it came to discipline.

27. Once a pilot like his dead father, Rabb has moved to lawyering as a result of a "tragic" (in the show's terms) "night vision problem." Innovative surgery is later used to rectify the problem, so that in "The Mission" (26 February 2002) he flies in Afghanistan. Even in the pilot episode a miniature version of this scenario of remasculinization is staged, when Rabb saves Cag. Another pilot pins gold wings on Rabb's uniform in a gesture of recognition.

28. Enloe, *Maneuvers*, 238.

29. In *JAG* and other popular representations of a gender-integrated military, it is civilian women who are typically inappropriately assertive, challenging military culture. The recurring character of an African American congresswoman, Bobbi Latham (Anne-Marie Johnson), in *JAG* performs this function: she is seen championing the cause of an officer accused of adultery (an episode which directly references the case of B-52 pilot Kelly Flinn).

30. It may not be coincidental that both this and the previous episode ("Dog Robber Part I") also involve Rabb's bringing Cag out of retirement for a delicate mission. Boone admits that he would not have agreed to the assignment a few months earlier, but that 9/11 has changed things. The episode also sees the regular character Gunny (Randy Vasquez) requesting assignment to active duty; in the changed context he needs to be where the action is.

31. As Laurie Schulze notes, "In order to be marketable, the concept for the TV movie has to be 'hot' or sensational, yet, it must be 'familiar' at the same time" ("Getting Physical," 37).

32. The director, Christopher Menaul, also directed *Prime Suspect* (1991), a tough British crime drama focused on a high-achieving woman in a hostile male police force.

7. CONFLICT OVER COMBAT

1. Basinger, *The World War II Combat Film*, 13.
2. Just as pragmatically, the huge commercial success of the comedy *Private Benjamin* the previous year is used to provide a reference point for audiences: "BEWARE PRIVATE BENJAMIN!"
3. See Beltrán "Más Macha."
4. The attack in which her hair is cut off by fellow recruits effectively enacts the nightmares she has been having concerning rape by military men. The sexual violence she fears from male soldiers is here replaced by violent punishment at the hands of her peers, an assault on her femininity replete with shots of gleeful, gloating faces.
5. Foley also challenges a white female cadet with a scathing assessment of her physical abilities and remarks suggesting that her father likely wanted a son.
6. Wiegman, *American Anatomies*, 138.
7. Tucker and Fried, "Do You Have a Permit for That?"
8. The film was the pilot for a short-lived series that aired during the 1983–84 season.
9. Enloe, *Maneuvers*, 238.
10. L. R. Williams, "Ready for Action," 173.
11. Williams discusses the potency of the scene for the star discourse relating to Moore as "shape-shifter" (ibid., 181).
12. Mace and Ross, *In the Company of Men*, 33.
13. Enloe, *Maneuvers*, 271.
14. Garber, *Vested Interests*, 24.
15. Burke, *Camp All-American*, 104.
16. Linville describes Walden as "only the ostensible center of the narrative" in a film that uses "her life and death as the occasion for male-centred tales of war" ("The Mother of All Battles," 107).
17. L. R. Williams, "Ready for Action," 180.
18. In 1991 Senator John Heinz and Congresswoman Barbara Boxer argued for a change in policy to avoid the posting of both parents at the same time.
19. Holm, *Women in the Military*, 441.

8. SCANDALOUS STORIES

1. Jeffords, "Performative Masculinities," 106.
2. Helen Benedict, "For Women Warriors, Deep Wounds, Little Care," *New York Times*, 26 May 2008.
3. Burke, *Camp All-American*, 51.
4. See Coulthard, "Killing Bill."
5. Projansky, *Watching Rape*, 102.

6. *Rough Treatment* is a British television drama, first transmitted on the ITV network on 28 and 29 May 2000.

7. Projansky, *Watching Rape*, 103.

8. Clover, *Men, Women, and Chainsaws*, 114–65.

9. Ibid., 60.

10. Clover, *Men, Women, and Chainsaws*, 143.

11. Reed, *The New Avengers*, 35.

12. Projansky, *Watching Rape*, 99.

13. Jeffords, "Performative Masculinities," 106, 112.

14. Jeffords writes that the film received only a test release in American cinemas, then proceeded to the video rental market (ibid., 102).

15. Ibid., 103.

16. Ibid., 114.

17. Francis Elliott, "Revealed: Half of RAF Women Are Victims of Sex Harassment," *The Independent on Sunday*, 23 January 2005, 1.

18. Daniela Nardini, who plays the role, established herself on British television in the short-lived but well-regarded BBC drama series *This Life* (1996–97). Anna, her tough, hard-drinking, but vulnerable character in that series, laid the ground for subsequent work as argumentative and independent characters; she won a BAFTA for her performance in 1998. *Rough Treatment's* director, Audrey Cooke, also worked on *This Life*.

19. British military culture is distinct from American military culture, although similar debates remain in evidence with respect to the distinction between combatant and noncombatant personnel; however, British military women have been deployed on active duty, as aggressors and peacekeepers, in Bosnia, Afghanistan, and Iraq. The journalist Kate Adie writes, "The Ministry has even grown circumspect about disclosing the percentage of women on operations, trying to give the impression that it's so routine that it's irrelevant" (*Corsets to Camouflage*, 239).

20. Clover, *Men, Women, and Chainsaws*, 122.

21. Projansky, *Watching Rape*, 113.

22. Nelson DeMille, *The General's Daughter* (New York: Warner, 1992), foreword.

23. Holm, *Women in the Military*, 441–42. DeMille's comments here are quite in line with the veterans' discourse associated with the Vietnam War in the 1990s, a discourse that seeks to speak about the suffering and sacrifice of individual soldiers unfairly neglected due to the unpopularity of the war itself. Soldiering is presented as a matter of following orders rather than a political activity; soldiers serving in Vietnam were not culpable for the administration's failings, and their bravery should be celebrated regardless of other concerns.

24. Projansky, *Watching Rape*, 117.

25. Mizejewski, *Hardboiled and High Heeled*, 59. Mizejewski describes the changes resulting from Congress passing "Title VII of the Civil Rights Act in 1972, pro-

hibiting discrimination in public law enforcement hiring. The next year, it passed the Crime Control Act, which mandated equal-opportunity employment policies for law enforcement agencies getting federal aid." As with military women, policewomen attracted male resentment, media attention, and uncertain attempts at incorporation within narrative fictions.

26. Indeed, as Mizejewski notes, the female investigator is a commercial asset; commenting on the 2003 season, she writes, "Clearly, the networks think a quick-thinking woman with a license and gun is a good prime-time risk" (*Hardboiled and High Heeled*, 11).

27. It is worth adding that in film and television texts, MPs are frequently presented as comically stupid and even brutish. Enforcing petty rules and regulations, they are regularly cast as figures to be outwitted by soldiers seeking to brawl, drink, or evade duty. In the television series *Private Benjamin*, it is the somewhat slow, by-the-book Winter who becomes an MP; she is delighted at the prospect of her new role and cracks enthusiastic jokes about high-pressure hoses. In *M*A*S*H* MPs are regularly deceived, bribed, or otherwise brought into the schemes of the unit's personnel.

28. While male soldiers are also subject to sexual assault and even rape, this is not a subject routinely explored in military fictions.

29. Projansky, *Watching Rape*, 175–78.

30. Mizejewski notes that the term *dick* emerged in slang to denote the penis, a detective, and a figure who watches (*Hardboiled and High Heeled*, 14–16).

31. Fuchs, Review of *Basic*.

32. From interviews included on the DVD.

33. "Tamzin Outhwaite: TV C.V.," *Radio Times*, 19–25 April 2003, p. 146.

AFTERWORD

1. See the director's statement on the film's website.

2. "Make it Hell," *Newsweek*, 17 May 2004, 26.

3. Enloe discusses this media usage of England in "Wielding Masculinity inside Abu Ghraib."

4. Giroux, "Education after Abu Ghraib."

5. Frank Rich, "The Disappearance of Abu Ghraib," *International Herald Tribune*, 22–23 January 2005, 10.

6. Burke, *Camp All-American*, 22.

7. Billie Mitchell, "The Creation of Army Officers," 37.

BIBLIOGRAPHY

Adie, Kate. *Corsets to Camouflage: Women and War.* London: Hodder and Stoughton, 2003.

Altman, Rick. *Genre: The Musical.* London: Routledge and Kegan Paul, 1981.

Ashley, Robert. Review of *G.I. Jane. Sight and Sound,* November 1997.

Auster, Albert. "*Saving Private Ryan* and American Triumphalism." *The War Film,* ed. Robert Eberwein. New Brunswick, N.J.: Rutgers University Press, 2004.

Barkalow, Carol, with Andrea Rabb. *In the Men's House: An Inside Account of Life in the Army by One of West Point's First Female Graduates.* New York: Poseidon, 1990.

Basinger, Jeanine. *A Woman's View: How Hollywood Spoke to Women, 1930–1960.* Hanover, N.H.: Wesleyan University Press, 1993.

———. *The World War II Combat Film: Anatomy of a Genre.* New York: Columbia University Press, 1986.

Bell-Metereau, Rebecca. *Hollywood Androgyny.* New York: Columbia University Press, 1985.

Beltrán, Mary. "Más Macha: The New Latina Action Hero." *Action and Adventure Cinema,* ed. Yvonne Tasker. London: Routledge, 2004.

Benedict, Helen. "The Private War of Women Soldiers." Salon.com, 7 March 2007.

Bogle, Donald. *Toms, Coons, Mulattoes, Mammies and Bucks: An Interpretive History of Blacks in American Films.* New York: Continuum, 1991.

Bragg, Rick. *I Am a Soldier Too: The Jessica Lynch Story.* New York: Alfred A. Knopf, 2003.

Burke, Carol. *Camp All-American, Hanoi Jane, and the High-and-Tight: Gender, Folklore and Changing Military Culture.* Boston: Beacon, 2004.

Butler, Ivan. *The War Film.* London: Tantivy, 1974.

Cadogan, Mary, and Patricia Craig. *You're a Brick, Angela! A New Look at Girls Fiction from 1839 to 1975.* London: Victor Gollancz, 1976.

Carl, Ann B. *A Wasp among Eagles: A Woman Military Test Pilot in World War II.* Washington: Smithsonian Institution Press, 1999.

Carruthers, Susan L. "Bodies of Evidence: New Documentaries on Iraq War Veterans." *Cineaste*, winter 2008, 26–31.

Christie, Agatha. *Taken at the Flood.* London: Fontana, 1961. (Originally published 1948.)

Christie, Ian. *Arrows of Desire: The Films of Michael Powell and Emeric Pressburger.* London: Faber and Faber, 1994.

Clover, Carol J. *Men, Women, and Chainsaws: Gender in the Modern Horror Film.* Princeton: Princeton University Press, 1992.

Cohan, Steven. *Masked Men: Masculinity and the Movies in the Fifties.* Bloomington: Indiana University Press, 1997.

Cohler, Deborah. "Keeping the Home Front Burning: Renegotiating Gender and Sexuality in U.S. Mass Media after September 11." *Feminist Media Studies* 6, no. 3 (2006), 245–61.

Collett Wadge, D., ed. *Women in Uniform.* London: Imperial War Museum, 2003. (Originally published 1946.)

Cooper, Michael L. *The Double V Campaign: African Americans and World War II.* Harmondsworth: Penguin, 1998.

Cornum, Rhonda. "Soldiering: The Enemy Doesn't Care If You're Female." *It's Our Military Too! Women and the U.S. Military*, ed. Judith Hicks Stiehm. Philadelphia: Temple University Press, 1996.

Costello, John. *Love, Sex and War: Changing Values 1939–1945.* London: Collins, 1985.

Coulthard, Lisa. "Killing Bill: Rethinking Feminism and Film Violence." *Interrogating Postfeminism: Gender and the Politics of Popular Culture*, ed. Yvonne Tasker and Diane Negra. Durham: Duke University Press, 2007.

Crockatt, Richard. "Citizenship and Identity in Time of War." *Citizenship and Identity: International Perspectives.* Occasional Paper, Clarke Center, Dickinson College, 7–9 April 1998.

Dale, Alan. *Comedy Is a Man in Trouble: Slapstick in American Movies.* Minneapolis: University of Minnesota Press, 2000.

D'Amico, Francine, and Laurie Weinstein, eds. *Gender Camouflage: Women and the U.S. Military.* New York: New York University Press, 1999.

Dick, Bernard F. *The Star-Spangled Screen: The American World War II Film.* Lexington: University of Kentucky Press, 1985.

Doherty, Thomas. "The New War Movies as Moral Rearmament: *Black Hawk Down* and *We Were Soldiers.*" *The War Film*, ed. Robert Eberwein. New Brunswick, N.J.: Rutgers University Press, 2004.

———. *Projections of War: Hollywood, American Culture, and World War II.* Revised ed. New York: Columbia University Press, 1999.

Eberwein, Robert, ed. *The War Film*. New Brunswick, N.J.: Rutgers University Press, 2004.

Ellis, Peter Beresford. *By Jove, Biggles! The Life of Captain W. E. Johns*. London: W. H. Allen, 1981.

Enloe, Cynthia. *Does Khaki Become You? The Militarization of Women's Lives*. London: Pandora, 1988. (Originally published 1983.)

———. "The Gendered Gulf." *Seeing Through the Media: The Persian Gulf War*, ed. Susan Jeffords and Lauren Rabinovitz. New Brunswick, N.J.: Rutgers University Press, 1994.

———. *Maneuvers: The International Politics of Militarizing Women's Lives*. Berkeley: University of California Press, 2000.

———. "The Politics of Constructing the American Woman Soldier." *Women Soldiers: Images and Realities*, ed. Elisabetta Addis, Valeria E. Russo, and Lorenza Sebesta. New York: St. Martin's, 1994.

———. "Wielding Masculinity inside Abu Ghraib: Making Feminist Sense of an American Military Scandal." *Asian Journal of Women's Studies* 10, no. 3 (2004), 89–102.

Escott, Beryl E. *Twentieth Century Women of Courage*. Thrupp, England: Sutton, 1999.

———. *The WAAF: A History of the Women's Auxiliary Air Force in the Second World War*. Buckinghamshire, England: Shire, 2003.

Faludi, Susan. *The Terror Dream: Fear and Fantasy in Post-9/11 America*. New York, Metropolitan Books, 2007.

Fischer, Lucy. *Shot/Countershot: Film Tradition and Women's Cinema*. London: BFI/Macmillan, 1989.

Freedman, Carl. "History, Fiction, Film, Television, Myth: The Ideology of *M*A*S*H*." *Southern Review* 26 (1990), 89–106.

Fuchs, Cynthia. Review of *Basic*. *Pop Matters* online, 28 March 2003.

Games, Naomi, Catherine Moriarty, and June Rose. *Abram Games: Graphic Designer. Maximum Meaning, Minimum Means*. Aldershot, England: Lund Humphries, 2003.

Garber, Marjorie. *Vested Interests: Cross-Dressing and Cultural Anxiety*. New York: Routledge, 1992.

Giroux, Henry A. "Education after Abu Ghraib: Revisiting Adorno's Politics of Education." *Cultural Studies* 18, no. 6 (2004), 779–815.

Glancy, Mark. *When Hollywood Loved Britain: The Hollywood "British" Film 1939–45*. Manchester, England: Manchester University Press, 1999.

Gledhill, Christine, and Gillian Swanson, eds. *Nationalising Femininity: Culture, Sexuality and British Cinema in the Second World War*. Manchester, England: Manchester University Press, 1996.

Goldstein, Joshua. *War and Gender: How Gender Shapes the War System and Vice Versa*. Cambridge: Cambridge University Press, 2001.

Gray Davidson, Osha. "A Wrong Turn in the Desert." *Rolling Stone*, 27 May 2004, 66.

Griggers, Cathy. "Thelma and Louise and the Cultural Generation of the New Butch Femme." *Film Theory Goes to the Movies*, ed. Jim Collins, Hilary Radner, and Ava Preacher Collins. New York: Routledge, 1993.

Gronnvoll, Marita. "Gender (In)visibility at Abu Ghraib." *Rhetoric and Public Affairs* 10, no. 3 (2007), 371–98.

Halberstam, Judith. *Female Masculinity*. Durham: Duke University Press, 1998.

Hallam, Julia. *Nursing the Image: Media, Culture and Professional Identity*. London: Routledge, 2000.

Harris, Carol. *Women at War: In Uniform 1939–1945*. Thrupp, England: Sutton, 2003.

Haynsworth, Leslie, and David Toomey. *Amelia Earhart's Daughters: The Wild and Glorious Story of American Women Aviators from World War II to the Dawn of the Space Age*. New York: William Morrow, 1998.

Heller, Dana. "States of Emergency: The Labors of Lesbian Desire in *ER*." *Genders OnLine Journal* 39 (2004), online.

Herbst, Claudia. "Shock and Awe: Virtual Females and the Sexing of War." *Feminist Media Studies* 5, no. 3 (2005), 311–24.

Hill, John. *Sex, Class and Realism: British Cinema 1956–1963*. London: British Film Institute, 1986.

Holland, Shannon L. "The Dangers of Playing Dress-up: Popular Representations of Jessica Lynch and the Controversy Regarding Women in Combat." *Quarterly Journal of Speech* 92, no. 1 (2006), 27–50.

Holm, Jeanne. *Women in the Military: An Unfinished Revolution*. 2nd ed. Novato: Presidio, 1992.

Howard, John W., III, and Laura C. Prividera. "Rescuing Patriarchy or Saving 'Jessica Lynch': The Rhetorical Construction of the American Woman Soldier." *Women and Language* 27, no. 2 (2004), 89–97.

Howell, Amanda. "Reproducing the Past: Popular History and Family Melodrama on *China Beach*." *Camera Obscura* 35 (1996), 158–84.

Jarrett-Macauley, Delia. "Putting the Black Woman in the Frame: Una Marson and the West Indian Challenge to British National Identity." *Nationalising Femininity: Culture, Sexuality and British Cinema in the Second World War*, ed. Christine Gledhill and Gillian Swanson. Manchester, England: Manchester University Press, 1996.

Jeffords, Susan. "Performative Masculinities, or, 'After a Few Times You Won't Be Afraid of Rape at All.'" *Discourse* 13, no. 2 (1991), 102–18.

———. *The Remasculinization of America: Gender and the Vietnam War*. Bloomington: Indiana University Press, 1989.

Jeffords, Susan, and Lauren Rabinowitz, eds. *Seeing Through the Media: The Persian Gulf War*. New Brunswick, N.J.: Rutgers University Press, 1994.

Jenson, Kimberly. *Mobilizing Minerva: American Women in the First World War*. Urbana: University of Illinois Press, 2008.

Johnston, Claire, and Paul Willeman, eds. *Frank Tashlin*. Edinburgh: Edinburgh Film Festival in association with *Screen*, 1973.

Karpf, Anne. *Doctoring the Media: The Reporting of Health and Medicine*. London: Routledge, 1988.

Kennedy, A. L. *The Life and Death of Colonel Blimp*. London: BFI, 1997.

King, Geoff. *Film Comedy*. London: Wallflower, 2002.

Kirkham, Pat. "Fashioning the Feminine: Dress, Appearance and Femininity in Wartime Britain." *Nationalising Femininity: Culture, Sexuality and British Cinema in the Second World War*, ed. Christine Gledhill and Gillian Swanson. Manchester, England: Manchester University Press, 1996.

Klein, Naomi. "The Year of the Fake." *Nation*, 26 January 2004, 10.

Knight, Arthur. *Disintegrating the Musical: Black Performance and American Musical Film*. Durham: Duke University Press, 2002.

Koppes, Clayton R., and Gregory D. Black. *Hollywood Goes to War: Patriotism, Movies and the Second World War from "Ninotchka" to "Mrs Miniver."* London: Tauris Parke, 2000. (Originally published 1987.)

Kumar, Deepa. "War Propaganda and the (Ab)uses of Women: Media Constructions of the Jessica Lynch Story." *Feminist Media Studies* 4, no. 3 (2004), 297–313.

Landay, Lori. *Madcaps, Screwballs, Con Women: The Female Trickster in American Culture*. Philadelphia: University of Pennsylvania Press, 1998.

Lant, Antonia. *Blackout: Reinventing Women for Wartime British Cinema*. Princeton: Princeton University Press, 1991.

LaPlace, Maria. "Producing and Consuming the Woman's Film: Discursive Struggle in *Now Voyager*." *Home Is Where the Heart Is: Studies in Melodrama and the Woman's Film*, ed. Christine Gledhill. London: BFI, 1987.

Levine, Elana. *Wallowing in Sex: The New Sexual Culture of 1970s American Television*. Durham, Duke University Press, 2007.

Linville, Susan. "'The Mother of All Battles': *Courage under Fire* and the Gender-Integrated Military.'" *Cinema Journal* 39, no. 2 (2000), 100–120.

Litoff, Judy Barrett, and David C. Smith. *We're in This War Too: World War II Letters from American Women in Uniform*. New York: Oxford University Press, 1994.

Lucia, Cynthia. *Framing Female Lawyers: Women on Trial in Film*. Austin: University of Texas Press, 2005.

Mace, Nancy, with Mary Jane Ross. *In the Company of Men: A Woman at the Citadel*. New York: Simon and Schuster, 2001.

Marlow, Joyce, ed. *The Virago Book of Women and the Great War*. London: Virago, 1998.

Meyer, Leisa D. *Creating GI Jane: Sexuality and Power in the Women's Army Corps During World War II*. New York: Columbia University Press, 1996.

Mitchell, Billie. "The Creation of Army Officers and the Gender Lie: Betty Grable or Frankenstein?" *It's Our Military Too! Women and the U.S. Military*, ed. Judith Hicks Stiehm. Philadelphia: Temple University Press, 1996.

Mitchell, Brian. *Women in the Military: Flirting with Disaster*. Washington: Regnery, 1998.

Mizejewski, Linda. *Hard Boiled and High Heeled: The Woman Detective in Popular Culture*. New York: Routledge, 2004.

Moore, Brenda L. "African-American Women in the U.S. Military." *Armed Forces and Society* 17, no. 3 (1991), 363–84.

———. "From Underrepresentation to Overrepresentation: African American Women." *It's Our Military Too! Women and the U.S. Military*, ed. Judith Hicks Stiehm. Philadelphia: Temple University Press, 1996.

Norman, Elizabeth M. *We Band of Angels: The Untold Story of American Nurses Trapped on Bataan by the Japanese*. New York: Simon and Schuster, 1999.

O'Day, Marc. "Beauty in Motion: Gender, Spectacle and Action Babe Cinema." *Action and Adventure Cinema*, ed. Yvonne Tasker. London: Routledge, 2004.

Paul, William. *Laughing Screaming: Modern Hollywood Horror and Comedy*. New York: Columbia University Press, 1994.

Pearce, Lynne, and Jackie Stacey, eds. *Romance Revisited*. London: Lawrence and Wishart, 1995.

Perkins, V. F. "Comedies." *Movie*, no. 5 (December 1962), 21–22.

Phillips, Anne. *Engendering Democracy*. Oxford: Polity, 1991.

Powell, Michael, and Emeric Pressburger. *The Life and Death of Colonel Blimp*, edited with introduction by Ian Christie. London: Faber and Faber, 1994.

Projansky, Sarah. *Watching Rape: Film and Television in Postfeminist Culture*. New York: New York University Press, 2001.

Purvis, June, ed. *Women's History: Britain, 1850–1945*. London: Routledge, 2000. (Originally published 1995.)

Quart, Barbara Koenig. *Women Directors: The Emergence of a New Cinema*. New York: Praeger, 1988.

Read, Jacinda. *The New Avengers: Feminism, Femininity and the Rape-Revenge Cycle*. Manchester, England: Manchester University Press, 2000.

Reeves, Connie L. "Invisible Soldiers: Military Nurses." *Gender Camouflage: Women and the U.S. Military*, ed. Francine D'Amico and Laurie Weinstein. New York: New York University Press, 1999.

———. "The Military Woman's Vanguard: Nurses." *It's Our Military Too! Women and the U.S. Military*, ed. Judith Hicks Stiehm. Philadelphia: Temple University Press, 1996.

Reiss, David S. *MASH: The Exclusive, Inside Story of TV's Most Popular Show*. Indianapolis: Bobbs-Merrill, 1983.

Robinson, Vee. *Sisters in Arms: How Female Gunners Defended Britain against the Luftwaffe.* London: Harper Collins, 1996.

Rogin, Michael. *Blackface, White Noise: Jewish Immigrants in the Hollywood Melting Pot.* Berkeley: University of California Press, 1998.

Rowe, Kathleen. *The Unruly Woman: Gender and the Genres of Laughter.* Austin: University of Texas Press, 1995.

Schulze, Laurie. "Getting Physical: Text/Context/Reading and the Made-for-Television Movie." *Cinema Journal* 25, no. 2 (1986), 35–50.

Seanz, Michael. "*China Beach*: U.S. War Drama." Website of the Museum of Broadcast Communications, n.d.

Solms, Virginia. "Duty, Honor, Country: If You're Straight." *It's Our Military Too! Women and the U.S. Military*, ed. Judith Hicks Stiehm. Philadelphia: Temple University Press, 1996.

Stiehm, Judith Hicks, ed. *It's Our Military Too! Women and the U.S. Military.* Philadelphia: Temple University Press, 1996.

Suid, Lawrence H. *Guts and Glory: Great American War Movies.* Reading, Mass.: Addison-Wesley, 1978.

Summerfield, Penny. "Women and War in the Twentieth Century." *Women's History: Britain, 1850–1945*, ed. June Purvis. London: Routledge, 2000. (Originally published 1995.)

Summers, Anne. *Angels and Citizens: British Women as Military Nurses 1854–1914.* Berks, England: Threshold, 2000.

Tasker, Yvonne. "Comic Situations/Endless War: *M*A*S*H* and War as Entertainment." *War Isn't Hell, It's Entertainment*, ed. Rikke Schubart, Fabian Virchow, Debra White-Stanley, and Tanja Thomas. Jefferson, N.C.: McFarland, 2009.

———. "Soldiers Stories: Women and Military Masculinities in *Courage under Fire*." *Quarterly Review of Film and Video* 19, no. 3 (2002), 209–22.

———. *Working Girls: Gender and Sexuality in Popular Cinema.* London: Routledge, 1998.

Thomas, David, and Ian Irvine. *Bilko: The Fort Baxter Story.* London: Hutchinson, 1985.

Torres, Sasha. "War and Remembrance: Televisual Narrative, National Memory, and *China Beach*." *Camera Obscura* 33, no. 4 (1994), 147–64.

Tucker, Lauren R., with Alan R. Fried. "Do You Have a Permit for That? The Gun as a Metaphor for the Transformation of G.I. Jane into G.I. Dick." *Bang Bang, Shoot Shoot! Essays on Guns and Popular Culture*, ed. Murray Pomerance and John Sakeris. Needham Heights, Mass.: Pearson Educational, 2000.

Vartanian, Carolyn Reed. "Women Next Door to War." *Inventing Vietnam: The War in Film and Television*, ed. Michael Anderegg. Philadelphia: Temple University Press, 1991.

Walker, Diana Barnato. *Spreading My Wings.* London: Grubb Street, 2003.

Waller, Jane, and Michael Vaughan-Rees. *Women in Uniform 1939–45*. London: Macmillan, 1989.

Wearing, Sadie. "Subjects of Rejuvenation: Aging in Postfeminist Culture." *Interrogating Postfeminism: Gender and the Politics of Popular Culture*, ed. Yvonne Tasker and Diane Negra. Durham: Duke University Press, 2007.

Wells, Helen. *Cherry Ames, Flight Nurse*. London: World Distributors, 1956. (Originally published 1945.)

Whatling, Clare. *Screen Dreams: Fantasising Lesbians in Film*. Manchester, England: Manchester University Press, 1997.

Wheelwright, Julie. *Amazons and Military Maids: Women Who Dressed as Men in the Pursuit of Life, Liberty and Happiness*. London: Harper Collins, 1989.

———. *The Fatal Lover: Mata Hari and the Myth of Women in Espionage*. London: Collins and Brown, 1993.

———. "'It Was Exactly Like the Movies!' The Media's Use of the Feminine During the Gulf War." *Women Soldiers: Images and Realities*, ed. Elisabetta Addis, Valeria E. Russo, and Lorenza Sebesta. New York: St. Martin's, 1994.

Wiegman, Robyn. *American Anatomies: Theorizing Race and Gender*. Durham: Duke University Press, 1995.

Williams, Kayla. *Love My Rifle More Than You: Young and Female in the U.S. Army*. London: Weidenfeld and Nicolson, 2006.

Williams, Linda Ruth. *The Erotic Thriller in Contemporary Cinema*. Edinburgh: Edinburgh University Press, 2005.

———. "Ready for Action: *G.I. Jane*, Demi Moore's Body and the Female Combat Movie." *Action and Adventure Cinema*, ed. Yvonne Tasker. London: Routledge, 2004.

Williams, Melanie. "'A Girl Alone in a Man's World': *Ice Cold in Alex* (1958) and the Place of Women in the 1950s British War Film Cycle." *Feminist Media Studies* 9, no. 1 (2009), 95–108.

Williamson, Catherine. "Swimming Pools, Movie Stars: The Celebrity Body in the Post-war Marketplace." *Camera Obscura* 38, no. 5 (1996), 4–29.

Wills, Nadine. "Women in Uniform: Costume and the 'Unruly Woman' in the 1930's Hollywood Musical." *Continuum: Journal of Media and Cultural Studies* 14, no. 3 (2000), 317–33.

Wise, Naomi. "The Hawksian Woman." (Originally published 1971.) *Howard Hawks: American Artist*, ed. Jim Hillier and Peter Wollen. London: British Film Institute, 1996.

Woll, Allen L. *The Hollywood Musical Goes to War*. Chicago: Nelson-Hall, 1983.

Young, Elizabeth. "Confederate Counterfeit: The Case of the Cross-Dressed Civil War Soldier." *Passing and the Fictions of Identity*, ed. Elaine K. Ginsberg. Durham: Duke University Press, 1996.

I Was a Male War Bride, 114, 139, 142–46, 154, 161

JAG, 216, 219–28, 256, 269
Jeffords, Susan, 256, 259–61
Johnstone, Shoshona, 214

Keep Your Powder Dry, 42–46, 49–51, 95, 136, 150, 152, 237
Kill Bill, 257
Korean War, 1, 21, 55, 77, 96, 100, 103, 131, 136, 146, 152, 175
Kosovo, 10, 211

Lant, Antonia, 9, 15, 35, 43, 46–47, 50–52, 58, 67
Legal drama, 216–20
Lesbianism, 37–39, 52, 70, 165, 222, 244, 256, 284 n. 30
Lieutenant Wore Skirts, The, 114, 139–40, 143, 145–47, 149
Life and Death of Colonel Blimp, The, 26–27, 55
Lioness, 278
Lone Star, 239
L-Word, The, 278
Lynch, Jessica, 212, 214–16, 251, 278–79

Marine Corps, 6, 232
Marine Raiders, 6, 55, 57, 59–62, 126
Marriage, 12, 54, 60–64, 79, 87–89, 97–100, 107, 113, 131–36, 142–43, 146–51, 161, 167, 184, 189–93, 223, 229, 239, 275
Masculinity, 11, 22, 50, 136, 142–43, 146–47, 153–59, 216–19, 224–29, 237; female, 4, 8–9, 24, 51–52, 63–64, 70, 87, 91, 114, 160, 181–83, 186, 190, 195–98, 221–22, 231–32, 240, 243–47, 273–78; military men and, 8, 10–11, 17, 27, 60–61, 114, 127–30, 140, 233, 239–40, 243, 259–68, 272–73

*M*A*S*H*, 174–79
*M*A*S*H* (TV), 12, 16, 73–74, 101–6, 108, 179–82, 187, 190, 192, 194, 196–99, 241
Matter of Life and Death, A, 55–56
Mechanised Transport Corps, 26
Meyer, Leisa D., 4–6, 25, 31–32, 38–41, 64
Military academies, 10–11, 103, 173, 207–10, 212, 247, 255, 256
Military culture, 17, 41, 206, 211–12, 218–19, 228–29, 235, 246–47, 256–58, 279–80
Military women: congressional debates on, 6, 25, 63; media coverage of, 6, 10, 13, 31–32, 78, 166–67, 203–16, 220, 223, 226, 231, 233, 240, 250, 262, 265–66, 272, 275, 278–79, 295 n. 1; military men and, 8, 93–96, 125–28, 159–63, 250–51; respectability of, 24–26, 31, 37–40, 49–51, 63–65, 68–69, 86, 88, 149, 197–98, 210, 263–66, 275–76; sexualization of, 5, 12, 15–16, 35–40, 67–70, 72–74, 97–98, 101–3, 105, 116–17, 123–25, 130, 132–35, 140, 147–48, 154, 157, 161–73, 176–79, 181–90, 198–99, 226, 240–41, 257, 273
Millions Like Us, 35
Ministry of Information, 25
Ministry of Labour, 9
Mizejewski, Linda, 268–69
Mobile women, 9, 27–28, 56, 65
Motherhood, 38, 94, 96, 100, 107, 110, 148, 206, 210–11, 220, 231, 239–41, 248–53, 278, 282–83 n. 8. *See also* Pregnancy
Musicals, 8, 113–37; blackface and, 128–30; female sexuality in, 118, 123–24, 132–33, 135–36; romance and, 119, 123–27, 130–36

Yvonne Tasker is professor of film studies in the School of Film and Television Studies at the University of East Anglia. Her books include *Interrogating Postfeminism: Gender and the Politics of Popular Culture*, with Diane Negra, (2007), *Action and Adventure Cinema* (2004), *Fifty Contemporary Film Directors* (2002, 2010), *Working Girls: Gender and Sexuality in Popular Cinema* (1998), and *Spectacular Bodies: Gender, Genre, and the Action Cinema* (1993).

Library of Congress Cataloging-in-Publication Data
Tasker, Yvonne, 1964–
Soldiers' stories : military women in cinema and television since World War II /
Yvonne Tasker.
p. cm.
Includes bibliographical references and index.
ISBN 978-0-8223-4835-1 (cloth : alk. paper)
ISBN 978-0-8223-4847-4 (pbk. : alk. paper)
1. Women soldiers in mass media. 2. Women and the military. 3. Women in motion pictures. 4. War films—History and criticism. I. Title.
PN1995.9.W6T375 2011
791.43′6581—dc22   2010049743